Strangers at the Bedside

OTHER BOOKS BY DAVID J. ROTHMAN

Politics and Power: The United States Senate 1869–1901

*The Discovery of the Asylum: Social Order and
Disorder in the New Republic*

On Their Own: The Poor in Modern America

(coedited with Sheila M. Rothman)

The Sources of the American Social Tradition

(coedited with Sheila M. Rothman)

Doing Good: The Limits of Benevolence

(with Willard Gaylin, Steven Marcus, and Ira Glasser)

Social History and Social Policy

(coedited with Stanton Wheeler)

*Conscience and Convenience: The Asylum and
Its Alternatives in Progressive America*

The Willowbrook Wars

(with Sheila M. Rothman)

STRANGERS AT THE BEDSIDE

*A History of How Law and
Bioethics Transformed Medical
Decision Making*

DAVID J. ROTHMAN

BasicBooks
A Division of HarperCollinsPublishers

Library of Congress Cataloging-in-Publication Data
Rothman, David J.
    Strangers at the bedside : a history of how law and bioethics
transformed medical decision making / David J. Rothman
        p.   cm.
    Includes bibliographical references and index.
    ISBN 0-465-08209-2 (cloth)
    ISBN 0-465-08210-6 (paper)
    1. Medicine—United States—Decision making—History.
2. Medicine—Research—United States—Decision making—
History.   3. Medical ethics—United States—History.   I. Title.
R723.5.R67   1991
610'.72—dc20   90-55598
                                                              CIP

To J.R.
For Doing Good

CONTENTS

ACKNOWLEDGMENTS

IN the course of research and writing, I received significant assistance from a number of individuals, and I am pleased to be able to acknowledge their contributions. I was fortunate enough to have exceptional guides to the world of medicine, and although they will dissent from some of the things said here, my debt to them is great. All on the faculty of the Columbia College of Physicians and Surgeons, they are: Henrik Bendixen, John Driscoll, Norman Kahn, Michael Katz, Edgar Leifer, Jay Meltzer, Harold Neu, and Keith Reemtsma. The two people most responsible for my joining the faculty, Thomas Morris and Donald Tapley, taught me all that they could about navigating in strange waters.

A grant from the National Endowment for the Humanities freed me from other responsibilities, and Daniel Jones (program officer for grant RO-21349-06) was particularly helpful. The Samuel and May Rudin Foundation provided matching funds as part of its ongoing support of the program at the Center for the Study of Society and Medicine. Neither foundation is responsible for the views expressed here, which, of course, means that in no way did they attempt to influence the direction or course of the research.

I have benefited, as have so many other researchers, from the knowledgeable staff of the National Archives, the National Institutes of

Health, the New York Academy of Medicine, and from the guidance of Richard Wolfe at the Countway Library of Medicine of Harvard University. I am also indebted to Daniel Fox and Ronald Bayer for their many valuable suggestions for strengthening the manuscript, and to Harold Edgar as well, although he remains convinced that historians' arguments cannot stand up to grueling cross-examination.

The idea for this book came as I prepared to deliver the University Lecture to the Columbia community, and in subsequent years, I had the opportunity to share ideas with colleagues at the University of Virginia (courtesy of John Fletcher), the University of California Medical School, San Francisco (Gunther Reisse), Cornell University (Sander Gilman), the University of Kansas Medical School (William Bartholome), and the University of Texas (William Winslade). A presentation to the annual meeting of the American Association for the History of Medicine and to the Smith Kline Beecham meeting on Controversies in Infectious Diseases (courtesy of Harold Neu) were also stimulating occasions.

Discussions with colleagues at the Center for the Study of Society and Medicine, Sherry Brandt-Rauf, Stephen Hilgartner, and Stephanie Kiceluk, helped me formulate and clarify my ideas. I benefited greatly from Robert Zussman's review of the manuscript and from his forthcoming work on medical decision making in adult intensive care units. Probably no one is more relieved at the appearance of this book than Nancy Lundebjerg, a most talented administrator in charge of the Center.

Martin Kessler, president of Basic Books, made certain that the upheavals that can sweep through publishing did not affect this book, and I am grateful to him for his confidence. My editor, Susan Rabiner, prodded and pushed the way excellent editors do, and unfailingly looked after the manuscript, and me.

Finally, I relish having one more occasion to recognize my ongoing obligations to Sheila Rothman. Her work on the history of patienthood (which is at the core of the National Endowment for the Humanities grant that we shared) will appear shortly, and again I was able to

ACKNOWLEDGMENTS

benefit from her knowledge, scholarly standards, and editorial skills. And this time, our children not only tolerated our shop talk but joined in, Matthew drawing on his experiences in photographing emergency medical care in New York City, Micol, on her personal interest in what it means to be a doctor. Put simply, they make it all worthwhile.

INTRODUCTION

Making the Invisible Visible

BEGINNING in the mid-1960s, the practice of medicine in the United States underwent a most remarkable—and thoroughly controversial—transformation. Although the changes have altered almost every aspect of the relationship between doctor and patient—indeed, between medicine and society—the essence can be succinctly summarized: the discretion that the profession once enjoyed has been increasingly circumscribed, with an almost bewildering number of parties and procedures participating in medical decision making. As late as 1969, the philosopher Hans Jonas could assert that "the physician is obligated to the patient and to no one else. . . . We may speak of a sacred trust; strictly by its terms, the doctor is, as it were, alone with his patient and God."[1] But even as he wrote, the image of a physician alone with a patient was being supplanted by one of an examining room so crowded that the physician had difficulty squeezing in and of a patient surrounded by strangers.

Well into the post–World War II period, decisions at the bedside were the almost exclusive concern of the individual physician, even when they raised fundamental ethical and social issues. It was mainly doctors who wrote and read about the morality of withholding a course of antibiotics and letting pneumonia serve as the old man's best friend, of considering a newborn with grave birth defects a "stillbirth" and sparing the parents the agony of choice and the burden of care, of

1

experimenting on the institutionalized retarded to learn more about hepatitis, or of giving one patient and not another access to the iron lung when the machine was in short supply. Moreover, it was usually the individual physician who decided these matters at the bedside or in the privacy of the hospital room, without formal discussions with patients, their families, or even with colleagues, and certainly without drawing the attention of journalists, judges, or professional philosophers. And they made their decisions on a case-by-case basis, responding to the particular circumstances as they saw fit, reluctant by both training and practice to formulate or adhere to guidelines or rules.

By the mid-1970s, both the style and the substance of medical decision making had changed. The authority that an individual physician had once exercised covertly was now subject to debate and review by colleagues and laypeople. Let the physician design a research protocol to deliver an experimental treatment, and in the room, by federal mandate, was an institutional review board composed of other physicians, lawyers, and community representatives to make certain that the potential benefits to the subject-patient outweighed the risks. Let the physician attempt to allocate a scarce resource, like a donor heart, and in the room were federal and state legislators and administrators to help set standards of equity and justice. Let the physician decide to withdraw or terminate life-sustaining treatment from an incompetent patient, and in the room were state judges to rule, in advance, on the legality of these actions. Such a decision might also bring into the room a hospital ethics committee staffed by an unusual cadre of commentators, the bioethicists, who stood ready to replace bedside ethics with armchair ethics, to draw on philosophers' first principles, not on the accumulated experience of medical practice.

Were all these participants not company enough, the physician in the ordinary circumstances of daily practice often encountered a new type of patient, particularly among young and better educated men, and even more frequently, women, who had assimilated a new message: rather than comply dutifully with your doctor's orders, be "alert to your responsibility in the relationship, just as you would in any other adult relationship where you are purchasing services."[2] In the 1950s, popular health care guides had carried such titles as "What to Do Until the Doctor Comes." The updated version might well be called: "What to Do After the Doctor Comes."

Without putting too fine a point on it, the critical period of change was 1966 to 1976. The transformation began when in 1966 a Harvard Medical School professor, Henry Beecher, exposed abuses in human experimentation. Then, in 1973, Congress, under the leadership of senators Walter Mondale and Edward Kennedy, established a national commission to explore medical ethics. The period closed with the New Jersey Supreme Court ordering doctors to yield to parental requests to remove twenty-two-year-old Karen Ann Quinlan from a respirator. The impact of these events, most generally framed, was to make the invisible visible. Outsiders to medicine—that is, lawyers, judges, legislators, and academics—penetrated its every nook and cranny, in the process giving medicine an exceptional prominence on the public agenda and making it the subject of popular discourse. This glare of the spotlight transformed medical decision making, shaping not merely the external conditions under which medicine would be practiced (something that the state, through the regulation of licensure, had always done), but the very substance of medical practice—the decisions that physicians made at the bedside.

The change was first manifested and implemented through a new commitment to collective, as against individual, decision making. There were standing committees to ensure that a researcher who would experiment with human subjects was not making a self-serving calculus of risks and benefits, and standing committees to review whether the physician who would withdraw treatment from a gravely ill newborn or, for that matter, from a terminally ill adult, was not idiosyncratic in his or her calculus of medical futility or judgment about a life not worth living. Second, a new formality came to characterize decision making. Written documentation was replacing word-of-mouth orders (or pencil notations to be erased later), as in the case of coding a patient DNR (do not resuscitate) so that if his heart stopped, the team would not make every last effort (through chemical and electrical stimulation) to revive him. This formality transformed the medical chart from an essentially private means of communication among doctors to a public piece of evidence that documented what the doctor had told, and heard from, the patient. Third, in a more subtle but no less critical

3

fashion, outsiders now framed the normative principles that were to guide the doctor–patient relationship. The critical pronouncements no longer originated in medical texts but in judicial decisions, bioethical treatises, and legislative resolutions. Outsiders, not doctors, defined the moral codes that were to guide physician behavior.

The causes and consequences of these extraordinary changes are the core concerns of this book. How did it happen that physicians, who had once ruled uncontested over their domain, came to confront committees, forms, general principles, and active patients? What were the roots of the idea, not very long ago unheard of, that "there is need to involve not only the medical profession, but lawyers, sociologists, moralists, and society at large" in the effort to resolve "complicated [medical] issues," for "the solutions will come only if society is willing to support the formal investigation by physicians, lawyers, sociologists and moralists"?[3] Why did this line become repeated so often and in such a variety of contexts as to become almost a truism? In a phrase, what brought new rules and new players to medicine?

In answering these questions, it will often be useful to contrast the perspectives and goals of physicians and nonphysicians, or outsiders as I call them. The designations are obviously broad, and for some purposes no doubt too broad. Medical specialists have often differed on policy issues from general practitioners, as anyone familiar with the history of the American Medical Association recognizes. And from 1966 to 1976, physicians were divided (albeit not evenly) among themselves on many of the substantive matters explored in this book. In almost every instance, it was physicians who assumed the role of whistleblowers and invited outsiders in. For example, Henry Beecher, a physician, exposed the abuse of discretion by individual researchers, and physicians such as Raymond Duff and William Bartholome lifted the curtain that surrounded neonatal decision making. But that said, in the debates over ruling medicine, the great majority of physicians who went on record, including the whistle-blowers, were deeply troubled about a loss of doctors' authority at the bedside and the expanded prerogatives of outsiders. The changes that came to medicine generally came over the strenuous objections of doctors, giving the entire process an adversarial quality.

On the other side, the outsiders who entered medicine ranged from lawyers to legislators to religion and philosophy professors. Although one would not have anticipated prior agreement among them on most subjects, they shared a goal of bringing new rules to medicine. Whether drawing on a tradition of predictability (in the law) or of first principles (in philosophy or religion), they joined together to create a new formality and impose it on medicine, insisting on guidelines, regulations, and collective decision making. They concurred on the need to reduce physicians' discretion and enhance patients' autonomy.

Given such disparate views and intentions, a twofold classification of doctors and outsiders makes sense. Although it can mask important distinctions, it helps us capture and explain the essence of a decade-long conflict. It conveys an image of a relatively well drawn battle line—which fits with the contours of the events.

I am also comfortable maintaining an insider–outsider distinction because in 1983 I became Professor of Social Medicine at Columbia's College of Physicians and Surgeons, even as I continued as professor of history in the university. My mandate from the medical school was to bring the methods and materials of the humanities and social sciences into its research and teaching curriculum. In a very personal way, then, I crossed the boundary and entered the world of medicine, in the process coming to appreciate just how different a world it is.

My assignment has been both exciting and difficult. Medicine has its own language, and it was disconcerting, almost humiliating, to arrive and listen to a group of twenty-six-year-olds carry on a conversation I could barely understand. "Dropping a crit," "flipping t waves," and "running v tach" were actions whose significance I neither recognized nor appreciated. Medicine also has its own brand of shoptalk; as I describe later, a first exposure to the "interesting case"—almost certain to involve devastating disease for the patient and many unknowns for the physician—was, even for someone who had investigated institutions for the retarded and prisons, emotionally draining and often too painful to share, at least with nonphysicians. But these experiences taught me firsthand that illness is highly segregated in this society, as are those who treat it.

I was struck again and again by the vast ignorance of colleagues and friends about the world of medicine. Although I was accustomed to exploring institutions that were sealed off from the general public, I had not imagined that hospitals belonged in this category. I was frequently asked questions that revealed a startling degree of distance and unfamiliarity: "Is an operating room really a theater, with rows of seats going up?" (No) "Do surgeons bring tape decks with them?" (Sometimes) "What do you wear on rounds?" (A suit, not a white coat)—and on and on, as though my questioners had never been inside a hospital or spoken to a doctor outside of an examining room. Of course, they had read all about respirators, transplants, and other high-technology interventions. But what they lacked was a feel for the enterprise, a sense of the actors and the routines. To judge from their reactions, I was a throwback to the anthropologists of the 1920s, an explorer of foreign parts, as though 168th Street in northern Manhattan was at one with the South Seas.

In truth, I sometimes shared this sensation. Surprise was, and remains, a constant feature of going on rounds. At one of my first sessions, I was startled to hear a resident inform a senior physician, just before we entered a patient's room, that the patient had "died" yesterday, but after having had his medications adjusted, was doing much better. Later that morning she related that another patient was making good progress: he had not "died" even once, and she was confident about his prospects. Surely I was on a magic island if death was reversible and resurrection commonplace. And even after I learned that to "die" was to suffer a cardiac arrest and undergo resuscitation, not all of the sense of mystery disappeared.

I was also unprepared for the grueling and continuous pace of medical practice, a pace that helps isolate physicians in their own universe. The day starts early (seven o'clock meetings are not uncommon), and ends late; one female physician confessed to me that she considered herself only part-time because family responsibilities (raising three children) allowed her to work only a forty-hour week. And time not devoted to practice or teaching is often spent keeping pace with the latest research findings in the medical journals; nothing is more common on rounds than for attending physicians or house staff to cite a recent article on the advantages and disadvantages of a particular drug or procedure. The physicians are alert to numbers, and findings from random clinical trials carry critical authority. But numbers alone do not rule, which brings us back to the issues at hand in the control of medicine.

Perhaps the most remarkable feature of clinical decision making is the extraordinary reliance on a case-by-case approach. No two patients, after all, are exactly alike; symptoms do not appear in the same pattern in the course of disease, and the results of tests do not always fall unambiguously into one category or another. Thus, medicine is as much art as science, and the clinical anecdote becomes highly relevant to treatment decisions. Because of uncertainty, clinicians value experience highly and are prepared to make decisions on the basis of a trial of one—that is, a patient treated some ten years ago whose case resembles the one today and who improved on a particular regimen. It is this resort to the anecdote that gives physicians the air of artists, even of magicians. In the face of confusing and contradictory symptoms, physicians can pull from a hat some case from the past and make their recommendation, often leading to the patient's recovery, albeit a baffling one.

Physicians, as I have learned, frequently bring this case-by-case approach into the consideration of social and ethical issues. Offer them a principle to consider (for example, that patients have the right to know their diagnosis), and they will often come up with a case (drawn from experience) that they believe undercuts and thereby negates the principle (for instance, the seeming inappropriateness of informing a seventy-five-year-old woman about to go off to her grandchild's wedding that she has an inoperable and slow-growing brain tumor). Describe a case in the ethics of decision making at the end of life that occurred at another hospital, and the physicians initially will try to obviate the problem by claiming that those doctors made egregious errors in their treatment (for example, this patient should never have needed a respirator in the first place). It is as though their ability to resolve the incident at hand absolves them of the need to formulate or respect general principles. If they can cite a case in which the proposed rule does not hold, then they have ostensibly discredited not only the rule but the search for rules. In short, clinicians start with the case at hand, and if they have their way, stop with the case at hand.

Outsiders from various disciplines seem far more prepared to seek out the general principle in deciding social and ethical questions. A legal, as opposed to medical, mind-set is much more likely to search for the rule that should be imposed on a particular case than to see how the case can be resolved without it. Those trained in history or in other disciplines in the humanities and social sciences share this orientation. The end point is not the individual case but the light it can shed on general phenomena. In history this often prompts an impatience with biography, at least to the degree that it invokes the details of one person's life that are irrelevant to the larger social or political context. Medicine, by contrast, is closer to biography than to history, or to put this point in medicine's language, to the case history. Most of what physicians write for lay audiences, whether it is a neurologist on aphasia or a surgeon on transplants, follows this pattern—focusing on the one exciting case, or a series of cases, and letting the one instance represent all.

Clinicians appear to be as uncomfortable with sociological analyses of the collective aspects of medical decision making and the structural underpinnings of medical institutions as they are with the humanists' search for general principles. Consider, for example, the case of infants who are being treated even when the overwhelming majority of physicians and nurses do not believe treatment should continue. Tell the head of a neonatal unit that such practices persist not because of some error or breakdown in communication but because of a collective ethos that is protreatment; explain that this structural element, not the particulars of each case, is probably shaping the treatment decision, and you probably will hear a firm denial that such a process could occur. The very idea that some underlying mechanisms might constrain or dictate action is altogether alien to a perspective that insists that each case is, and must be, considered on its own merits.[4]

This perspective is transmitted from one generation of physicians to the other, not in so many words but in the very organization of medical school education. In clinical teaching the case approach is sacrosanct, and anyone who would bring social and ethical issues into the curriculum must adopt the same style. To begin with the general (What does "patient autonomy" mean?) and then move down to the particular (What are the implications for terminating treatment?) is to lose one's audience at the outset. Rather, one must start with the particular, with the specifics of a case and hope (distractions fielded) that one gets to the general point. In fact, many medical schools long resisted the formal teaching of ethics, not because they believed that ethics could not be taught, but because it had to be taught at the bedside, by starting with the individual case. This type of approach, which I call *bedside ethics*, essentially meant teaching by example, by role modeling, by students taking cues from practicing physicians. Students were not to learn ethics by studying principles but by watching senior physicians resolve individual situations and then doing likewise. It is as though medical decision making begins and ends (or more precisely, should begin and end) with the dyad of the doctor and the patient alone in the examining room.

These biographical details and disciplinary outlooks help explain my approach in this book. They suggest, first, how alien rules are to medical decision making and how dogged and persistent an effort to alter this orientation would have to be. Second, although a doctor–outsider distinction may seem rudimentary, both scholarship and experience have persuaded me how real and powerful it is—so much so that in some ways this book represents my attempt to understand why a medical school would ask me (and the requests now extend, obviously, to many others) to cross over and enter its domain.

Perhaps most important, these observations make clear that from the start my own predilection strongly favored bringing rules to medicine. What I did not, however, fully appreciate at the outset was that by 1983 many of the critical battles had already been fought and a number of victories won. Thus, I immediately became a member of the institutional review board to oversee the conduct of human experimentation; I helped the medical director of the neonatal unit organize a bioethics committee, on which I took a seat; I helped a team of physicians who were conducting in vitro fertilization set up guidelines; and I sat with the heart transplant team as they pondered procedures for selecting recipients. Of course, I and the other committee members encountered resistance from colleagues. But it soon became apparent to me that what was needed most was not an insistence on bringing rules to medicine but a careful analysis of how the transformation in medical decision making had occurred.

• • •

9

The causes of this sweeping transformation are as far-reaching as its implications. To understand the origins and outcomes of the disputes over ruling medicine requires tracing developments within both medicine and society, a reckoning that takes into account physician behavior and more diffuse public attitudes. For in many ways, the conflicts come down to an erosion in trust, to a decline in the deference given to doctors and to their professional judgments. To grapple with such delicate and elusive sentiments as trust and deference requires scrutinizing both sides of a relationship—what doctors did and what outsiders did—to make traditional ties and procedures seem inadequate and obsolete.

Surprisingly, the story opens in the laboratory, not the examining room. A series of exposés of practices in human experimentation revealed a stark conflict of interest between clinical investigators and human subjects, between researchers' ambitions and patients' well-being. This perception undercut an older confidence in the exercise of medical discretion and gave the regulation of clinical research a special prominence on the public agenda. The ethics of experimentation attracted the concern not only of those within medicine (particularly at the National Institutes of Health and the Food and Drug Administration), but an array of outsiders, most notably politicians and academics (law professors, philosophers, and sociologists), who had previously paid scant attention to medical issues. In fact, the agitation over human experimentation quickly became linked to the rights movements that were gaining strength in the 1960s, largely because the great majority of research subjects were minorities, drawn from the ranks of the poor, the mentally disabled, and the incarcerated. This linkage ensured that the rights of research subjects (or, conversely, the felt need to restrict the discretion of the researcher) would not only capture but hold public attention.

The result was an entirely new system of governance for human experimentation. Federal regulations required mechanisms for collective decision making, thereby abridging the once considerable freedom of the investigator. No less important, human experimentation gave an entirely new weight to the idea of consent, to making certain that the subject understood the nature of the experiment and voluntarily agreed to participate. This unprecedented reliance on the mechanism of consent reflected not so much an abstract commitment to the importance of the principle of consent as a deeply felt need to protect vulnerable individuals from single-minded, overeager investigators.

Attitudes and practices initially formulated to cope with laboratory practices, quickly, if unpredictably, spread to bedside practices, and understanding the dynamics will take us through the second half of this book. The analysis begins with the altered social position of medicine in the post–World War II decades, with the fact that the doctor became a stranger and the hospital a strange place. As the social distance between doctor and patient, and between hospital and community, enlarged, a sense of trust eroded. When one could no longer assume that the physician shared the same set of values as the patient, it seemed vital to devise and implement new mechanisms, preferably formal or even rigid, to further patients' particular wishes. It became appropriate to post on hospital walls a copy of the Patient Bill of Rights, as though the facility were a factory and its users, rank-and-file labor. Even more notably, as doctor and hospital moved apart from patient and community, the practical wisdom that the practitioner had accumulated over years of clinical experience seemed less impressive and relevant than the wisdom that the philosopher or lawyer had accumulated through the study of first principles. In effect, bedside ethics gave way to bioethics.

The impact of these structural changes was intensified and propelled forward by a series of extraordinary innovations in medical practice. Almost immediately upon the heels of the exposés in human experimentation came the breakthrough in organ transplantation, first with kidneys and then most dramatically, in 1968, with hearts. Transplantation appeared to put the physician, like the researcher, in a position of conflict of interest with the patient. Taking a heart from one desperately ill patient to give to another raised the frightening prospect that a physician eager to save one life might sacrifice another. Transplantation also raised troubling questions about how best to distribute scarce resources—conventional wisdom on triage was no help—and prompted a Harvard committee, made up mostly of physicians, to attempt, unilaterally, to redefine the criterion for death by making the brain, not the heart, the determining organ. Every one of these issues swelled the ranks of outsiders who became concerned with medicine, to the point that Congress created a national commission—dominated by lay, not medical, members—to explore, first, the ethics of human experimentation and, later, all of medical ethics. And every one of these issues made it seem all the more necessary to bring collective and formal procedures to medical decision making, reinforcing the growing sense that medical decisions should not be left to the discretion of individual physicians.

The story culminated in a newborn nursery and an adult intensive care unit: Beginning with the death of a retarded newborn at the Johns Hopkins University Hospital because his parents refused to permit life-saving surgery and reaching it apogee in the case of Karen Ann Quinlan, perhaps the most famous patient in recent medical history, the license to decide questions of life and death shifted from the profession to the polity, from the hidden recesses of the hospital intensive care unit and one of medicine's best-guarded secrets to the open courtroom and everyday conversation. After Quinlan, medical decision making became the province of a collection of strangers, with judges, lawyers, ethicists, and legislators joining doctors at their patients' bedside.

As would be expected, these developments have generated many polemics, evenly divided between laypeople denouncing medical arrogance for not letting Grandma die a peaceful and quick death, and physicians complaining that the new rules undercut the delivery of good medical care and force them to badger dying patients with unnecessary questions. Consumer newsletters urge patients to assert themselves, and medical newsletters run banner headlines proclaiming that "OUTSIDERS SHOULD STAY OUT OF MEDICINE." Nostalgia mixes with anger and recriminations: Where is yesterday's family doctor? Where is yesterday's grateful patient?

The changes have also produced a more substantial body of analysis, most of it focusing on medical economics and medical technologies. Ostensibly, new rules came to medicine because care was too expensive and physicians too powerful. That both these considerations are important is beyond dispute; some regulatory measures were bound to be imposed on medicine when the bill for national health care skyrocketed from $19 billion in 1960 to $275 billion by 1980 (and on to $365 billion and 10 percent of the gross national product by 1985). It is not surprising to find the federal government—in an effort to control Medicare costs—empowering review committees to disallow reimbursements for unnecessary, long hospital stays, and to find corporations—attempting to limit expenditures on fringe benefits—insisting on the right to review recommendations to treat an employee. By the same token, technological advances have been so heady that many outsiders have deep fears (and fantasies) about their abuse. When respirators and dialysis machines could keep the dying alive for weeks, months, or years, there was bound to be widespread concern about medicine doing more than anyone might want it to do.

But neither economics nor technology required so basic a reordering of the balance between doctor and patient. There is no iron clad formula dictating what percentage of resources an advanced industrial society should devote to health care; and were the totality of the story cost containment, there would have been no reason to create oversight committees for research or to formalize DNR procedures. So too, had other considerations not intervened, one could imagine trusting the expert in the technology to determine the appropriate use of the technology. Why not let those who understand the mechanics of respiration decide when to connect or disconnect the respirator? Why not let those who are able to defy death be the ones to define death? In short, costs and technology are highly relevant to the new posture toward medicine and medical decision making, but they alone cannot explain it. Indeed, an erosion of trust may well have been a precondition for economic and technological regulation. It was because doctors were strangers that they could not be trusted with the respirator. It was because hospitals were strange institutions that their costs and practices had to be monitored.

To present the history of a change is inevitably to raise questions on the merits of the change. Was the cure worse than the disease? Did bringing new rules to medicine prove more mischievous than helpful? In the following pages I frame initial answers to these questions— although perhaps not as directly and unequivocally as some might hope. Still, to understand the elements that propelled the movement forward is to come away, I believe, convinced of its necessity and validity, albeit with significant qualifications and concerns.

One final caution: The history traced here is an ongoing one, and judgments about intended and unintended consequences are bound to be premature. The field of medicine is now buffeted by the winds of change—let one issue float up, and it is immediately blown away by yet another issue. For a time, all that anyone wanted to talk about were the new federal reimbursement formulas ("Is There Life after DRGs?" was the title of one lecture). Then the concern shifted to quality control (Can patient care and hospital budgets survive interns getting a full night's sleep?), and then focused on the treatment of AIDS (What degree of risk should a physician be required to accept? How far should AIDS patients be allowed to go in choosing their own drug regimens?). Each issue prompted the call for new rules, committees, and guidelines, and each has brought still more participants (from data retrieval specialists to AIDS activists) into medicine. Thus, it is much too early to offer final verdicts, but not too early to remember just how recently medicine and medical decision making became so central a subject in public and policy discourse. I can only hope, as do many other historians, that an analysis of the origins of a change can help us—doctors, patients, and citizens alike—to direct and enhance the change.

CHAPTER 1

The Nobility of the Material

C HANGE began with a whistle-blower and a scandal.

In June 1966, Henry Beecher, Dorr Professor of Research in Anesthesia at Harvard Medical School, published in the *New England Journal of Medicine (NEJM)* his analysis of "Ethics and Clinical Research" and thereby joined the ranks of such noted muckrakers as Harriet Beecher Stowe, Upton Sinclair, and Rachael Carson.[1] As has so often happened in the course of American history, a publication like *Uncle Tom's Cabin, The Jungle,* or *Silent Spring* will expose a secret—whether it be the violation of the slave family, the contamination of food, or the poisoning of the environment—so compellingly as to transform public attitudes and policy. Beecher's article fits in this tradition. Its devastating indictment of research ethics helped inspire the movement that brought a new set of rules and a new set of players to medical decision making.[2]

The piece was short, barely six double-columned pages, and the writing terse and technical, primarily aimed at a professional, not a lay, audience. Beecher tried (not altogether successfully) to maintain a tone of detachment, as though this were a scientific paper like any other. "I want to be very sure," he insisted, "that I have squeezed out of it all emotion, value judgments, and so on."[3] Even so, its publication created a furor both inside and outside the medical profession.

At its heart were capsule descriptions of twenty-two examples of

15

investigators who had risked "the health or the life of their subjects" without informing them of the dangers or obtaining their permission. No citations to the original publications or names of the researchers appeared. Beecher did give the editors of the *NEJM* a fully annotated copy, and they vouched for its accuracy; he steadfastly refused all subsequent requests for references. Publicly, he declared that his intention was not to single out individuals but to "call attention to widespread practices." Privately, he conceded that a colleague from the Harvard Law School had advised him that to name names might open the individuals to lawsuits or criminal prosecution.[4]

The research protocols that made up Beecher's roll of dishonor seemed flagrant in their disregard of the welfare of the human subjects. Example 2 constituted the purposeful withholding of penicillin from servicemen with streptococcal infections in order to study alternative means for preventing complications. The men were totally unaware of the fact that they were part of an experiment, let alone at risk of contracting rheumatic fever, which twenty-five of them did. Example 16 involved the feeding of live hepatitis viruses to residents of a state institution for the retarded in order to study the etiology of the disease and attempt to create a protective vaccine against it. In example 17, physicians injected live cancer cells into twenty-two elderly and senile hospitalized patients without telling them that the cells were cancerous, in order to study the body's immunological responses. Example 19 involved researchers who inserted a special needle into the left atrium of the heart of subjects, some with cardiac disease and others normal, in order to study the functioning of the heart. In example 22, researchers inserted a catheter into the bladder of twenty-six newborns less than forty-eight hours old and then took a series of X rays of the bladders filling and voiding in order to study the process. "Fortunately," noted Beecher, "no infection followed the catheterization. What the results of the extensive x-ray exposure may be, no one can yet say."

Beecher's most significant, and predictably most controversial, conclusion was that "unethical or questionably ethical procedures are not uncommon" among researchers—that is, a disregard for the rights of human subjects was widespread. Although he did not provide footnotes, Beecher declared that "the troubling practices" came from "leading medical schools, university hospitals, private hospitals, governmental military departments ... governmental institutes (the National Institutes of Health), Veterans Administration Hospitals and industry." In short, "the basis for the charges is broad." Moreover, without attempting any numerical estimate of just how endemic the practices were among researchers, Beecher reported how dismayingly easy it had been for him to compile his list. An initial list of seventeen examples had been easily expanded to fifty (and winnowed down to twenty-two for publication). He had also examined 100 consecutive studies that were reported on in 1964 "in an excellent journal; 12 of these seemed unethical." He concluded, "If only one quarter of them is truly unethical, this still indicates the existence of a serious problem."

At a time when the media were not yet scouring medical journals for stories, Beecher's charges captured an extraordinary amount of public attention. Accounts of the *NEJM* article appeared in the leading newspapers and weeklies, which was precisely what he had intended. A circumspect whistle-blower, he had published his findings first in a medical journal without naming names; but at the same time, he had informed influential publications (including the *New York Times*, the *Wall Street Journal*, *Time*, and *Newsweek*) that his piece was forthcoming. The press reported the experiments in great detail, and reporters, readers, and public officials alike expressed dismay and incredulity as they pondered what had led respectable scientists to commit such acts. How could researchers have injected cancer cells into hospitalized senile people or fed hepatitis viruses to institutionalized retarded children? In short order, the National Institutes of Health (NIH), the major funder of research in the country, was getting letters from legislators asking what corrective actions it intended to take.[5]

Beecher, as he fully expected, infuriated many of his colleagues, and they responded angrily and defensively. Some, like Thomas Chalmers at Harvard, insisted that he had grossly exaggerated the problem, taking a few instances and magnifying them out of proportion.[6] The more popular objection (which can still be heard among investigators today) was that he had unfairly assessed 1950s practices in terms of the moral standards of a later era. To these critics, the investigators that Beecher had singled out were pioneers, working before standards were set for human investigation, before it was considered necessary to inform subjects about the research and obtain their formal consent to participation. The enterprise of human investigation was so novel that research ethics had been necessarily primitive and underdeveloped.

However popular—and, on the surface, appealing—that retort is, it not only fails to address the disjuncture between public expectations and researchers' behavior but is woefully short on historical perspective. If the activity was so new and the state of ethics so crude, why did outsiders shudder as they read about the experiments? However tempting it might be to short-circuit the history, neither human experimentation nor the ethics of it was a recent invention. Still, Beecher's critics were not altogether misguided: there was something substantially different about the post–World War II laboratories and investigators. If researchers were not as morally naïve as their defenders would suggest, they occupied a very special position in time. They had inherited a unique legacy, bequeathed to them by the World War II experience.

Thus, for many reasons, it is important that we trace, however briefly, this history, particularly in its most recent phases. In no other way can we understand how investigators could have designed and conducted the trials that made up Beecher's roster. And in no other way can we understand the gap between the investigators' behavior and public expectation, a gap that would produce not only wariness and distrust but also new mechanisms for governing clinical research. These attitudes and mechanisms spread, more quickly than might have been anticipated, from the laboratory to the examining room. A reluctance to trust researchers to protect the well-being of their subjects soon turned into an unwillingness to trust physicians to protect the well-being of their patients. In the new rules for research were the origins of the new rules for medicine.

Until World War II, the research enterprise was typically small-scale and intimate, guided by an ethic consistent with community expectations.[7] Most research was a cottage industry: a few physicians, working alone, carried out experiments on themselves, their families, and their immediate neighbors. Moreover, the research was almost always therapeutic in intent; that is, the subjects stood to benefit directly if the experiments were successful. Under these circumstances, the ethics of human investigation did not command much attention; a few scientists, like Claude Bernard and Louis Pasteur, set forth especially thoughtful and elegant analyses. But for the most part, the small scale and poten-tially therapeutic character of the research seemed protection enough, and researchers were left to their own conscience, with almost no effort to police them. To be sure, not everyone's behavior matched the stan-dard or lived up to expectations. By the 1890s, and even more fre-quently in the opening decades of the twentieth century, some investigators could not resist experimenting on unknown and unknow-ing populations, particularly inmates of orphanages and state schools for the retarded. But at least before World War II such practices were relatively infrequent.

The idea of judging the usefulness of a particular medication by actual results goes back to a school of Greek and Roman empiricists, but we know little about how they made their judgments and whether they actually conducted experiments on human beings. The medieval Arab medical treatises, building on classical texts, reflect an apprecia-tion of the need for human experiments, but again the record is thin on practice. Scholars like the renowned Islamic scientist and philoso-pher Avicenna (980–1037) recommended that a drug be applied to two different cases to measure its efficacy, and he also insisted that "the experimentation must be done with the human body, for testing a drug on a lion or a horse might not prove anything about its effect on man." However, he offered no guidance about how or on whom such experiments should be conducted.[8]

If earlier practices remain obscure, a number of ethical maxims about experimentation do survive. Maimonides (1125–1204), a noted Jewish physician and philosopher, counseled colleagues always to treat pa-tients as ends in themselves, not as means for learning new truths. A fuller treatment of research ethics came from the English philosopher and scientist Roger Bacon (1214–1292). He excused the inconsisten-cies in therapeutic practices among contemporary physicians on the following grounds: "It is exceedingly difficult and dangerous to per-form operations on the human body, wherefore it is more difficult to work in that science than in any other. . . . The operative and practical sciences which do their work on insensate bodies can multiply their experiments till they get rid of deficiency and errors, but a physician cannot do this because of the nobility of the material in which he works; for that body demands that no error be made in operating upon

it, and so experience [the experimental method] is so difficult in medicine."[9] To Bacon the trade-off was worth making: the human body
was so noble a material that therapeutics would have to suffer deficiencies and errors.

Human experimentation made its first significant impact on medical
knowledge in the eighteenth century, primarily through the work of
the English physician Edward Jenner, and his research on a vaccination
against smallpox exemplifies both the style and technique that would
predominate for the next 150 years. Observing that farmhands who
contracted the pox from swine or cows seemed to be immune to the
more virulent smallpox, Jenner set out to retrieve material from their
pustules, inject that into another person, and see whether the recipient
could then resist challenges from small amounts of smallpox materials.
In November 1789 he carried out his first experiment, inoculating his
oldest son, then about a year old, with swinepox. Although the child
suffered no ill effects, the smallpox material he then received did produce an irritation, indicating that he was not immune to the disease.[10]

Jenner subsequently decided to work with cowpox material. In his
most famous and successful experiment, he vaccinated an eight-year-
old boy with it, a week later challenged him with smallpox material,
and noted that he evinced no reaction. No record exists on the interaction between Jenner and his subject save Jenner's bare account: "The
more accurately to observe the progress of the infection, I selected a
healthy boy, about eight years old, for the purpose of inoculation for
the cow-pox. The matter . . . was inserted . . . into the arm of the boy
by means of two incisions."[11] Whether the boy was a willing or unwilling subject, how much he understood of the experiment, what kind
of risk–benefit calculation he might have made, or whether his parents
simply ordered him to put out his arm to please Mr. Jenner remains
unknown. Clearly, Jenner did the choosing, but do note the odd change
in style from the active "I selected" to the passive "the matter was . . .
inserted." All we can tell for certain is that the boy was from the
neighborhood, that Jenner was a man of standing, that he chose the
boy for the experiment, and that smallpox was a dreaded disease. Still,
some degree of trust probably existed between researcher and subject,
or subject's parents. This was not an interaction between strangers, and
Jenner would have been accountable had anything untoward happened.

Word of Jenner's success spread quickly, and in September 1799 he received a letter from a physician in Vienna who had managed to obtain some vaccine for his own use. His first subject, he told Jenner, was "the son of a physician in this town." Then, encouraged by his initial success, he reported, "I did not hesitate to inoculate . . . my eldest boy, and ten days afterwards my second boy." In this same spirit, Dr. Benjamin Waterhouse, professor of medicine at Harvard, learned of Jenner's work and vaccinated seven of his children; then, in order to test for the efficacy of the procedure, he exposed three of them to the disease at Boston's Smallpox Hospital, with no ill effects. Here again, colleagues and family were the first to share in the risks and benefits of research.[12]

Even in the premodern era, neighbors and relations were not the only subjects of research. Legends tell of ancient and medieval rulers who tested the efficacy of poison potions on condemned prisoners and released those who survived. Much better documented is the example of Lady Mary Wortley Montagu, wife of the British ambassador to Turkey, who learned about Turkish successes in inoculating patients with small amounts of the smallpox material to provide immunity. Eager to convince English physicians to adopt the procedure, she persuaded King George I to run a trial by pardoning any condemned inmate at the Newgate Prison who agreed to the inoculation. In August 1721, six volunteers were inoculated; they developed local lesions but no serious illness, and all were released. As science went, the trial was hardly satisfactory and the ethics were no better—the choice between death or enrollment in the experiment was not a freely made one. But such ventures remained the exception.[13]

For most of the nineteenth century, research continued on a small scale, with individual physicians trying out one or another remedy or procedure on a handful of persons. Experimentation still began at home, on the body of the investigator or on neighbors or relatives. One European physician, Johann Jorg, swallowed varying doses of seventeen different drugs in order to analyze their effects; another, James Simpson, searching for an anesthesia superior to ether, inhaled chloroform and awoke to find himself lying flat on the floor.[14] In what is surely the most extraordinary moment in nineteenth-century human experiments, Dr. William Beaumont conducted his famous studies on "The

Physiology of Digestion" on the healed stomach wound of Alexis St. Martin. There was a signed agreement between them, though not so much a consent form (as some historians have suggested) as an apprenticeship contract; but even this form testified to the need for investigators to obtain the agreement of their subjects. St. Martin bound himself for a term of one year to "serve, abide, and continue with the said William Beaumont . . . [as] his covenant servant"; and in return for board, lodging, and $150 a year, he agreed "to assist and promote by all means in his power such philosophical or medical experiments as the said William shall direct or cause to be made on or in the stomach of him."[15]

The most brilliant researcher of the century, Louis Pasteur, demonstrates even more vividly just how sensitive investigators could be to the dilemmas inherent in human experimentation. As he conducted laboratory and animal research to find an antidote to rabies, he worried about the time when it would be necessary to test the results on people. In fall 1884 he wrote to a patron deeply interested in his work: "I have already several cases of dogs immunized after rabic bites. I take two dogs: I have them bitten by a mad dog. I vaccinate the one and I leave the other without treatment. The latter dies of rabies: the former withstands it." Nevertheless, Pasteur continued, "I have not yet dared to attempt anything on man, in spite of my confidence in the result. . . . I must wait first till I have got a whole crowd of successful results on animals. . . . But, however I should multiply my cases of protection of dogs, I think that my hand will shake when I have to go on to man."[16]

The fateful moment came some nine months later when there appeared at his laboratory door a mother with her nine-year-old son, Joseph Meister, who two days earlier had been bitten fourteen times by what was probably a mad dog. Pasteur agonized over the decision as to whether to conduct what would be the first human trial of his rabies inoculation; he consulted with two medical colleagues and had them examine the boy. Finally, he reported, on the grounds that "the death of the child appeared inevitable, I resolved, though not without great anxiety, to try the method which had proved consistently successful on the dogs." By all accounts, Pasteur passed several harrowing weeks as he oversaw the administration of twelve inoculations to the boy. ("Your father," Madam Pasteur wrote her children, "has had another bad night; he is dreading the last inoculations on the child. And yet there can be no drawing back now.") By mid-August, Pasteur relaxed, "confident of the future health of Joseph Meister" and the validity of his findings.[17] The extraordinary caution with which Pasteur approached human experimentation, even when it might save a life, was a standard that not all of his successors would maintain.[18]

The most significant formulation of research ethics in the nineteenth century was the work of Claude Bernard, professor of medicine at the College of France. Bernard conducted pioneering research in physiology, discovering, among other things, the essential role of glycogen in fueling muscle movement. In addition, he composed an exceptionally astute treatise on the methods of experimentation, including the ethics of experimentation. Fully cognizant of and generally comfortable with the traditions in human experimentation—"morals do not forbid making experiments on one's neighbor or one's self"—Bernard set down the maxim that he believed should guide practices: "The principle of medical and surgical morality," he wrote in 1865, "consists in never performing on man an experiment which might be harmful to him to any extent, even though the result might be highly advantageous to science, i.e., to the health of others." To be sure, Bernard did allow some exceptions; he sanctioned experimentation on dying patients, including feeding a condemned woman larvae of intestinal worms without her knowledge to learn whether the worms developed in her intestines after her death. "As experiments of this kind are of great interest to science and can be conclusive only on man, they seem to be wholly permissible when they involve no suffering or harm to the subject of the experiment." But Bernard made eminently clear that scientific progress did not justify violating the well-being of any individual.[19]

Bernard's writing is so celebrated today—his maxims have undoubtedly been repeated more often in the past 20 years than in the prior 100—that it is particularly important to affirm that he was not unique among contemporaries in voicing or acting on such sentiments. Let one obscure example suffice. In 1866, J. H. Salisbury, an American professor of physiology, was eager to test a theory that linked malarial fever to vapors arising from stagnant pools, swamps, and humid low grounds. (He was correct in associating such settings with malaria; his mistake was making vapors, rather than mosquitoes, the agent that spread the disease.) Accordingly, he filled six tin boxes with "decidedly malarious dying prairie bog, transported them to a district some five miles away from the malaria area, and placed them on the sill of an open second-story window of the bedroom of two young men." He instructed them to keep the box on the sill and the window open. On the twelfth and fourteenth days of the experiment one and then the other of the men came down with the fever; Salisbury repeated the experiment a second time with three more young men, and two of them contracted the fever. Although he wanted very much to continue, he stopped his research: "On account of . . . the difficulty of obtaining the consent of parties for experiments, I have been unable to conduct this part of the examination further." Clearly, the neighbors were convinced that the odors from his box caused malaria, and they would no longer consent to put themselves at risk—a judgment that Salisbury understood and did not attempt to subvert.[20]

In fact, by the nineteenth century, common law recognized both the vital role of human experimentation and the need for physicians to obtain patients' consent. As one English commentator explained in 1830: "By experiments we are not . . . speaking of the wild and dangerous practices of rash and ignorant practitioners . . . but of deliberate acts of men from considerable knowledge and undoubted talent, differing from those prescribed by the ordinary rules of practice, for which they have good reason . . . to believe will attend to the benefit of the patient, although the novelty of the undertaking does not leave the result altogether free of doubt." The researcher who had consent was "answerable neither in damages to the individual, nor on a criminal proceeding. But if the practitioner performs his experiment without giving such information to, and obtaining the consent of his patient, he is liable to compensate in damages any injury which may arise from his adopting a new method of treatment."[21] In short, the law distinguished carefully between quackery and innovation; and so long as the investigator had obtained the agreement of the subject, research was a legitimate, protected activity.

With the new understanding of germ theory in the 1890s and the growing professionalization of medical training and research in the 1900s, the sheer amount of human experimentation increased. Clinical trials of new therapeutic agents became much more frequent, even before the 1935 introduction of sulfonamides. Over this period, the intimate link between investigators and subjects weakened, although the relatively small scale and essentially therapeutic character of the research continued.

Subjects were now more likely to be a group of patients in a particular hospital rather than neighbors or kin. Physicians administered a new drug to a group of sick patients and compared their rates of recovery with past rates among similar patients or with those of other patients who did not have the drug. (Random and blind clinical trials, wherein a variety of patient characteristics are carefully matched and where researchers are purposely kept ignorant of which patient receives a new drug, were still in the future.) Thus, in Germany physicians tested antidiphtheria serum on thirty hospitalized patients and reported that only six died, compared to the previous year at the same hospital when twenty-one or thirty-two died.[22] In Canada, Banting and Best experimented with insulin therapy on diabetic patients who faced imminent death, and took recovery as clear proof of the treatment's efficacy.[23] So too, Minot and Murphy tested the value of a liver preparation against pernicious anemia by administering it to forty-five patients in remission, who all remained healthy so long as they took the treatment. The normal relapse rate was one-third, and three patients who stopped treatment on their own accord relapsed.[24] It is doubtful that many of these subjects received full information about the nature of the trial or formally consented to participate. But they probably were willing subjects, ready to gamble, even if they understood neither the odds nor the nature of the game, since the research had therapeutic potential and they were in acute distress or danger.

As medicine became more scientific, some researchers did skirt the boundaries of ethical behavior in experimentation and started elevating medical progress over the subject's welfare. But often as not, hostile public reactions made clear that they were perilously close to violating the norms. Probably the most famous experiment in this zone of ambiguity was the yellow fever work of the American army surgeon Walter Reed. In some ways, he demonstrated a genuine sensitivity to the ethics of experimentation; in other ways, he anticipated all too clearly the abuses that were to follow.

Reed's goal was to identify the source of transmission of yellow fever, which was taking a terrible toll among North and South Americans. When he began his experiments, mosquitoes had been identified as crucial to the transmission, but their precise role was still unclear. "Personally," Reed wrote from Cuba, "I feel that only can experimentation on human beings serve to clear the field for further effective work."[25] In time-honored tradition, members of the research team first subjected themselves to the mosquito bites; but it soon became apparent that larger numbers of volunteers were needed, and the team adopted a pull-them-off-the-road approach. No sooner was the decision made to use volunteers than a soldier happened by. "You still fooling with mosquitoes?" he asked one of the doctors. "Yes," the doctor replied. "Will you take a bite?" "Sure, I ain't scared of 'em," responded the man. And with this feeble effort to inform a subject about the nature of the experiment, "the first indubitable case of yellow fever . . . to be produced experimentally" occurred.[26]

As Reed's project came to rely on growing numbers of human subjects, its procedures became more formal. After two of the team's members died of yellow fever from purposeful bites, the rest, who had not yet contracted the disease, including Reed himself, decided "not to tempt fate by trying any more [infections] upon ourselves. . . . We felt we had been called upon to accomplish such work as did not justify our taking risks which then seemed really unnecessary." Instead, Reed asked American servicemen to volunteer, which some did. He also recruited Spanish workers, drawing up a contract with them: "The undersigned understands perfectly well that in the case of the development of yellow fever in him, that he endangers his life to a certain extent but it being entirely impossible for him to avoid the infection during his stay on this island he prefers to take the chance of contracting it intentionally in the belief that he will receive . . . the greatest care and most skillful medical service." Volunteers received $100 in gold, and those who actually contracted yellow fever received a bonus of an additional $100, which, in the event of their death, went to their heirs.[27]

Reed's contract was traditional in its effort to justify the research by citing benefits for the subjects—better to be sick under Reed's care than left to one's own devices. But the contract was also innovative, in that intimacy gave way to a formal arrangement that provided an enticement to undertake a hazardous assignment, and the explanation in subtle ways distorted the risks and benefits of the experiment. Yellow fever endangered life only "to a certain extent"; the likelihood that the disease might prove fatal was unmentioned. So too, the probability of contracting yellow fever outside of the experiment was presented as an absolute certainty, an exaggeration to promote subject recruitment.

Although the press had no knowledge of the contract, it did keep an eye on the research, prepared to render judgments about appropriate risks and benefits. Just how uneasy journalists were with nontherapeutic research protocols is evident from the headlines that local Cuban newspapers ran about Reed's work. "HORRIBLE IF TRUE!" declared one of them, and the accompanying story reported on "a rumor ... so horrible" about Spanish immigrants being shut up at night in special quarters into which "are released a large number of mosquitos who have bitten individuals suffering from yellow fever. . . . If the workman is taken sick and dies the experiment has demonstrated its effectiveness." Such research, the article concluded, constituted "the most monstrous case of humanitarian ... savagery which we have been witness to." Even more notable, after Reed and his team, but not all other investigators, were convinced that the mosquito was the agent that transmitted yellow fever, some of Reed's colleagues wanted to continue the experiments in order to identify the dangerous insect strains more precisely. An article in the *Washington Post* took them to task, urging that the human experiments be halted because it would be unconscionable to continue putting people at risk now that "all are agreed that the mosquito does the business."[28] In sum, Reed was at once candid and self-serving, and the public had little difficulty distinguishing between the two.

Some human experiments in the pre–World War II period did cross the boundaries of acceptable ethics and might well have been included on Beecher's list. A number of researchers in the United States and elsewhere could not resist using incompetent and institutionalized populations for their studies. So captive and compliant a group of people seemed ideal, from a purely experimental perspective, for testing new treatments. The Russian physician V. V. Smidovich (publishing in 1901 under the pseudonym Vikenty Veeressayev) cited more than a dozen experiments, mostly conducted in Germany, in which unknowing patients were inoculated with microorganisms of syphilis and gonor-rhea.[29] When George Sternberg, the surgeon general of the United States in 1895 (and a collaborator with Walter Reed), wanted to test the efficacy of a preparation that might immunize against or treat smallpox, he ran experiments "upon unvaccinated children in some of the orphan asylums in . . . Brooklyn."[30] Dr. Joseph Stokes, of the Department of Pediatrics at the University of Pennsylvania School of Medicine, and two colleagues analyzed the effects of "intramuscular vaccination of human beings . . . with active virus of human influenza" by experimenting on the residents of two large state institutions for the retarded.[31]

The work of Hideyop Noguchi is another notable case in point. An associate member of the Rockefeller Institute for Medical Research, Noguchi investigated the ability of a substance he called "luetin," an extract from the causative agent of syphilis, to diagnose syphilis. Just as Clemens von Pirquet had demonstrated in 1907 that the injection of a small amount of tuberculin into the skin could indicate a tubercular condition, Noguchi hoped to prove that an injection of a small amount of luetin could indicate a syphilitic condition. After carrying out animal experiments that demonstrated to his satisfaction that luetin could not transmit the disease, he moved to human experimentation. With the cooperation of fifteen New York physicians, Noguchi tested some 400 subjects, mostly inmates in mental hospitals and orphan asylums and patients in public hospitals. Two hundred fifty-four of them were syphilitic; the remainder, his "various controls," included 456 normal children and 190 adults and children suffering from such diseases as tuberculosis and pneumonia. Before administering luetin to these subjects, Noguchi and some of the physicians did first test the material on themselves, with no ill effects. But no one, including Noguchi, informed the subjects about the experiment or obtained their permission to do the tests.[32]

Noguchi did have his justifications: First, the test was safe, as shown by his own participation. Second, it ostensibly was therapeutic, in that it might detect hidden cases of syphilis among the subjects. But the arguments were patently weak and certainly did not ward off a strong outcry, at least from some quarters of the public. The antivivisectionists, in particular, saw in this research a confirmation of their fear that a disregard for the welfare of animals would inevitably engender a disregard for the welfare of humans. Under the title "What Vivisection Invariably Leads To," one pamphleteer asked, "Are the helpless people in our hospitals and asylums to be treated as so much material for scientific experimentation, irrespective of age or consent?" And if the research was so risk-free, asked a leader of the movement, "might not the Rockefeller Institute have secured any number of volunteers by the offer of a gratuity of twenty or thirty dollars?" The press soon joined in. The *New York Times* ran the story under the banner, "THIS OUTRAGE SHOULD BE PUNISHED"; and the president of the Society for the Prevention of Cruelty to Children wanted to see criminal charges brought against Noguchi. U.S. Senator Jacob Gallinger of New Hampshire, an antivivisectionist sympathizer, called for a commission to investigate practices in New York hospitals and to enact legislation that would punish investigators who conducted such experiments. So too, the Committee on Protection of Medical Research of the American Medical Association asked editors of medical journals to examine papers submitted for publication, imploring them, "In any case of diagnosis or treatment when the procedure is novel or might be objected to, let the fact be stated that the patient or his family were fully aware of and consented to the plan."[33]

In the end, neither Noguchi's research nor the other experiments on the retarded or the mentally ill produced prosecutions, corrective legislation, or new professional review policies. Violations were too few; nontherapeutic research on captive populations was still the exception. And when the public learned about such incidents, objections quickly arose, reflecting a widely shared sense of what was fair and unfair in human experimentation. Had these norms held sway even as the methods of research changed, Beecher might not have been compelled to write his article.

CHAPTER 2

Research at War

THE transforming event in the conduct of human experimentation in the United States, the moment when it lost its intimate and directly therapeutic character, was World War II. Between 1941 and 1945 practically every aspect of American research with human subjects changed. For one, a cottage industry turned into a national program. What were once occasional, ad hoc efforts by individual practitioners now became well-coordinated, extensive, federally funded team ventures. For another, medical experiments that once had the aim of benefiting their subjects were now frequently superseded by experiments designed to benefit others—specifically, soldiers on the battlefront. For still another, researchers and subjects were more likely to be strangers to each other, with no necessary sense of shared purpose or objective. Finally, and perhaps most important, the common understanding that experimentation required the agreement of the subjects—however casual the request or general the approval—was often superseded by a sense of urgency that overrode the issue of consent.

The fact that all these characteristics first appeared in wartime, as a critical part in the battle against totalitarianism, helped ensure that they would not provoke public opposition. Neither the growing distance between researcher and subject nor the inattention to principles of consent sparked critiques or expressions of distrust. To the contrary, all these characteristics were viewed as a necessary and admirable element in the home-front effort. Later we will discuss the impact of the German atrocities, but well into the 1960s, the American research community considered the Nuremberg findings, and the Nuremberg Code, irrelevant to its own work.

In the summer of 1941, President Franklin Roosevelt created the Office of Scientific Research and Development (OSRD) to oversee the work of two parallel committees, one devoted to weapons research, the other to medical research. The need for a Committee on Medical Research (CMR) had been apparent for well over a year. The government had been sponsoring weapons research through a central agency that coordinated the work of researchers all over the country, but the chiefs of the military services could not agree on how to organize the medical research wing and lacked guiding precedents. They finally decided to establish one master agency to supervise the two activities, and thus began what Dr. Chester Keefer, one of the mainstays of the CMR, later described as "a novel experiment in American medicine, for planned and coordinated medical research had never been essayed on such a scale."[1]

Over the course of World War II the CMR recommended some 600 research proposals, many of them involving human subjects, to the OSRD for funding. The OSRD, in turn, contracted with investigators at some 135 universities, hospitals, research institutes, and industrial firms to conduct the investigations. The accomplishments of the CMR effort required two volumes to summarize (the title, *Advances in Military Medicine*, does not do justice to the scope of the investigations), and the list of publications that resulted from its grants takes up seventy-five pages. All told, the CMR expended some $25 million (a sum that pales in comparison to what the National Institutes of Health eventually spent in the 1960s), but at the time it was extraordinary.[2] In fact, the work of the CMR was so important that it supplied not only the organizational model but the intellectual justification for creating in the postwar period the National Institutes of Health. The CMR came to represent the promise of what coordinated, well-funded efforts could accomplish for scientific progress—what medical research could do for the betterment of humanity.

The health problems that confronted American soldiers and threatened to undermine their combat efficiency (and combat efficiency was the criterion) were obvious to the CMR staff, who sought quick, effective solutions. They wanted not so much to support basic research but to achieve immediate clinical payoffs. The major concerns were dysentery, influenza, malaria (in the Pacific theater), wounds, venereal diseases, and physical hardships (for example, sleep deprivation, exposure to frigid temperatures). Creating effective antidotes required skill, luck, and numerous trials with human subjects, and the CMR staff oversaw the effort with extraordinary diligence. Because it was wartime, the agency underwrote protocols that in a later day (and an earlier one as well) would have produced considerable protest. But its directors deftly managed the problem. Knowing just when to proceed aggressively or cautiously, they enhanced both the scientific and social reputation of medical research.

One primary CMR target was dysentery. Battlefront conditions did not allow for standard hygienic procedures against contaminated water and food or contagion from other carriers, and dysentery was especially debilitating to a fighting corps. No effective inoculations or antidotes existed, and the CMR wanted researchers to move ahead vigorously on both fronts. Outbreaks of the disease in so many different environments made it likely that a variety of bacteria caused the infection, and hence a vaccine would have to be effective against a great number of potentially dangerous organisms. To make matters still worse, the organisms themselves were known to be highly toxic. This meant, noted one researcher, that "inoculation . . . in adequate amounts [to create immunity] may induce such severe local and general reactions as to make general application among troops impractical."[3]

Even before facing up to these formidable problems, investigators had to find a research site. Since animal experiments would yield only limited information, sooner or later the researchers would need a setting in which to test a vaccine or an antidote on humans. The obvious location was the least satisfactory—drugs could not be evaluated in the field, on soldiers at the battlefront. The preparations might be too toxic, and besides, side effects and efficacy could not be measured under gunfire. A substitute setting would have to be found, and it did not take researchers long to identify one. Stuart Mudd, one of the leading researchers on this project for the CMR, suggested the order of things: First, "specific prophylactis by properly chosen antigenic fractions should be thoroughly explored in the laboratory." Then the agents should be tested in "institutions such as asylums," where dysentery was often rampant. This was precisely the order followed—research first on animals, then on orphans in asylums and on the retarded in institutions.[4]

No researcher and no one at CMR ever commented on the irony that to simulate the filth and lack of hygiene at the battlefront one only had to go to caretaker institutions. Rather, the fact was accepted and reported matter-of-factly: "In certain civilian institutions," noted the CMR summary volume, "where outbreaks of dysentery are not uncommon, opportunities have been furnished to observe the effect of the vaccines under approximately field conditions." Indeed, researchers scored points with the CMR for being able to get into institutions. Thus, a CMR official praised one investigator because "he has . . . access to various state institutions where facilities for study of dysentery are unexcelled."[5]

Among the most important subjects for the dysentery research were boys and girls between the ages of thirteen and seventeen in the Ohio Soldiers and Sailors Orphanage. CMR contract 293 went to doctors Merlin Cooper and B. K. Rachford of the Cincinnati Children's Hospital to attempt to immunize the children against dysentery with "killed suspensions of various types of shigella group of bacteria." The team injected different suspensions in different ways, some subcutaneously, some intramuscularly, and some intravenously; it also mixed the dysentery vaccine with the standard typhoid vaccine to learn whether the combination enhanced efficacy. All the experiments carried serious side effects, with the intravenous injections causing the most severe reactions. On 12 March 1943, ten boys were injected with ten million dysentery bacteria: "The systematic reaction," reported the team, "was profound and began within less than 30 minutes. It was essentially the same in all of the boys. The skin was pale and ashy grey in color. The blood pressure was not altered but the temperature sky-rocketed to 105°F and up in spite of measures to counteract the rise. Severe pounding headache and a constricting type of backache were almost universal complaints. The bulbar conjunctivae were hyperemic. Rapidly, nausea, vomiting and watery diarrhea ensued. Fever persisted for 24 hours and when it subsided the subjects were exhausted. By the second day all had recovered." The ten boys had an average maximum temperature of 104.6 degrees.[6]

Although the boys did appear to have built up an immunity against dysentery (measured not by direct challenge but by laboratory tests on their blood), the severity of their reaction ruled out the vaccine. The researchers then considered whether substituting subcutaneous for intravenous injections would, in their language, "hit the target." They experimented with injecting enough inoculant to give the subjects a very sore arm, "with the thought that an inflammatory reaction might break a barrier and permit a little antigen to trickle through the blood stream toward the target." To this end, they took several boys in whom "the dosage was increased cautiously until it appeared that systematic reaction, local reaction, or both were limiting factors."[7] Then, with the dose level established, they inoculated another group of ten boys subcutaneously with the vaccine, but the subjects still averaged fevers of 102 degrees, which was too severe a reaction to permit general use.

The team also tested a potential vaccine by injecting it subcutaneously in a group of girls at the Home. They experienced less swelling on their arms than did the boys, but their systemic responses were just as extreme: "Nausea, abdominal pain, headache, vomiting and on one occasion, diarrhea were observed. In one girl the reaction was unusually severe. . . . This subject became nauseated 3 hours after the injection and vomited repeatedly during the ensuing 17 hours." Although the project could not produce a safe vaccine, the researchers remained optimistic, noting that they had used very high dosages in order to make certain that they were getting substantial responses. Their final report explained that among the children at the asylum "many reactions should be classified as severe. However, there is no evidence to warrant the inference that successful immunization of human beings cannot be accomplished with dosages of vaccine too low to yield severe reactions. In these experiments dosage was purposefully raised as high as was considered safe in order to facilitate technically the measurements of heterologous immunity."[8] In other words, they had elevated the dosages to demonstrate the potency of the agent, whatever the side effects on the children.

Residents at other custodial institutions, particularly for the mentally retarded, also served as subjects for dysentery vaccine experimentation. Researchers considered them less-than-ideal candidates, not because they were incapable of giving consent but because the researchers did not know whether the condition of retardation altered reactions to the vaccine. Nevertheless, CMR-sponsored dysentery projects were conducted at the Dixon (Illinois) Institution for the Retarded and at the New Jersey State Colony for the Feeble-Minded.[9] So too, investigators evaluated the efficacy of sulfonamide preparations against dysentery by using ward patients at public hospitals for their subjects, with no information conveyed or consents obtained. Once again, the research carried significant dangers to the subjects, for the drugs under investigation could cause extensive kidney damage.[10] Indeed, James Watt, of the U.S. Public Health Service, and Sam Cumins, a resident in medicine and pathology at the Shreveport (Louisiana) Charity Hospital, published (in the widely read *Public Health Reports*) findings that included 6 deaths among 238 cases of sulfonamide-treated patients in their protocols. Although the death rate appeared lower among treated than nontreated populations, there is no indication that the subjects or their relatives had any idea that they were part of an experiment— and a risky one at that. Here is but one example:

Case 3— Twenty-month-old colored female admitted with a history of severe diarrhea. The culture was positive. . . . The patient was treated with sulfamethazine and 3 days later the temperature and clinical findings showed definite improvement. However, at the end of this time the temperature began to rise. Sulfonamide was discontinued as urinary findings indicated definite kidney damage. The patient's fever remained at a high level. Progressive toxicity ensued with oliguria. The patient died on the eighth hospital day. Death due to toxic nephritis presumably resulting from the sulfonamide used. The colon showed healing ulcerations of the mucosa.[11]

This research project, like the others, did not produce an effective vaccine or antidote. The preparations were either too potent or too weak to do any good. That most of the subjects were the institutionalized retarded or that consent was ignored did not seem to create problems, at least to judge by the silence both in the CMR and in the press. The overarching consideration was that dysentery was such a peril to the fighting soldiers that researchers on the home front had to do everything to eradicate it.

Probably the most pressing medical problem that the CMR faced right after Pearl Harbor was malaria, "an enemy even more to be feared than the Japanese."[12] Not only was the disease debilitating and deadly, but the Japanese controlled the supply of quinine, one of the few known effective antidotes. Chemists had discovered the antimalarial actions of pentaquine, but the complications, including stomach pains and diminished mental competence, were unacceptable. The CMR leaders hoped that further research would establish an effective dosage with fewer side effects or that researchers might uncover new and less toxic therapeutic agents.

Malaria, unlike dysentery, seldom occurred in the United States, so researchers had no ready sites for drug trials. After testing antidotes on animals, they would next have to transmit the disease to human subjects and then measure the efficacy of their interventions. But where were they to find subjects to participate in such protocols? The answer, with no one dissenting, was the state mental hospitals and prisons.

Dr. Alf Alving of the University of Chicago, under CMR grant 450, organized a sixty-bed clinical unit for drug testing at the Manteno (Illinois) State Hospital. The subjects were psychotic, back-ward patients whom researchers purposely infected with malaria through blood transfusions and then gave experimental antimalarial therapies. Alving's reports made no mention of any effort to obtain their consent, but the very choice of psychotic inmates demonstrates how irrelevant such concerns were. He did hire a psychiatrist to spend "between four and six hours a week discussing the psychiatric aspects of the patients we deal with at Manteno." But the assignment was to explain the subjects to the researchers, not to interpret the experiment for the subjects.[13]

Dr. Alving and other investigators relied still more heavily on prisoners to meet their research needs. Through the cooperation of the commissioner of corrections of Illinois and the warden at the Stateville penitentiary (better known as Joliet), reported Dr. Alving, "one entire floor of the prison hospital and a portion of a second floor have been turned over to the University of Chicago to carry out malarial research. Approximately 500 inmates have volunteered to act as subjects." Some were infected via mosquito bites (a mode of transmission that was more dangerous than blood transfusion) and then given pentaquine, a "promising" drug regimen. Researchers then correlated the severity of the malaria challenge (moderate, severe, extraordinarily severe), with the drug regimen, relapse rate, and side effects, which included nausea, vomiting, changes in the heartbeat rhythm (depression of T waves), fever, and blackouts. In the course of these trials, one prisoner died, suffering a heart attack after several bouts of high fever. The researchers insisted the death was unrelated to the malaria experiments, but worried about attracting other volunteers. However, the incident had no adverse impact. "We heard through the grapevine," Dr. Alving reported to Washington, "that there was considerable argument for a day or two. The end result, howeyer, was quite astonishing. We have had quite a number of new volunteers who were converted to the worth-whileness of experimental work."[14]

Whether these prisoners were truly capable of volunteering for the experiments was not broached by the researchers, the CMR, prison officials, or the press. Almost all the commentary was congratulatory, praising the wonderful contributions that the inmates were making to the war effort. Press releases from Washington lauded the inmates' willingness to volunteer and without a promise of reward, "accept full responsibility for any ill effects, aware of the risk and discomfort . . . and knowing, too, that . . . there is a real hazard involved." Furthermore, they said, "these one-time enemies to society appreciate to the fullest extent just how completely this is everybody's war."[15]

The CMR also supported a major research effort to create a vaccine against influenza. Although not as threatening as malaria, respiratory ailments were "the cause of the greatest amount of disability" among soldiers, and of all the infections, influenza was the most feared. It not only had the highest mortality rate, but could again reach the catastrophic epidemic levels of 1919. As the CMR reported, the "memory of the great pandemic of influenza that occurred toward the end of World War I and realization of its disastrous effects stimulated, at the very beginning of mobilization, the investigation of all possible methods for the control of this disease."[16]

One team, under the direction of Dr. Werner Henle of the University of Pennsylvania Medical School and Philadelphia's Children's Hospital, conducted extensive research on vaccines against influenza A and B. His bimonthly reports to the CMR described his progress in preparing the inoculant and the arrangements made to test them on several hundred residents both at the nearby state facility for the retarded (Pennhurst) and the correctional center for young offenders. The protocols typically involved administering the vaccine to the residents and then three or six months later purposely infecting them with influenza (by fitting an aviation oxygen mask over their face and having them inhale a preparation of the virus for four minutes). The team also infected control groups with the virus, but not the vaccine, in order to compare the different rates of infection. As was to be expected with influenza, those who contracted the disease suffered fever (up to 104 degrees), aches, and pains.[17] Although the vaccines often did provide protection, they were not always free of side effects. As with the malaria preparations, researchers experimented with different preparations. One group of women residents at Pennhurst were injected with an influenza vaccine in a mineral oil base, and many of them developed nodules at the injection site that persisted for six to eighteen months; one had such a severe abscess as to require surgery.[18]

A second team working on influenza vaccines was led by Dr. Jonas Salk, who would later develop the first antipolio vaccine. This group took its human subjects from among the residents of Michigan's Ypsilanti State Hospital and followed essentially the same design as the Henle team: inoculate a group (for example, the "102 male residents of a single ward . . . [who] ranged in age from 20 to 70 years") with the vaccine and later challenge them with the virus; select a comparable group of residents for controls and infect them with the virus without the benefit of the vaccine.[19] The reports from the Salk team, published in such prestigious publications as the *Journal of Clinical Investigation*, accurately identified the subjects, and the researchers fully described the findings: "In the unvaccinated group, 11, or 41%, . . . had temperatures of 100 or more and 6, or 22%, had temperatures of 101 or above. In the 69 vaccinated individuals, 7, or 10%, had temperatures between 100 and 100.9."[20]

Pleased with these preliminary results, Salk and his team turned the entire Ypsilanti Hospital, with its 2,000 residents, into a research site, adding as well the 5,700 patients at the nearby Eloise Hospital and Infirmary. Half received the vaccine, and the other half a placebo. Blood analysis indicated immunities among the inoculated, but the best evidence of efficacy came a year later when, by chance, an epidemic of influenza broke out at Ypsilanti. To the researchers' satisfaction, those inoculated had a significantly lower incidence of the disease.

After these successes, the Office of the Surgeon General of the U.S. Army arranged for the vaccine to be tested on enrollees in the Army Specialized Training Program at eight universities and a ninth unit made up of students from five New York medical and dental colleges. "With the approval of the appropriate authorities," but with no mention of what the subjects were told about the experiment, the teams inoculated 6,263 men and injected 6,211 others with a placebo. Able to keep close track of them for follow-up studies, the researchers learned that 7 percent of the controls, as compared to only 2 percent of the inoculated, had contracted influenza within a year. The research begun on the institutionalized mentally ill and continued on recruits and students produced the desired result: an effective influenza vaccine.[21]

It was not just the success or failure of any single experiment, however, that gave CMR in particular and medical research in general such a favorable standing with the public during World War II. Closely associated with these enterprises were the efficient production and distribution of penicillin (many people mistakenly credited the war effort with the discovery of penicillin), and the CMR deserves much of the praise. Its staff helped develop and allocate the "miracle drug," promoting not only cures but morale on the war front and the home front.

It was the CMR that met the challenge posed by the renowned British pathologist Howard Florey during his visit to the United States in the summer of 1941 and his demonstration on the antibacterial properties of the penicillin mold. The problem was how to produce sufficient penicillin without sacrificing its potency. Under CMR superintendence, private drug companies began the cumbersome manufacturing process. By December 1942 enough of the drug was available to test it on 90 cases, and by December 1943, 700 cases. Thus, what might have been the most devastating medical problem confronting the armed services—death from wound infections—turned out to be altogether manageable. By June 1944 enough penicillin was available to treat all the wounded in the Normandy invasion.

The system devised by the CMR between 1942 and 1944 was successful in meeting military needs and collecting data on efficacy. Most of the drug went to ten general and military hospitals where a specially trained medical officer supervised its use and reported on outcomes. Lesser amounts went to twelve hospitals to test for efficacy against gonorrhea. (This was probably the source of the widely repeated but apocryphal tale of a medical officer who administered his only vial of penicillin to the soldier who was "wounded" in the brothel, not to the one wounded in the battlefield, because the brothel victim would return sooner to the front lines). Although the CMR records are silent on what, if anything, patients were told before receiving penicillin, the early trials typically involved the gravely ill who had failed on other therapies. Thus, in April 1943 a small group of battle casualties who had contracted osteomyelitis were being cared for without success at the Bushnell General Hospital in Brigham, Utah. A bacteriologist at the hospital wrote Chester Keefer about his own futile attempts to make enough penicillin to treat the men; Keefer then arranged to send him a limited supply of the drug from his own stores. The soldiers underwent a "remarkable" recovery, and the efficacy of penicillin against this type of infection was established.[22]

The CMR also kept some reserves of the drug to dispense on a case-by-case basis for civilian use. Any physician who believed that his patient required penicillin was to send full details of the case to the CMR, and Keefer then evaluated the request. His criterion was straightforward: he allotted the drug to patients with a deadly disease who demonstrated no satisfactory response to alternative therapies and for whom there was reason to believe penicillin might prove effective. Thus, patients with staphylococcal meningitis or puerperal fever received the drug, whereas those with tuberculosis or leukemia did not. Word of pencillin's effectiveness spread, and newspaper stories all over the country heralded the miracles that the drug performed—in one town it saved a dying child, in another, an almost moribund woman who had just given birth. Medical research became identified with miracles, and medical researchers with miracle makers.

• • •

Whenever the wartime research goals raised issues that might have aroused public opposition, the CMR directors handled the situation skillfully and delicately. They recognized the limits of CMR's maneuverability, thereby maintaining an almost perfect record of support. Two examples amply demonstrate their techniques, one involving research into the effects of hardship conditions on combatants, the other involving efforts to find a cure for gonorrhea.

Of all the research that the CMR supported, none fit more closely with wartime needs than survival under hardship conditions. The Nazi investigations produced some of the most horrific experiments conducted on concentration camp inmates and testified to at Nuremberg. The CMR, in this instance, did not violate the dignity or the rights of subjects. Where one might have expected the greatest disparity between war goals and protection of human subjects, none occurred.

The medical issues were as obvious as they were unexplored: If a group of sailors were shipwrecked and ended up on a raft with a limited supply of water, ought they to supplement their supply by drinking some amount of salt water? What ration kit would provide soldiers in very hot (or cold) climates with an optimum nutritional balance? How did heat (or cold or altitude) affect the performance of physical tasks? The subjects for CMR-sponsored research on such topics came from the ranks of conscientious objectors (COs) who believed that by enrolling as subjects, they were not primarily serving the military machine but humanity, that they were contributing to an effort not to destroy but to save lives. For this research, investigators did not use inmates of mental hospitals or institutions for the retarded, probably not for ethical reasons but because the experiments required competent and cooperative subjects. Since the measure of the effects of heat and nutrition would be performance, they wanted subjects capable of carrying out routine tasks under normal conditions.

The COs were formally under the jurisdiction of the Selective Service Administration, which in 1943 decided to allow them to volunteer for research work, either as subjects or as laboratory assistants. COs were also affiliated with a national service organization, generally, the American Friends (Quakers), the Mennonites, or the National Service Board for Religious Objectors. Hence, an investigator who wanted to use a CO in his research first had to approach the CMR and then contact both the Selective Service Administration and the CO's particular service organization. He had to compose two very different letters, one to the CMR explaining how the research would further the war effort and another to the CO's organization explaining how it would promote the well-being of humanity—and most researchers proved adept at fulfilling the dual assignment. The process was cumbersome but well worth the bother. With trained personnel so scarce, well-educated and diligent COs not only contributed to the project as cooperative subjects but as skilled assistants and administrators. The net effect of all these procedures was to put the survival research under the closest scrutiny, with government agencies, private organizations, and the subjects themselves fully informed about the experiments. The process also protected the COs from coercion, for a request for assistance went to the service organization, not directly to the individual, and the CO had to come forward and express his willingness to volunteer.

Those who did volunteer drank various mixtures of saltwater and fresh water and then had their weight checked and urine analyzed. (The findings confirmed the Ancient Mariner's view that sea water was of no benefit.) They subsisted on 500 grams a day, some with water alone, others with different foodstuffs. (Here the lesson was to stock lifeboat kits not with the standard chocolate and biscuits but with more easily digested glucose and fat.) Others sat on rooftops exposed to wind and frigid temperatures and then had their physiological responses measured; or sat in sweltering rooms, became dehydrated, and then performed simple tasks to test their efficiency; or sat in low-pressure chambers, simulating conditions at different altitudes and then underwent psychological and physiological testing. The research proceeded smoothly: the investigators pleaded for more COs, the Selective Service sought assurances that the COs were not getting off too lightly, and the COs completed their assignments and even remained with the teams afterward, satisfied that they had respected their scruples and served their nation.[23]

With even greater attention to the potential for public opposition, the CMR researchers sought a prevention and cure for gonorrhea. However intense the pressure for results, the CMR would not risk a scandal. It conducted a remarkably thorough and sensitive discussion of the ethics of research and adopted procedures that satisfied the principles of voluntary and informed consent. Indeed, the gonorrhea protocols contradict blanket assertions that in the 1940s and 1950s investigators were working in an ethical vacuum.

Everyone in the CMR and in the Surgeon General's Office recognized the threat of gonorrhea to military efficiency. In February 1943, Dr. J. Earle Moore, the chairman of the Subcommittee on Venereal Diseases for the National Research Council, informed the CMR that each year 350,000 military personnel were likely to contract fresh infections of gonorrhea. He noted, "Assuming an average loss of time of 20 days per infected man (the actual figure for Army in recent years to 1941 was 35–45 days, for Navy 10–15 days), this will account for 7,000,000 lost man days per year, the equivalent of putting out of action for a full year the entire strength of two full armored divisions or of ten aircraft carriers." Thomas Parran, the surgeon general, noted that gonorrhea not only weakened the armed services but also "represented a serious threat to the health and efficiency of our defense workers."[24] The problem, in short, was nothing to smirk about.

Nor was the problem easy to resolve. As of 1942 no one had been able to induce gonorrhea in animals, and therefore all the testing of preventives and cures would require human subjects. (That penicillin was soon to resolve the issue could not, of course, be known.) Investigators were eager to tackle the assignment but questioned the ethical, legal, and political implications. In October 1942, Dr. Moore informed Dr. Richards, the chairman of the CMR, that he had recently received a letter from Dr. Charles Carpenter, of the University of Rochester School of Medicine, who wanted to "work out a human experiment on the chemical prophylaxis of gonorrhea. He has asked me to supply him with a statement that in my opinion such human experimentation is desirable. . . . I have pointed out to Dr. Carpenter that I could not make such a statement without the approval of higher authority. May I ask you to supply me with the attitude of the Committee on Medical Research toward human experimentation in general, and toward the particular problem of human experimentation in the chemical prophylaxis of gonorrhea."[25]

Richards promised to bring the question immediately to the full committee: "In the meantime I have confidence that the Committee will support me in the statement that human experimentation is not only desirable, but necessary in the study of many of the problems of war medicine which confront us. When any risks are involved, volunteers only should be utilized as subjects, and these only after the risks have been fully explained and after signed statements have been obtained which shall prove that the volunteer offered his services with full knowledge and that claims for damages will be waived. An accurate record should be kept of the terms in which the risks involved were described." As for gonorrhea research, the CMR would have to rely on "the judgment of the Responsible Investigator, supplemented by the judgment of the committee in whose field the investigator is proceeding." Three weeks later Richards informed Moore that the CMR fully endorsed his position on human experimentation; all legal responsibility for damages rested with the investigator and his institution, but "arrangements can be made whereby both he and the Institution can be protected by insurance."[26]

Thus encouraged, Dr. Carpenter, and several other investigators as well, submitted grants to the CMR for gonorrhea research on human subjects. The protocols were elaborate and sophisticated both in terms of scientific method and protection of human subjects. In order to study the efficacy of oral and topical preventive treatments, Carpenter intended to divide volunteers into three categories: one group would take sulfonamide compounds by mouth and then be exposed to the infection; a second would be exposed to the infection, after which topical agents would be applied to the genital tract; a third would serve as controls, infected but not given any oral or topical protection. Carpenter proposed to conduct the research on prisoners, for they offered the advantage of being under complete control during the necessary observation period and out of contact with women. He informed the CMR that negotiations were already under way with prison officials in Georgia.

The CMR carefully reviewed the proposal in and out of house. The referees approved of the science and many, like Dr. R. E. Dyer, the director of the National Institutes of Health, expressly approved of the ethics: "The outline of methods to be employed seems adequate to insure a definite answer and to safeguard the volunteers."[27] But some reviewers were apprehensive about possible legal repercussions. The head of the American Medical Association (AMA), for example, was concerned that an unscrupulous lawyer might learn about the project, bring suit, and try to discredit all medical research. Taking such possibilities seriously, the CMR heads set out to make certain that every contingency had been considered and to marshal full support.

To these ends, it sponsored a day-long meeting on 29 December 1942 that brought together representatives from the military services, state health departments, and interested researchers. The group not only reviewed the protocols and explored potential legal liabilities (for example, might a state law against maiming oneself be invoked against the volunteers?) but also scrutinized a "Proposed Plan of Procedure in the Study of Chemical Prophylaxis in Human Volunteers among Prison Inmates," which was to guide all the researchers.

The proposed plan specified precisely which prisoners would be ineligible to volunteer (for instance, those who were chronically ill, had a history of rheumatic fever, or had negative reactions to sulfonamides). It also specified the protocol for transmitting the infection: a nonsulfonamide-resistant strain with a low thermal death point was to be applied for five minutes. The proposed plan also included a two-page, single-spaced "Statement of Explanation of the Experiment and Its Risks to Tentative Volunteers"—in effect, a consent form:[28]

The study which we plan to carry on here, and for which we have asked your cooperation, is concerned with gonorrhea. You may also know this disease as the 'clap,' 'strain,' or the 'running ranges.' Some of you have had the infection at some time in the past and you know it did not make you seriously sick. Recently a simple, dependable treatment has been discovered which consists of a drug taken in the form of pills.

What we propose to try now is to develop certain methods of *preventing* the disease. . . . Gonorrhea causes a great loss of time in the Army and Navy. . . . It is not possible to use animals for this purpose because they are not susceptible to gonorrhea. Therefore, we are calling on you for your cooperation. This is one way in which you can specifically help in the war effort. The benefits will not be limited to the armed forces . . . and it is very likely that you and your families might later profit from them.

In the first place, I want to assure you that so far as we are able to discover, there is no reason to expect any injury from this treatment, but one cannot predict with positiveness that the result in all cases will be the same. . . .

Most patients with gonorrhea can be cured within 5 to 10 days with modern treatment without experiencing discomforts or complications. A few patients with gonorrhea do not respond to modern treatment methods (probably less than 1 in 10). These patients can usually be cured by older methods, which, however, require more time to get results. A few of the patients who are treated by these older methods develop certain complications in the lower genital tract which, in most instances, are ultimately cured. In very rare instances patients treated by the older methods develop complications which involve the joints, the eyes, and other organs.

A very small percentage of patients treated by modern methods experience discomfort while taking the medication. This may consist of a tired sensation or a slight headache, but these symptoms never become serious if the patient is observed daily by the physician. Fever, skin rash, nausea, and vomiting rarely occur but do disappear rapidly when the treatment is stopped. Other reactions have been reported which involved the blood, joints, kidneys, liver, and nervous system, but these reactions have been so rare that the possibility of their occurrence is extremely remote.

Before we can accept you as part of our group, it is necessary to obtain written permission from you.

Although the document exaggerated the potential benefit of the research to the subjects and too blatantly tried to persuade them to make their contribution to the war effort, it noted the potential complications and accurately assessed the research risks. In all, it satisfied the need to inform and protect human subjects.

The CMR staff continued to move circumspectly, reviewing the proposed research with city and state health officers, prison officials, heads of major research organizations, and legal advisors. Overwhelming support for the investigations emerged, and the consensus was that using prisoners was the only feasible and acceptable option. As Dr. Moore told Dr. Richards, civilians would not have submitted to the sexual isolation and medical supervision for the necessary six months, military personnel could not have been kept from active duty for so long, and "inmates of institutions for the feeble-minded or insane" could not have been used because it would have been "clearly undesirable to subject to any experimental procedure persons incapable of providing voluntary consent."[29] A few reviewers, like Frank Jewett, the president of the National Academy of Science, questioned whether prisoners were capable of giving voluntary consent to an experiment, but most others were persuaded that the benefits of the research outweighed whatever doubts anyone might have.[30] Thomas Parran summed up the prevailing view: "The utilization of human subjects who voluntarily submit themselves to experimentation may properly be compared to the research which enabled Doctor Walter Reed and his co-workers to discover the method of transmission of yellow fever."[31]

The aftermath of these deliberations was not as interesting as the deliberations themselves. The CMR staff voted to support the research; but then, to be certain that the protocols violated no state laws, they proposed using prisoners in federal penitentiaries. James Bennett, the director of the federal system, was eager to cooperate and to help enroll subjects. "We cannot obligate the government," he informed Dr. Moore, "insofar as reduction of sentence for those who volunteer is concerned. It is believed, however, that the U.S. Board of Parole would be willing to give each subject . . . due credit and consideration for his willingness to serve his country in this manner when he becomes eligible for parole." The administrative hurdles cleared, a major project began at the U.S. penitentiary at Terre Haute, Indiana, but the investigators soon terminated it because "not any of the exposure techniques employed proved capable of producing disease with a consistency considered to be adequate for a study of experimental prophylaxis."[32] Shortly thereafter, the curative role of penicillin was established, obviating the need for additional research.

At first glance, the record of human experimentation during World War II constitutes a curious mixture of high-handedness and forethought. The research into dysentery, malaria, and influenza revealed a pervasive disregard of the rights of subjects—a willingness to experiment on the mentally retarded, the mentally ill, prisoners, ward patients, soldiers, and medical students without concern for obtaining consent. Yet, research into survival under hardship conditions and into gonorrhea was marked by formal and carefully considered protocols that informed potential subjects about the risks of participation.

Behind these differences lies the evaluation of the CMR administrators and researchers about the likely response to specific investigations. When they sensed the possibility of an adverse public reaction, they behaved cautiously. Giving gonorrhea to prisoners might have raised a storm of protest from a variety of sources, some objecting to prisoners injuring themselves, others objecting to efforts to protect the promiscuous from the consequences of their immorality; since the protocol might, therefore, have ended up on the front page of a newspaper or in a courtroom, the CMR directors were scrupulous about building a scientific consensus on the importance of the project and protecting the rights of the volunteers. As a result of these calculations and actions, the research community secured public acceptance of a new kind of medical research and human experimentation.

Most of the time, however, the CMR and the research community were confident that their work would not be questioned—that their research on dysentery, malaria, and influenza using incompetent and incarcerated subjects would pass community scrutiny. Why, then, did officials who understood the need to make subjects' participation informed and voluntary in occasional cases find it so easy to disregard the requirements in most other cases? How could they say in the case of gonorrhea that it was "clearly undesirable to subject to any experimental procedures persons incapable of providing voluntary consent," and then go ahead and do precisely that in the case of dysentery and malaria?

The answer begins with an appreciation of the fact that the first widespread use of human subjects in medical research occurred under wartime conditions. First, a sense of urgency pervaded the laboratories. Time was of the essence when combat soldiers were under the immediate threat of disease. A campaign mentality inevitably affected not only the theaters of war but the theaters of research, justifying every shortcut or elimination of time-consuming procedures. The presumption was full speed ahead, *except* where negative fallout was most likely.

But why were informing a subject about an experiment and obtaining consent defined as time-consuming, instead of necessary, measures? Because, in the second instance, wartime conditions brought a reliance on such procedures as the draft, forced military duty, and assignment to combat—and these new facts of life inevitably affected the mind-set of researchers. Every day thousands of men were forced to face death, whether or not they understood the campaign, the strategy, or the cause. Since these investigations were integral to the military effort, the rules of the battlefield seemed to apply to the laboratory. Researchers were no more obliged to obtain the permission of their subjects than the Selective Service was to obtain the permission of civilians to become soldiers. One part of the war machine conscripted a soldier, another part conscripted an experimental subject, and the same principles held for both.

Moreover, the use of mentally incompetent people as research subjects seemed to be in accord with popular expectations of sacrifices to be made on the home front. All citizens were—or were supposed to be—contributing to the war effort, even at great personal cost and inconvenience. By this standard, it was reasonable to expect the mentally ill and retarded to make their contributions too, albeit involuntary ones. It was ever so easy to believe that if these handicapped individuals could somehow have understood the nature of the request, if they could have had a momentary flash of competence and been asked whether they wished to join the experiment and further the war effort, they would have agreed. Hence, to enroll them in research was not to violate their rights but to exercise a substituted judgment: Were they competent, they would have volunteered for the project.

It requires little historical imagination to recognize the appeal of this line of argument in a society mobilized for war. Since the mentally ill and retarded had the same stake as all other citizens in an Allied victory, it seemed altogether appropriate that they be called on to perform whatever services they could. And at a time when the social value attached to consent had so frequently to give way before the necessity of conscription and obedience to orders, there was little reason for medical researchers to worry about using incompetent human subjects. Some people were ordered to face bullets and storm a hill; others were told to take an injection and test a vaccine. No one ever said that war was fair, or that it should be fairer for the incompetent than the competent.

To make this same point in traditional philosophical terms, wartime inevitably promotes teleological, as opposed to deontological, positions. The greatest good for the greatest number is the most compelling precept to justify sending some men to be killed so that others may live— and this ethic has little difficulty in defending the use of the institutionalized retarded or mentally ill for experimentation. Of course, the investigations were to be scientifically sound, and to have passed all the appropriate animal tests; but these criteria met, it appeared acceptable to test the interventions on humans, including those unable to give consent.

In sum, the lessons that the medical researchers learned in their first extensive use of human subjects was that ends certainly did justify means; that in wartime the effort to conquer disease entitled them to choose the martyrs to scientific progress. They learned, too, that the public would accept such decisions, and that so long as the researchers were attentive to potential areas of dispute, the support for research was considerable. All of this constituted an intellectual legacy that researchers would not forget, even when peacetime conditions returned.

CHAPTER 3

The Gilded Age of Research

THE twenty years between the close of World War II and the appearance of Henry Beecher's exposé witnessed an extraordinary expansion of human experimentation in medical research. Long after peace returned, many of the investigators continued to follow wartime rules. Utilitarian justifications that had flourished under conditions of combat and conscription persisted, and principles of consent and voluntary participation were often disregarded. This was, to borrow a phrase from American political history, the Gilded Age of research, the triumph of laissez-faire in the laboratory. Yet between 1945 and 1965 very few investigators or their funders took note of the changed circumstances. The thrust of public policy was not to check the discretion of the experimenter but to free up the resources that would expand the scope and opportunity for research.

The driving force in post–World War II research, including both intellectual direction and financial support, was provided by the National Institutes of Health. Created in 1930 as an outgrowth of the research laboratory of the U.S. Public Health Service, the NIH did not assume its extraordinary prominence until 1946.[1] When the Committee on Medical Research, along with the other wartime organizations, was about to be phased out, many scientists and political leaders (but not all) found the prospect of the federal government abdicating its research role simply unthinkable.[2] So vital an activity could not be permitted to regress to the prewar condition of limited and haphazard support by private foundations and universities.[3]

It was not difficult to make the case for transforming the NIH into the peacetime CMR. In the fall of 1945, Vannevar Bush, the director of the Office of Scientific Research and Development, laid out plans for a Program for Postwar Scientific Research in a report entitled "Science, the Endless Frontier." Bush first listed the achievements of medical research over the past two hundred years and then noted the "spectacular" record during World War II. He recounted the victories over smallpox, typhoid, tetanus, yellow fever, and infectious diseases, noting first the discovery of the sulfa drugs and then, of course, penicillin. Medicine, he insisted, was on the verge of its most heroic explorations, and at such a moment it would be foolhardy to close off the "frontiers" of science by ending federal support.

To judge by congressional reactions as well as press comments, Bush's appeal struck a responsive chord. Although disputes broke out about the appropriate division of authority between the government and the investigator, and among the various federal agencies, there was significant agreement on the need for a federal investment in research.[4] "World medicine," noted one editorial, "appears to be approaching the threshold of a brilliant new era of discovery in which some of mankind's most dreaded diseases may be wiped out." And the proof of the assertion was in the "miracle drug"—penicillin. It unleashed the imagination of both the general public and the research community, so that no prediction of progress, however grandiose, seemed fanciful. In the fall of 1945, Alexander Fleming, who had discovered the antibacterial properties of the penicillin-producing mold, toured the United States, received a hero's welcome, and delivered the same exhilarating message: "We are only at the beginning of this great study. . . . We can certainly expect to do much toward reducing the sum total of human suffering."[5] Political figures echoed his refrain: "We have found the cause of a number of epidemic diseases and have practically conquered them," declared Louisiana's Senator Joseph Ransdell. "May we not expect the same kind of success against the so-called degenerative diseases if we work hard enough?"[6] And his heady optimism bore directly on the prospects for a strengthened NIH, for Ransdell was one of the Senate's strongest supporters of the new program. The press, too, invoked the wartime experience and the benefits of penicillin to buttress the case for an expanded NIH. "This seems to be the golden age of chemotherapy," commented the *New York Times*. "It is sad to realize that had it not been for the war, penicillin might not yet have been placed in the hands of physicians, and that we need something more than the natural curiosity of the research scientist to speed discovery that means so much to mankind."[7]

If the general well-being of humanity was not reason enough to justify federal support of research, then national self-interest was. In 1945, unlike 1919, there was little sense that the Allies had won a war to end all wars; hence, those concerned with defense strategies, like Secretary of the Navy James Forrestal, strongly endorsed expansion of the NIH. The United States, he argued, had been foolish not to fund medical research between the two wars and dared not repeat the error.[8] "A future aggressor," concurred editorial writers, "will move even more swiftly than Hitler did. Two oceans will not give us time to establish another OSRD. Continuous systematic research is an evident necessity. It may be regarded as a kind of military insurance."[9]

Thus, in 1945, the lesson learned from both the battlefield and the laboratory was to reorganize the NIH along the lines of the CMR and fund it generously—in effect, involve an army of investigators from universities and hospitals in the war against disease and await the impressive results. With World War II just behind and with medical research so closely linked to national security, discussions about federal research policy inevitably invoked war metaphors: Given the high stakes, the campaign was to be an all-out battle against disease. Researchers reinforced and reflected this attitude: With the potential for incredible breakthroughs so great, all—and one means *all*—methods of investigation were legitimate.

The results of this mandate were apparent first in the spectacular growth of the NIH. Congress gave the NIH not only the responsibility but the budgetary resources to expand on the work of the CMR. In 1945 the appropriation to NIH was approximately $700,000. By 1955 the figure had climbed to $36 million; by 1965, $436 million; and by 1970, $1.5 billion, a sum that allowed it to award some 11,000 grants, about one-third requiring experiments on humans. As a result of this largess, NIH was able both to run an extramural program like the CMR had done, making grants to outside investigators, and to administer an internal, intramural research program of its own. In 1953, NIH opened its Clinical Research Center, in which investigators appointed to its own staff coordinated patient treatment with medical research. Those who worked at the Bethesda site during the "halcyon days" of the 1950s, to quote the NIH deputy director during that period, J. D. Rall, were overwhelmed by the "awesome immensity of the place and diversity of research interests."[10] Indeed, the scope and significance of NIH operations were such that through the 1980s, practically every chairman of a basic science department in major American medical schools was at some point in his career an NIH fellow or NIH grant recipient.

The Clinical Center was a 500-bed research hospital that admitted patients on referral when their disease fit with the particular investigatory interests of one of the seven NIH institutes. The focus was mainly, but not exclusively, on chronic diseases, including arteriosclerosis, rheumatoid arthritis, leukemia, and schizophrenia. Every patient admitted was part of a formal research study—a research subject—but the NIH, at least before 1965, never put the matter quite so baldly. Instead, it blurred the lines between research and therapy. The Clinical Center, as its patient brochures and handbooks explained, would "benefit all people by adding to our storehouse of knowledge . . . [and] at the same time . . . provide the best possible medical and nursing care." The center's "team of experts [was] working for your better health and for new knowledge." The facility also admitted a group of volunteers drawn from religious and service organizations to serve as normal controls in some of the projects. The NIH materials hastened to assure them, as they did the patients, that their well-being came first: "The normal control is not 'experimented upon' without regard to his individual welfare. . . . The welfare of the patient takes precedence over every other consideration."[11]

The Clinical Center, however, instituted almost no formal procedures or mechanisms to ensure that patients' best interests were not sacrificed to the researchers' own agendas. The center did not, in the first instance, educate patients to be alert to possible conflicts of interest or to question the researcher closely about the protocol. The material that specifically addressed "The Patient's Part in Research at the Clinical Center" invoked the ethos of the traditional doctor–patient therapeutic relationship and essentially asked the patient to trust the researcher: "Just like the family doctor, the physician in the Clinical Center has a professional and moral obligation to do everything possible to benefit the patient. . . . The primary purpose of the Clinical Center is medical research in the interest of humanity, and this purpose is achieved at no sacrifice of benefit to the individual." That an NIH researcher was many things but assuredly *not* a family physician, or that the well-being of humanity and the well-being of a patient might diverge, were issues the NIH would not confront.

The Clinical Center set neither formal requirements to protect human subjects nor clear standards for its investigators to follow in making certain that subjects were well informed about the research protocols. As a result, the hallmark of the investigator–subject relationship was its casualness, with disclosure of risks and benefits, side effects and possible complications, even basic information on what procedures would be performed, left completely to the discretion of the individual investigator.[12] Thus, patients at the National Heart Institute were asked to sign a general consent form before undergoing surgery; but, as its director, Donald Fredrickson, later observed, explaining the procedures to the patients was "by no means universal." One reason for the omission, Fredrickson explained, was that researchers were convinced their protocols involved no significant risk to the patient; in their view, since the experiments did not depart markedly from standard practice and represented only a minor variant on major therapeutic or diagnostic interventions, the details were too trivial to justify disclosure. But Fredrickson added a second consideration, without noting the inherent contradiction between the two points: the investigators feared that discussing the research aspects in detail would "unduly alarm the patient and hinder his reasonable evaluation of procedures important to his welfare." Thus, the cardiac surgery service had its patients sign only a standard surgical consent form, even though, as Fredrickson conceded, the procedures might be anything but standard. For example, "during the surgery, research procedures are sometimes performed, such as . . . application of tiny metal clips to the heart for post-operative measurements, etc." So too, on the diagnostic cardiology unit: "Neither the details of all measurements or procedures carried out during catheterization nor a complete recital of each specific hazard is given the average patient."[13] The conclusion seems inescapable that it was not so much the subjects' well-being but the researchers' needs that kept the communication between them to a minimum.

Moreover, NIH investigators were not obliged by internal rules or their own sense of propriety to consult with colleagues in order to make certain that their evaluation of risks was not biased by an eagerness to do the research. They were not required to obtain another investigator's opinion, let alone approval, on whether the protocol was truly nothing more than a minor deviation from standard practice. To be sure, NIH did have a Medical Board Committee composed of representatives of each of the institutes and the Clinical Center staff, and NIH officials maintained that "any nonstandard, potentially hazardous procedure, or any involving normal subjects receives appropriate group consideration before it is undertaken." However, as one deputy director explained, "It is not necessary to present each project to any single central group." Investigators who wanted a consultation on whether their protocol involved "potential hazard to the life or well-being of the patient" had the option of seeking the advice of the Medical Board Committee; but if the investigators believed that their protocols were not hazardous, they were free to proceed. The choice was the investigator's alone and so, not surprisingly, the board was rarely consulted. Nor were informal consultations a regular practice. The Heart Institute, for example, had been without a director from 1953 to 1961. The result, according to Fredrickson, was "a sense of 'hopelessness' on the part of the Clinical Associates and some lack of dispassionate review of the conduct of some of the more routine aspects of research and clinical care."[14]

Researchers at the other NIH institutes were equally casual. Patients might receive a general description of the protocols, but the specifics were not often spelled out. Some investigators asked for a signature on a general release form; others noted in the chart that they had discussed the issues with the patient. NIH, however, had no fixed methods or requirements to make certain that the subject received an explanation of the procedures, indicated an understanding of them, and voluntarily consented to participate. Dr. Robert Cohen, the director of clinical investigations for the National Institute of Mental Health, reported that "in only a small percentage" of cases did patients sign a specific consent form, and even then, "the negative aspects of therapy" were not usually stipulated and recorded on the forms. His counterpart at the National Cancer Institute noted that some colleagues followed a formal procedure and others an informal one, and that they could not agree among themselves about either the style or the substance of the investigator–subject communication.[15] Thus, the Cancer Institute had no uniform policy about consent other than a general understanding that the researcher should somehow obtain it.

Peer review of NIH research protocols followed this same pattern. Officially, patient care at the Clinical Center was the joint responsibility of clinicians and researchers, and institute directors contended that consultations between them at the bedside or in committees ensured high-quality medical care and research. Ostensibly, colleagues were judging the scientific value and ethical soundness of each other's work. However, no regulations existed to ensure a timely or effective implementation. In some institutes, group consideration of research proposals took place at ward rounds conducted by the chief of service; in others, the branch chiefs and the scientific director of the institute met to discuss a particular project. But such sessions were unscheduled and infrequent, and in the absence of a formal system, everyone conceded that some research could slip through the cracks. When the clinical director of the Cancer Institute was asked, "Is it possible for a physician on the staff to do a procedure that is essentially new or different before it has been reviewed either by group consideration or by the service head?" he responded "that it is possible, that it is unlikely, and that it is assumed that senior investigators will discuss continually with their immediate superiors their current research efforts."[16] NIH officials in the 1950s clearly were unready to acknowledge that assumptions and practice might well diverge, or that explicit guidelines and procedures might seal the cracks. Left to themselves, they were ready to let the researchers handle decision making.

This policy reflected, first, a faith at the Clinical Center that the researcher–subject relationship was identical to the doctor–patient relationship.[17] In medical investigations, as in medical therapy, the well-being of patients (even if they were now subjects), was paramount.

Holding to such a premise, the Clinical Center directors unhesitatingly transferred the discretion that the physician enjoyed in the examining room directly to the investigator in the laboratory. In fact, the only time that NIH required formal review and approval of a human experimentation protocol by its Medical Board Committee was with research involving normal volunteers. NIH treated normal subjects differently precisely because they did not fit into the traditional doctor-patient relationship. Since the subjects were not sick, the researcher could not invoke a clinical model of responsibility, and NIH here—but only here—thought it necessary to go beyond a trust in the investigator's judgment.

Second, the Clinical Center assumed that researchers who were concerned about the ethics of a particular protocol would on their own initiative consult with colleagues. Peer review, however ad hoc, would provide the necessary checks; professionals would be self-regulating. The alternative—to insist on precise explanations to patients and to obtain their formal consent—seemed but an empty ritual to the NIH research community. Laypeople had neither the scientific knowledge nor emotional capability, especially when they were acutely ill, to understand protocols. "The usual patient," as one of the directors put it, wants "to avoid the necessity of grappling with painful facts related to his own welfare. He prefers (and in a real sense he has no other choice) to depend on an overriding faith that the physician and institution will safeguard his interests above any other consideration." At the Clinical Center particularly, he continued, "patients feel that they have ... gained an opportunity that is open to relatively few."[18] These patients were not about to question or oppose the physician's judgment. The patient was to trust the physician, whether in the guise of researcher or therapist, and that was the sum of the matter.

At least some NIH chiefs recognized that other, very different considerations accounted for the softness of the procedures—namely, an enormous intellectual and emotional investment in research and the shared conviction that the laboratory would yield up answers to the great mysteries of disease. Since the researcher, not the clinician, controlled the NIH structure and occupied the positions of leadership in its hierarchy, the absence of regulations reflected researchers' preferences to keep their laboratory work unfettered. "At NIH," observed Dr. Phillipe Cardon (a psychiatrist, not a bench researcher), "taking care of patients is not by and large considered to be as challenging, important, or rewarding as is doing a clinical experiment. . . . If we were more interested in taking care of patients than in research, we wouldn't be here. It is unrealistic to expect most very good investigators also to be very good physicians (or vice versa)." Cardon himself was not overly concerned about the implications of this fact, for he, at least, trusted the researcher to "judge the relative values of right and wrong" and abide by the appropriate limits in "putting patients 'in jeopardy' for the public good." Still, he asked, "In clinical research, is the means utilized justified by the ends?"[19] His own answer seemed to be a qualified yes, provided that the peril was not too great and the potential public benefit considerable.

Raising the issue as Cardon did at once enlightened and troubled some of his NIH colleagues. "We are on the defensive," responded one of them, "because, whether we like it or not, we have in some senses utilized the concept of the end justifies the means." Each of us here, observed another, knows that "it is easy to get carried away with the importance of one's own research." Still others conceded that researchers had a "special angle of vision" (others might say a self-interest) that could lead them to minimize the risks of an experiment to the subject when the benefits to humanity seemed extraordinary. These worries, however, did not dictate NIH policy. Rather, a confidence in the ultimate value of research fostered and justified a hands-off policy that left investigators with the sole discretion to determine risks and benefits. The final word went to one institute director who concluded: "Society would be in peril if we did not do clinical research."[20]

The NIH was so committed to this position that it would not devise procedures or guidelines to govern the extensive extramural research that it supported. By 1965 the NIH extramural program was the single most important source of research grants for universities and medical schools, by NIH estimates supporting "between 1,500 and 2,000 research projects which, by their titles, indicate presumptive experimentation involving man." Nevertheless, grant provisions included no stipulations about the conduct of human experimentation, and NIH

internal memoranda noted that it treated applications "for clinical research the same as for other research." NIH staff did find that many
investigators, "without formal requirements for such information . . .
may describe . . . local practices concerning the provision for informed
consent, and other matters relating to professional ethical considerations." Reviewers, too, on their own initiative would "often deliberate
ethical questions in relation to grants." However, such submissions
were voluntary and the discussions random. "There is little attempt,"
NIH officials reported, "to develop consensus as to what clinical research practices should be, or even to define what is the nature of the
ethical issues at stake."[21]

The universities made little effort to fill the gap. In 1960, Dr. Louis
Welt, of the University of North Carolina School of Medicine, one of
the handful of people then interested in the ethics of human experimentation, asked some eighty university departments of medicine about
their practices and guidelines. He reported that of the sixty-six responding departments "only eight have a procedural document and
only 24 have or favor a committee to review problems in human experimentation."[22] Shortly thereafter, a newly established Law–Medicine
Research Institute at Boston University conducted a similar survey and
confirmed Welt's findings. Only nine of fifty-two departments of medicine had a formal procedure for approving research involving human
subjects, and only five more indicated that they favored this approach
or planned to institute such procedures. Twenty-two departments did
have a peer-review committee, but with merely an advisory role.[23]

Both of these surveys revealed a widespread conviction that ethical
considerations in research were best left to the judgment of the investigators. They were in the best position to calculate the risks and benefits to the subjects, to share information they thought appropriate,
and ultimately to decide whether the subjects were voluntarily and
knowingly agreeing to participate in the experiment. The medical research community, noted the Boston University survey, has "a general
skepticism toward the development of ethical guidelines, codes, or sets
of procedures concerning the conduct of research." Welt not only
reached the same conclusion but agreed with it: "A committee cannot
take responsibility. . . . This must always be in the hands of the individual investigators." Consultations with colleagues could be useful,

but "responsibilities return to their rightful place in the minds and hearts of the investigators."[24]

Granted, no profession invites regulation, and individuals, whether they work at the bench or the desk, prefer to be left alone on the assumption that they will behave ethically. Medical researchers and their institutions (from the NIH to almost all university medical schools and teaching hospitals), however, viewed the investigator's prerogative as sacrosanct, and that fact requires explanation. Perhaps any highly motivated group would have reacted in this same fashion, magnifying the importance of their own work so as to minimize the sacrifices that others would have to make for it, but few commentators called them to task. No less puzzling, in the immediate postwar decades, this delegation of authority to the researcher did not spark significant opposition or debate from outside medicine. Neither Congress nor the academy nor the media urged that human experimentation be subjected to the oversight of committees or be responsive to formal principles and codes defining the rights of subjects.[25]

The response to human experimentation might well have been otherwise. After all, the Nuremberg tribunal in 1945 and 1946 cast a shadow over the entire field of human experimentation. Revelations about the atrocities that the Nazis committed—for instance, putting subjects to death through prolonged immersion in subfreezing water to learn the limits of bodily endurance or castrating them in order to study the effects of X rays on the genitals—might have sparked a commitment in the United States to a more rigorous regulation of research. So too, the American research effort during the war may have raised questions and spurred closer oversight. Some might have suggested that Americans had come close to following the dictum, proclaimed by Hitler in 1942, that "as a matter of principle, if it is in the interest of the state, human experiments were to be permitted," that it was unacceptable for "someone in a concentration camp or prison to be totally untouched by the war, while German soldiers had to suffer the unbearable." This was, in fact, the line of argument that the defense attorney for the Nazi doctors pursued at the Nuremberg trial. With the research on American prisoners at question, he asked that the court "not overlook the fact that particularly during the last years, even outside Germany, medical experiments were performed on human beings who undoubtedly did not volunteer for these experiments."[26]

The Nuremberg Code, the set of standards on ethical research that emerged from the tribunal, might have served as a model, even if a slightly flawed one, for American guidelines. Its provisions certainly were relevant to some types of medical research that had been (and still were) under way in the United States. The opening provision of the Nuremberg Code declared: "The voluntary consent of the human subject is absolutely essential. This means that the person involved should have legal capacity to give consent." By this principle, the mentally disabled were not suitable subjects for research—a principle that American researchers did not follow. Moreover, the Code insisted that the research subject "should be so situated as to be able to exercise free power of choice," which rendered questionable the American practice of using prisoners as research subjects. The Nuremberg Code also declared that human subjects "should have sufficient knowledge and comprehension of the elements of the subject matter involved as to make an understanding and enlightened decision." Thus, American practices notwithstanding, persons mentally disabled by illness or retardation were not to be enrolled.

Yet, with a few exceptions, none of these issues received sustained analysis in the United States in the immediate postwar period. Neither the horrors described at the Nuremberg trial nor the ethical principles that emerged from it had a significant impact on the American research establishment. The trial itself did not receive extensive press coverage. Over 1945 and 1946 fewer than a dozen articles appeared in the *New York Times* on the Nazi research; the indictment of forty-two doctors in the fall of 1946 was a page-five story and the opening of the trial, a page-nine story.[27] (The announcement of the guilty verdict in August 1947 was a front-page story, but the execution of seven of the defendants a year later was again relegated to the back pages.) Over the next fifteen years only a handful of articles in either medical or popular journals took up Nuremberg.

In part, this silence may have represented a postwar eagerness to repress the memory of the atrocities. But more important, the events described at Nuremberg were not perceived by researchers or commentators to be directly relevant to the American scene. The violations had been the work of Nazis, not doctors; the guilty parties were Hitler's henchmen, not scientists. Francis Moore, a professor of surgery at Harvard Medical School and a pioneer in kidney transplantation, was especially sensitive to ethical issues in experimentation and was ahead of most of his colleagues in recognizing the dilemmas in human experimentation. But even as he decried the German atrocities, he distanced science and non-Germans from them. The "horrible nightmares of Dachau and Belsen will ever stand in the conscience of all men," he told a symposium on drug research in 1960. But the lesson had to remain "most especially in the conscience of Germans"; further, "the tragedy of this intentional suffering and torture can never be erased, but one of the ironic tragedies of the human experimentation by the German 'scientists' was that no good science of any sort came from any of this work."[28]

Madness, not medicine, was implicated at Nuremberg. Few people noticed that many of the German perpetrators were university-trained and university-appointed researchers or that many of them possessed first-rate medical credentials and had pursued notable careers. Instead, the prevailing view was that they were Nazis first and last; by definition, nothing they did, and no code drawn up in response to them, was relevant to the United States.[29]

Other articles that addressed the Nuremberg trial drew from it not the lesson that the state should regulate experimentation but quite the reverse—that the state should not interfere with medicine. Nuremberg became a stick with which to beat the idea of "socialized medicine," not the occasion to oversee research.[30] The logic of the argument was that the atrocities were the result of government interference in the conduct of research (and here, the distinction between the Nazi government and all other governments was lost). Science was pure—it was politics that was corrupting. Hence, state control over medicine through regulations that intruded in the private relationship between doctor and patient or investigator and subject were likely to pervert medicine.

Even an incident notorious enough to capture headlines and expose the unregulated character of human experimentation had a minimal impact on the mood of benign neglect. In 1962, when Senator Estes Kefauver was winding up a long and only modestly successful campaign to regulate drug company prices, the thalidomide scandal broke.

The drug, widely prescribed in Europe for pregnant women at risk for spontaneous abortion or premature delivery, was in the process of being evaluated for safety by the Food and Drug Administration (FDA). One official, Francis Kelsey, dissatisfied with the quality of the European test results, delayed approval, and in the interim the link between thalidomide and birth defects (typically, warped or missing limbs) became established. Although a major catastrophe had been averted, some 20,000 Americans, of whom 3,750 were of childbearing age and 624 were reported as pregnant, had already taken thalidomide on an experimental basis, that is, as part of the drug company protocols. However, the precise number of recipients was unknown and their identification incomplete, mostly because the companies and the prescribing physicians who were conducting the trials kept very sloppy records. Kefauver took full advantage of the scandal to clinch the case for greater regulation, and as a direct result, Congress empowered the FDA to test drugs not only for safety (an authority it had held since 1938) but for efficacy as well.

In the course of the hearings and debates on the bill, the senators learned, to the amazement of some of them, that patients who had received experimental drugs in these clinical trials did not always know that they were participating in an experiment. Many of the subjects who had taken thalidomide had had no idea that they were part of a drug trial and had not given their consent. New York's Senator Jacob Javits, profoundly disturbed by this situation, proposed an amendment to the Kefauver bill that would have compelled the secretary of Health, Education and Welfare (HEW) to issue regulations that "no such [experimental] drug may be administered to any human being in any clinical investigation unless . . . that human being has been appropriately advised that such drug has not been determined to be safe in use for human beings."[31] One might have thought that the desirability and fairness of such a regulation were indisputable; surely subjects in an experiment should be told that a drug is not demonstrably safe and asked whether they wish to take it. Yet the debates that followed were anything but mild, and the Javits amendment did not survive for long in its original form. As late as 1962, even so elementary a protection of human subjects could not win approval, and the reasons clarify why regulating medical research appeared unacceptable.

Javits cogently argued his case. He assured colleagues that he was not opposed to human experimentation and fully appreciated its critical role in medical progress ("I feel deeply that some risks must be assumed"). Nevertheless, "experimentation must not be conducted in a blind way, without people giving their consent. . . . [Otherwise,] where is the dignity, the responsibility, and the freedom of the individual?" These arguments notwithstanding, Javits recognized that the amendment was running into trouble, and attempted to salvage it by changing the language from the secretary "shall" to the secretary "may" issue such regulations; in its weakened form, intervention became discretionary, not obligatory, and allowed for as many exceptions as the secretary might wish. Javits also made clear that his proposal would affect only the administration of drugs whose safety was not known; he was not asking that patients be informed about all drugs physicians prescribed for them.[32]

Nevertheless, Javits could not persuade his colleagues to impose so elementary a requirement on researchers. First, the senators responded with extreme caution because they consistently confused experimentation with therapy and the investigator with the physician. And just as this blurring of the lines committed the NIH to a hands-off policy, so it undercut a regulatory response from Congress. Senators feared that compelling physicians to inform a patient about an experimental drug would also compel them to inform a patient about a diagnosis that was fatal; in order to get patients to take the new drug, the doctor would have to tell them that they were suffering from a life-threatening illness. For example, Colorado's Senator John Carroll, claimed to be generally sympathetic to the Javits amendment: "I believe that under normal circumstances, when a man . . . goes to a doctor, that man has a right to know if he is to be given untested medicine. . . . I firmly believe every human being has a right to know whether he is being treated with experimental medicine . . . that he is to be used as a guinea pig." Why, then, oppose the amendment? Because with a "strict, mandatory, prenotification requirement, we might prevent the doctor from helping his patients in times of extreme emergency." Or as Mississippi's Senator James Eastland insisted: "It might be an experimental drug, a single injection of which would provide him with a chance to live." The debate even slipped over into the case of the coma patient, in the process revealing the senators' inability to distinguish between the competent and the incompetent patient, and between an emergency and a nonemergency situation. Thus, one senator objected to the proposal because it would keep a comatose patient from getting potentially life-saving drugs: "How could he be notified that an experimental drug is being used?"[33]

In the Senate, as in the Clinical Center and countless university hospitals as well, the ethos of the examining room cloaked the activities of the laboratory, and the trust accorded the physician encompassed the researcher. Lawmakers were no more able than NIH officials to distinguish the human subject from the patient, so that efforts to regulate experimentation—however reasonable—were translated into attempts to regulate therapy, which were still considered unnecessary and intrusive. For any change to occur, it would first be necessary to differentiate the researcher from the doctor and the laboratory from the examining room.

Moreover, the confusion of experimentation with therapy reflected an extraordinary optimism about the prospects of innovation. The hearings may have been deeply affected by thalidomide, but when it came to regulating research, the senators saw every new drug as a potential penicillin. They hesitated to intervene in research because they assumed that experiments were likely to prove successful and the drugs under investigation would turn out to be therapeutic wonders. Through the course of the debate the senators frequently posed their hypothetical cases about experimental drugs in terms of the new, miraculous injection, the life-saving pill, the prescription that would revive the near-dead. They measured the impact of regulation not by calculating risks but by exaggerating benefits. Fantasies, not nightmare cases, ruled: the researcher who had a miracle cure for a deadly disease or who could awaken the comatose patient ought not to be burdened or bridled with administrative regulations.

Starting from such premises, it is small wonder that Congress proved unwilling to say cleanly and simply that researchers must obtain the permission of their subjects before conducting drug experiments. The Javits amendment finally emerged in the legislation as a request to the secretary of HEW to promulgate regulations so that investigators dispensing experimental drugs would obtain the consent of their subjects "except where they deem it not feasible or, in their best professional judgment, contrary to the best interests of such human beings."[34] The qualifications took the heart out of the resolution, granting investigators broad discretion to decide when such vague considerations as feasibility or best interest were being served.

Between 1945 and 1965 an occasional academic conference or organization attempted a sophisticated analysis of the issues in human experimentation—the deliberations of the Law–Medicine Research Institute at Boston University are one such example. The more typical approach, however, is exemplified by the National Society for Medical Research (NSMR). Founded to counter the campaigns of antivivisectionists, the NSMR, in 1959, for the first time devoted a conference to "Clinical Research—Legal and Ethical Aspects." Persuaded that "the law has not kept pace with modern medical developments," the conference attendees produced several useful analyses, including one on the weaknesses of the Nuremberg Code and another on the value of peer review in human experimentation. But the most notable characteristic of the 1959 conference—indeed, of much of the literature on ethics and human experimentation between 1945 and 1965—was its calmness. The discussions made the problems seem more conceptual than actual, more academically interesting than pressing. There was no sense of crisis, of lives at stake, or of trusts violated, and no hint of scandal. When Dr. Louis Welt discussed the difficulty of obtaining a noncoerced consent, the group he focused on was medical students, not prisoners or the mentally disabled. When a colleague reviewed human experimentation at the NIH Clinical Center, he found its guiding principles altogether adequate (requiring "only slight modification in light of experience") and made no comment about actual practices.[35]

When discussants glimpsed a conflict of interest between the researcher and the subject, or between the principle of the greatest good for the greatest number and the rights of the individual, they grew distinctly uncomfortable and moved either to smooth over differences or to make certain that the research enterprise was not seriously hampered. Thus, the NSMR's 1959 conference report made the ordering of priorities clear: "The standards for health research on human subjects should recognize the imperative need for testing new procedures,

materials and drugs on human subjects as essential to the public interest. The protection of personal rights of individuals . . . can co-exist
with the public necessity to use people—sick or well—as subjects for
health research." The primary goal was testing new procedures, and
the rights of individuals would coexist with it. The conference report
did declare that experiments on minors or on the incompetent should
have the approval of parents or guardians and should "also significantly benefit or may reasonably benefit the individual." But, probably
aware of how far World War II practices had departed from this
standard, the authors added a critical qualification: "There may perhaps be justification in the absence of this requirement in a national
emergency or for an experiment of utmost importance. Here, the avail-
ability of certain persons, not able to consent personally, may constitute
a strategic resource in terms of time or location not otherwise obtain-
able." Although the report conceded that "the Nazis hid behind this
rationalization . . . [and] such justifications should not even be considered except in the most dire circumstances," still it gave retrospective
approval to the wartime researchers and prospective approval to investigators on the brink of findings of "utmost importance."[36]

In this same spirit, several international medical organizations in the
postwar decades published guidelines for human experimentation, expanding on the Nuremberg Code. Most of these efforts, however, did
not involve American groups; and with the exception of a few researchers who made this a field of special study, the codes captured little
attention in the United States and had minimal impact on institutional
practices.[37] The American Medical Association (AMA), which spoke
for the interests of general practitioners, rather than specialists or medical investigators, did frame a research code, but the stipulations were
vague and lacked any reference to means of enforcement. The code
required the voluntary consent of the human subject but said nothing
about what information researchers should impart; who, if anyone,
should monitor the process; or what the ethics were of conducting
research on incompetent subjects, such as the institutionalized mentally
disabled. The code did condemn experiments on prisoners, expressing
explicit "disapproval of the participation in scientific experiments of
persons convicted of murder, rape, arson, kidnapping, treason or other
heinous crimes."[38] But its aim was to protect public safety, not inmates'

rights. The AMA believed that parole boards were treating prisoner-volunteers too generously, giving them early release as a reward for assuming medical risks, and thus returning hardened criminals to the streets too quickly.[39]

In all, American researchers in the immediate post–World War II period ran their laboratories free of external constraints. The autonomy they enjoyed in conducting human experiments was limited only by their individual consciences, not by their colleagues, their funders, their universities, or any other private or public body. How the investigators exercised this discretion, the record they compiled, became the focus of Henry Beecher's analysis. What we find there is a case study of the dangers of leaving medical science on its own.

CHAPTER 4

The Doctor as Whistle-blower

THE career of Henry Beecher provided few clues that he would be the one to expose in most compelling fashion how the researchers in the post–World War II decades abused their discretion. Unlike many whistle-blowers, Beecher stood at the top of his profession. Although the family name is a famous one in American history—his kin included Harriet Beecher Stowe, the "little lady" that Lincoln credited with bringing on the Civil War, and Henry Ward Beecher, the minister who was exceptionally influential until being disgraced by an adulterous affair—Henry's branch had not prospered. He grew up in Kansas in very modest circumstances and graduated from the University of Kansas. Talented and ambitious, he worked his way through Harvard Medical School, trained in general medicine, and then joined the Harvard faculty and the staff of the Massachusetts General Hospital (MGH). Beecher was so highly regarded that when in the late 1930s Harvard and the MGH sought to professionalize the field of anesthesiology, they gave him the assignment. He did a masterful job, coming to hold the Dorr Professorship of Research in Anesthesia and to chair the department.[1]

What prompted Beecher to analyze the conduct of human experiments and to go public with his findings? Anesthesiologists do have a reputation for being the fifth column within medicine. Beecher belonged to the specialty that daily watches colleagues perform in the operating room and then discusses their relative strengths and weaknesses. He was also something of a maverick who delighted in controversy and conflict. In 1954, for example, he was senior author of "A Study of the Deaths Associated with Anesthesia and Surgery," a paper framed in highly judgmental terms. Its purpose was to determine "the extent of the responsibility which must be borne by anesthesia for failure in the total care of the surgical patient." Others would have called this an investigation of comparative mortality with anesthetic agents. The major finding was that the use of the new and very popular anesthetic agent curare was associated with a significantly higher death rate, and Beecher hoped, again in contentious fashion, that "the study itself, by directing attention to these matters, would lead to sharper criticism of existing practices with improvement in them," which it did.[2]

Beecher's concern for research ethics also drew on his personal experiences. He was both a committed investigator and one who was fully prepared to use his laboratory skills to promote societal ends. His major interest in the 1940s and 1950s was the effects of drugs on pain, performance, and perceptions, a field which he pioneered. Given the obvious military relevance of the subject, Beecher worked closely with the U.S. Army during World War II and continued the collaboration into the opening years of the cold war. He explored such questions as which narcotic was best administered to wounded soldiers in combat, and he also alerted the military to the importance of what he called "the second great power of anesthesia," that is, its potential as a truth-telling serum. In short, Beecher learned firsthand about research in the service of society and in the process may have become sensitive to how slippery a slope he was on.

The most important consideration, however, was Beecher's commitment to good science, that is, to well-designed and properly constructed research protocols. He was among the first to insist on the need for controls in drug experiments, convinced that in no other way could the investigator eliminate the placebo effect and accurately measure the efficacy of a new drug. Beecher's most lasting contribution as a researcher was to establish how the very act of taking a drug, whatever its potency, led some patients to improve; he calculated that "of the average pain relief produced by a large dose of morphine treating severe pain, nearly half must be attributed to a placebo." Hence, if the outcomes for one group taking a medication were not compared to outcomes for a similar group taking a placebo, the efficacy of a drug could not be known. "The scientist as well as the physician," insisted Beecher in 1959, "is confronted with a bewildering array of new agents launched with claims sometimes too eagerly accepted by a compassionate physician trying to help a patient in trouble. The properly controlled, quantitative approach holds the only real hope for dealing with the oncoming flood of new drugs."[3] Thus, Beecher's sharpest fear was that research of dubious ethicality might impugn the legitimacy of experimentation, discrediting the prime force bringing progress to medicine. Bad ethics would undercut the pursuit of good science, and the result would be widespread ignorance and old-fashioned quackery.[4]

When Beecher first addressed research ethics in the late 1950s, only a handful of others shared his concern, and not until the mid-1960s did his ideas capture widespread attention. The breakthrough occurred in March 1965 at a conference on drug research at Brook Lodge, Wisconsin, sponsored by the Upjohn pharmaceutical company. Beecher delivered a paper on the ethics of clinical research, which went beyond discussions of general principles to cite specific cases. Although he did not name individual investigators, he discussed specific research protocols, all published, whose ethics disturbed him. His use of real cases caught the media's attention, and both the *New York Times* and the *Wall Street Journal* ran lengthy accounts of his talk.[5] Colleagues, too, evinced an unusual interest in his remarks, by no means all of it friendly or favorable. "I really was subjected to a most humiliating experience," Beecher told a friend about the aftermath of the Brook Lodge meeting. In particular, he reported, Dr. Thomas Chalmers and Dr. David Rutstein, both colleagues at the Harvard Medical School, "called a press conference to refute what I said without finding out whether or not I could be present. They made prepared statements and the meeting was terminated before I had an opportunity to do so. Chalmers charged me with being an irresponsible exaggerator. Rutstein stood up there with him and did not dissent."[6] Beecher seemed somewhat surprised by so agitated a response, but he immediately moved to defend his position and, judging by the way he threw himself into the task, relished the opportunity.

Beecher's strategy was to turn the Brook Lodge presentation into a professional journal article that documented the ethical dilemmas in human experimentation by describing actual research protocols. He had no trouble accumulating some fifty examples of what he considered investigations of dubious ethicality, and in August 1965, he submitted the article (again without footnotes to the cases) to the *Journal of the American Medical Association (JAMA)*. In a covering letter he told the editor, John Talbott, that the manuscript represented "about ten years of as careful thought as I am capable of doing. It has been read by a great many individuals, including the president of the Massachusetts Medical Society, who, though appalled by the information, agree that it should be published, and the sooner the better. I do hope you will find this suitable for publication in the Journal . . . the finest place for it to appear, in my view. It is rather long. I do not believe it can be shortened significantly and carry the same message, which so urgently needs to be disseminated." After Talbott responded that he was sending it out for review, Beecher wrote again to emphasize how important it was that *JAMA* publish the piece: "Last year I gave an oral presentation at a closed medical meeting and the reverberations from that are still continuing. . . . Unquestionably the shoe pinched a lot of feet."[7]

In October, Talbott rejected the article, informing Beecher that neither of two reviewers favored publication. One insisted that "the story could be told in twenty-five per cent of the space, illustrated by ten items with references rather than forty-eight items without references." The other found it so "poorly organized [that] frankly, I was surprised that a thoughtful physician of Doctor Beecher's stature expected you to review this manuscript. Should the decision be to revise, I would be interested in seeing the revision provided it is well prepared and eliminates nine-tenths of the examples." Apparently not eager to get involved in publishing so controversial a piece, Talbott noted that Beecher had twice expressed an unwillingness to make substantial deletions and did not give Beecher the option of changing his mind or making revisions. He thought it best to have Beecher "start afresh with another editorial board."[8]

Beecher then turned to the *New England Journal of Medicine (NEJM)*. He submitted a slightly revised and fully annotated copy, and Dr. Joseph Garland and two of his assistants (the "brain trust," he called them) reviewed it case by case; they recommended omitting about half the protocols, apparently not so much for reasons of space but because they did not find all the examples equally compelling. Some author–editor give-and-take went on, but Beecher accepted their recommendations and was not unhappy to have the piece, in his view, "understate the problem."[9]

Conscious that the *NEJM* did not enjoy the *JAMA*'s circulation, Beecher notified the press about its forthcoming publication and at the same time warned John Knowles, the head of the MGH, that "a considerable amount of controversy" might ensue. "I have no doubt that I shall come in for some very heavy criticism. For the sake of the Hospital, I have tried to make certain that the material is as thoughtful, as accurate and as unexaggerated as possible."[10]

Beecher's indictment was powerful, arousing, as classic exposés do, a sense of disbelief that such practices had continued for so long without either scrutiny or sanction. A sample of three conveys the style of the twenty-two.

Example 16. This study was directed toward determining the period of infectivity of infectious hepatitis. Artificial induction of hepatitis was carried out in an institution for mentally defective children in which a mild form of hepatitis was endemic.... A resolution adopted by the World Medical Association states explicitly: "Under no circumstances is a doctor permitted to do anything which would weaken the physical or mental resistance of a human being except from strictly therapeutic or prophylactic indications imposed in the interest of the patient." There is no right to risk an injury to 1 person for the benefit of others.

Example 17. Live cancer cells were injected into 22 human subjects as part of a study of immunity to cancer. According to a recent review, the subjects (hospitalized patients) were "merely told they would be receiving 'some cells'— ... the word cancer was entirely omitted."

Example 19. During bronchoscopy a special needle was inserted through a bronchus into the left atrium of the heart. This was done in an unspecified number of subjects, both with cardiac disease and with normal hearts. The technique was a new approach whose hazards were at the beginning quite unknown. The subjects with normal hearts were used, not for their possible benefit but for that of patients in general.[11]

The investigations that made up Beecher's roster of dishonor differed in methods and goals. The researchers in some explored physiologic responses (as in example 19); in others, they attempted to learn more about a disease (examples 16 and 17); in still others, they tested new drugs (example 4) or withheld a drug of known efficacy to test an alternative (example 1). All the examples, however, endangered the health and well-being of subjects without their knowledge or approval. Only two of the original fifty protocols, Beecher reported, so much as mentioned obtaining consent, and he doubted that even they had gone very far in that direction: "Ordinary patients will not knowingly risk their health or their life for the sake of 'science.' Every experienced clinician knows this. When such risks are taken and a considerable number of patients are involved, it may be assumed that informed consent has not been obtained in all cases." Perhaps, he was later asked, the investigators had actually obtained consent but neglected to mention it in their publications? Beecher found it fanciful to believe (as in example 1) that a group of soldiers with strep throat would knowingly participate in an experiment in which they would be denied penicillin and face the risk of contracting rheumatic fever: "I have worked on the ward of a large hospital for 35 years, [and] I know perfectly well that ward patients will not . . . volunteer for any such use of themselves for experimental purposes when the hazard may be permanent injury or death."[12]

Beecher's cases did not represent only a few bizarre examples; rather, his catalogue described how mainstream investigators in the period from 1945 to 1965 exercised their broad discretion. This fact emerges from a review of the original publications from which Beecher took his twenty-two examples—the first such review since the *NEJM* editors accepted the article for publication. (See Appendix A for complete citations to the twenty-two cases.)

Comparing the original twenty-two articles with Beecher's published account makes clear in the first instance that the strength of Beecher's indictment does not emanate from its methodological sophistication or scientific character. The selection was impressionistic, even arbitrary, not part of a random survey or systematic inquiry. Beecher himself considered the cases to be no more than apt examples, protocols that he knew about or had discovered as he read the *Journal of Clinical*

Investigation or the *NEJM*. Not surprisingly, then, the list of twenty-two has many idiosyncrasies: fully half of the studies involved research into cardiovascular physiology (examples 6 through 13 and 19 through 21), and two of the studies (examples 15 and 19) were carried out in England. But however haphazard the selection process, Beecher was singling out mainstream science—indeed, science on the frontier. To judge by such criteria as each researcher's professional affiliation, the sources of funding, and the journal of publication, these were typically protocols from leading investigators in leading institutions, working on some of the most important questions in medicine. Beecher was describing the clinical ethics of elite researchers, those already in or destined to be in positions of authority.

Beecher's twenty-two examples were current, all drawn from the immediate postwar period. One of the papers appeared in 1948, thirteen appeared between 1950 and 1959, and eight between 1960 and 1965. The journals were prestigious: six of the papers appeared in the *NEJM* (examples 1, 4 through 6, 14, and 16), five in the *Journal of Clinical Investigation* (examples 8, 10, 13, 15, 20), two in the *JAMA* (examples 2 and 9), and two in *Circulation* (examples 19 and 20). The funders of the research (which numbered more than twenty-two, since some projects received multiple support) included the U.S. military (the surgeon general's office or the Armed Forces Epidemiology Board), five projects; the National Institutes of Health, five projects; drug companies (including Merck and Parke, Davis and Company), three projects; private foundations, eight projects; and other federal offices (including the U.S. Public Health Service and the Atomic Energy Commission), three projects. Clearly, this was not research in tiny labs carried out by eccentric physicians.

Perhaps most telling were the auspices under which the research projects were conducted. Thirteen of the twenty-two examples came from university medical school clinics and laboratories: Case Western Reserve University (examples 1 and 2); the University of California Center for Health Sciences, Los Angeles (example 5); Harvard Medical School and its affiliated hospitals, including Peter Bent Brigham Hospital and Children's Hospital (examples 6, 9, 13, and 19); the University of Pennsylvania (example 7); Georgetown and George Washington Universities (example 8); Ohio State University (example 12); New

York University (example 16); Northwestern University (example 18); and Emory and Duke Universities (example 21). Three of the projects were conducted at the Clinical Center of the NIH (examples 10, 11, and 20).

The credentials of the principal investigators were one more indication of their importance. The younger ones were often research fellows, some in medicine (Case Western Reserve, example 1), others in surgery (Harvard, example 6); or postdoctoral or exchange fellows (NIH, examples 7 and 14). In two cases the more senior people were professors (NYU, example 16; Cornell, example 17). Among the junior researchers, a number were beginning to make their mark in the world of research and later went on to illustrious careers, becoming national leaders in medicine, chairmen of major departments, and winners of major awards, often for the very research that Beecher had cited.

Dr. Saul Krugman conducted the research described in Beecher's example 16, the purposeful infection with hepatitis of residents at the Willowbrook State School for the Retarded. After his Willowbrook investigations of 1956 through 1972, Dr. Krugman became the chairman of the pediatrics department at New York University and the winner, in 1972, of the Markle Foundation's John Russell Award. The citation praised Krugman for demonstrating how clinical research ought to be done. In 1983, Dr. Krugman also won the Lasker Prize, probably the highest award given for research in this country, just a notch below the Nobel Prize.

Dr. Chester Southam was the investigator in Beecher's example 17. An associate professor of medicine at the Cornell University Medical School and the chief of the section on clinical virology at the Sloan-Kettering Institute for Cancer Research, he was in charge of the research involving the injection of cancer cells into elderly and senile patients. In 1967, Dr. Southam was elected vice-president of the American Association for Cancer Research, and in 1968 he became its president.[13]

Examples 10 and 11, studies in heart physiology on patients at the NIH Clinical Center, involving "a mercury-filled resistance gauge sutured to the surface of the left ventricle" and "simultaneous catheterization of both ventricles," were conducted in 1957 and 1960 by Dr. Eugene Braunwald, then a researcher in cardiology at the NIH. (Dr.

Braunwald's is the only name to appear three times on the Beecher roll—principal investigator in these two cases, and one of the four authors of the paper in example 20.) In 1967, Dr. Braunwald won the Outstanding Service Award of the Public Health Service and in 1972, the Research Achievement Award of the American Heart Association. In 1972 he became Hersey Professor and chairman of the Department of Medicine at Peter Bent Brigham Hospital, Harvard Medical School, and he later headed the Department of Medicine at Beth Israel Hospital as well.

How is the behavior of these investigators to be understood? It will not suffice to claim that they were simply less moral or trustworthy than their colleagues. They were too well supported, too integral to the research establishment, and, ultimately, too much honored to characterize as aberrant or deviant. The idea that these particular experiments raised complicated ethical issues beyond the state of the field is no more persuasive. In practically every one of the twenty-two cases, it was self-evident that the subjects would not benefit directly from the research and might even be harmed. Neither Krugman's retarded subjects nor Southam's senile ones nor Braunwald's cardiac ones would have been better off for having participated in the protocols.

It also seems too narrow an explanation to place all the blame on raw personal ambition—the desire to get grants, win promotions, capture the prize. Undoubtedly, these considerations motivated some of the researchers, and Beecher himself, although he did not address the question directly, suggested this motivation. He stressed in particular the new and massive infusion of research funds through the NIH and the intensified research ethos in the postwar period. "Medical schools and university hospitals are increasingly dominated by investigators," he observed. "Every young man knows that he will never be promoted to a tenure post . . . unless he has proved himself as an investigator," and this at a time when "medical science has shown how valuable human experimentation can be in solving problems of disease and its treatment."[14] However valid his point, it does not explain why the research community evinced no difficulty with these protocols, why no scientist who read Krugman's publications in the 1950s protested, and why no department that reviewed the work of these researchers with-held promotion on the grounds of unethical behavior.

A better entry point for understanding how investigators and their colleagues justified these protocols is the impact of the World War II experience, because the exceptional protocol of the pre-1940 period became normative. Clinical research had come of age when medical progress, measured by antidotes against malaria, dysentery, and influenza, was the prime consideration, and traditional ethical notions about consent and voluntary participation in experimentation seemed far less relevant. A generation of researchers were trained to perform, accomplish, and deliver cures—to be heroes in the laboratory, like soldiers on the battlefield. If researchers created effective vaccines, diagnostic tests, or miracle drugs like penicillin, no one would question their methods or techniques.

This orientation survived into the postwar years, not simply because a license granted is not easily revoked, but because the laboratory achievements were so remarkable. Having been given extraordinary leeway, the researchers delivered extraordinary products: an array of antibiotics, including a cure for tuberculosis; a variety of drugs for treating cardiac abnormalities; a new understanding of hepatitis. Given this record, who would want to rein in such talent and creativity, to intrude and regulate behavior inside the laboratory? Surely not a senate committee that was investigating a drug scandal, let alone the NIH, whose extramural grants were funding the research. How much wiser to trust to the researcher and await one breakthrough after another.

Most of the researchers in Beecher's protocols were the heirs to this wartime tradition, although they had not actually participated in the war effort or held Committee on Medical Research (CMR) contracts. Of the thirty-two American investigators, only eight had been born before 1920 (of whom four had seen military service); of the twenty-four others, seventeen were born between 1921 and 1929, and seven between 1931 and 1934. They were, in other words, the products of medical and scientific training in the immediate postwar period, trained to think in utilitarian terms and ready to achieve the greatest good for the greatest number.

It is no coincidence that this cohort of investigators took as their research subjects persons who were in one sense or another devalued and marginal: they were either retarded, institutionalized, senile, alcoholic, or poor, or they were military recruits, cannon fodder for battles in a war against disease. These social characteristics at once reflected and promoted a utilitarian calculus among researchers, encouraging them to make the same judgments in the 1950s and early 1960s as their predecessors had made in the 1940s.

Beecher had relied on the logic of the situation—the patients' presumed unwillingness to put themselves at jeopardy—to argue that the researchers had not actually obtained consent from their subjects. Had he scrutinized the types of patients enrolled in the protocols more closely, he could have clinched his point, for in practically every instance, they lacked either the opportunity or the ability to exercise choice. The research subjects in examples 1 and 2 were soldiers in the armed forces; in example 3, charity patients; in examples 4 and 16, the mentally retarded; in examples 6 and 22, children or newborns; in examples 9 and 17, the very elderly; in example 12, the terminally ill; in examples 13 and 15, chronic alcoholics with advanced cases of cirrhosis. The subjects in examples 8, 10, 11, and 20 were patients in the Clinical Center, where, as we have noted, patients were generally not informed about the research procedures that accompanied treatment interventions. In fact, these four examples (involving catheterization and strain-gauge studies) were the very ones that Donald Fredrickson had cited, when he headed the Clinical Center's Heart Institute, to demonstrate that NIH patients were kept ignorant of protocols.

The incompetence of many of these subjects had enabled the researchers to assert all the more confidently their right to exercise discretion and to substitute their own judgment. Because the subjects could not understand the intricacies of a scientific protocol, the investigators felt justified in taking matters into their own hands. To Chester Southam, it was unnecessary to offer explanations to elderly and senile patients about injections of cancer cells because they would become frightened and because he knew, supposedly, that no danger existed. Some of this calculation may have reflected the laboratory version of the old clinical saw that a minor operation is an operation being performed on someone else. But Southam and other investigators were convinced that their procedures, however daring or invasive, actually carried little risk. (Little risk, but some: When Southam was later asked why, if the procedure was so harmless, had he not injected the cancer cells into his own skin, he replied that there were too few skilled cancer researchers around.) So too, Eugene Braunwald may have reasoned that it was unnecessary to obtain the permission of Clinical Center patients to insert a strain gauge on cardiac vessels or to measure cardiac functioning with a catheter because he reckoned the risks to be minimal.[15] And in this spirit, Saul Krugman reasoned that feeding live hepatitis viruses to Willowbrook residents was acceptable not only because the disease was already endemic there but because he considered the Willowbrook strain of the virus to be mild, posing no threat to the well-being of the children.[16]

After minimizing the question of risks, the researchers confidently asserted that the potential benefits were enormous. Southam conducted his experiments in the belief that the reactions of an already debilitated patient to foreign cancer cells would cast new light on the immunological system and bring him close to a cure for cancer. Was Southam an unethical researcher? Hardly, in his view. He aimed to become one of humanity's great benefactors. Behind Krugman's Willowbrook research was a conviction that he could do more good for more people if he could conquer hepatitis. Was Krugman taking advantage of the institutionalized retarded? Hardly. Whatever vaccines he produced would protect them against a disease to which they were particularly exposed. So too, Braunwald was undoubtedly convinced that his studies would be of enormous gain to all heart patients, which turned out to be correct. Was Braunwald ignoring the rights of the desperately sick at the Clinical Center? No, for the more he learned about cardiovascular functioning, the better those patients would be served.

A powerful exposé is often more able to identify a problem than to propose effective or imaginative solutions, and Beecher's contribution was no exception. He was too committed a researcher to so much as dally with the thought of abolishing human experimentation and was even reluctant to regulate it in ways that might hamper its operation. He was exceptionally ambivalent about the implications of his own findings and, at least initially, very reluctant to use them as basis for new departures. First, Beecher doubted the ability of a formal code of ethics to shape researchers' behavior. He did not believe "that very many 'rules' can be laid down to govern experimentation in man. In most cases these are more likely to do harm than good. Rules are not going to curb the unscrupulous."[17] Second, he was skeptical of the value of making the consent process itself more elaborate and trusting informed patients to look after their own best interest. After all, patients were too inclined to accede to physicians' requests, with or without well-intentioned explanations.

At the same time, however, Beecher, as much as any single figure, undercut the assumptions that were so critical to the hands-off policy at NIH and elsewhere: that the physician and the investigator were one and the same, and that the trust patients afforded to doctors should be extended to researchers. In one of his first major discussions of research ethics, an article in *JAMA* in 1959 on "Experimentation in Man," Beecher painstakingly differentiated between the two roles, subverting the idea that the ethical tradition in medicine was sufficient to produce ethical behavior in research. The two activities were "different in their procedures, in their aims, and in their immediate ends." The physician's exclusive concern was with the well-being of one particular patient; his ethical obligations were clear and uncomplicated (or at least relatively so): to do all in his power to advance the well-being of the patient. The investigator, on the other hand, was in a much more complicated position. His aim was to advance knowledge that would benefit society; his overriding allegiance was to his protocol, to a class of patients, if you will, not to the individual subjects in his protocol.

Beecher feared that a commitment to the general good as against the individual good might easily legitimate ethically dubious research, and he feared such a prospect especially because of the lessons of Nuremberg, which he was among the first to explicate. Perhaps he was conscious of the atrocities because of his earlier work with the army; in his papers are copies of then-classified German research reports, mostly dealing with the effects of exposure, which he may have evaluated, at the army's request, for their scientific value. Whatever the reason, he insisted: "Any classification of human experimentation as 'for the good of society' is to be viewed with distaste, even alarm. Undoubtedly all sound work has this as its ultimate aim, but such high-flown expressions . . . have been used within recent memory as cover for outrageous acts. . . . There is no justification here for risking an injury to an individual for the possible benefit to other people. . . . Such a rule would open the door wide to perversions of practice, even such as were inflicted by Nazi doctors on concentration-camp prisoners. . . . The individual must not be subordinated to the community. The community exists for man."[18]

On a less profound level, Beecher also distinguished the researcher from the physician by outlook and ambition. Doctors might let monetary concerns guide their actions, making treatment decisions in order to increase their incomes, but such behavior was immediately recognized as patently unethical. Investigators, however, were caught up in a system of promotions and grant getting that so emphasized research results as to obfuscate research ethics. The physician who lined his pockets at his patients' expense was condemned, whereas the researcher who produced new findings by disregarding the rights of his subjects might well win scientific prizes. Researchers knew they had to publish in order not to perish by being denied academic advancement and government funding; everyone recognized that tenure came only to those who proved themselves superb investigators, whatever their ethics. This environment nullified a concept of identity of interest between researcher and subject.

Yet the power of this critique notwithstanding, Beecher wavered, reluctant to recommend new rules or methods of regulation. He did have a short list of dos and don'ts for investigators: no use of prisoners of war for research, extreme caution about conducting research on laboratory personnel or medical students (who might feel obliged to consent because of their positions), but an allowance to do research on prisoners and volunteers if they gave consent. Beecher was also prepared to implement some type of "group decision supported by a proper consultive body," although he offered no details on how it might be organized or administered. But his final word on the researchers who conducted the twenty-two protocols was a variation on the theme of "they knew not what they did." He noted, with more rhetorical flourish than evidence or accuracy, that their "thoughtlessness and carelessness, not a willful disregard of the patient's rights, account for most of the cases encountered." Armed with such a formulation, he comfortably asserted that "calling attention ... will help to correct abuses present." He maintained such an old-fashioned faith in the integrity of the individual researcher that, after weighing all the alternatives, he concluded: "The more reliable safeguard [is] provided by the presence of an intelligent, informed, conscientious, compassionate, responsible investigator."[19]

In the end, Beecher's responses highlight the strengths and weaknesses of the insider's exposé. Without his courage, the movement to set new rules for human experimentation would have proceeded on a much slower track. Few others had the scientific knowledge and ethical sensibilities to call into question medical researchers' ethics. But at the same time, with such knowledge and sensibility came both forgiveness (investigators know not what they do) and paternalism (subjects can never understand what investigators do). Left to Beecher, the reaction to the scandals would have been an appeal to professional trust and responsibility, as though consciousness-raising could solve the problem.

CHAPTER 5

New Rules for the Laboratory

EVEN the most sensational exposé will not necessarily spark fundamental alterations in public attitudes or policy. Media attention is fickle and the competition for front-page coverage or a few minutes on the evening news so intense that even egregious scandals may fade from attention. Further, countless ways exist for those in authority to explain problems away, from blaming a few bad apples to assuring everyone that the deficiencies have already been corrected. But not all exposés disappear without a trace. They may affect those so high in power as to generate critical changes (Watergate) or reveal conditions so substandard as to shock the conscience (a hellhole of an institution for the retarded), or describe conditions so frightening in their implications as to rivet attention (images of a silent spring). Human experimentation had elements in common with all of these, helping to ensure that its scandals would produce structural change.

A number of investigators certainly attempted to minimize the problem. Some insisted, as we have seen, that Henry Beecher's cases were aberrations; although no one dared to make the point so bluntly, other researchers undoubtedly believed it proper to trade off the rights of highly marginal groups for the sake of scientific progress, to keep the World War II model operational and out of mothballs. After all, strictly utilitarian principles could justify the experiments of a Saul Krugman; the retarded, it could be argued, did not have all that much to lose when compared to the societal gains if the research produced a vaccine against hepatitis. And Beecher himself exemplified how difficult it was to break out of an older, hands-off model of maintaining a faith in the integrity of the investigator and minimizing the implications of a conflict of interest with the subject. Nevertheless, the scandals deeply affected public attitudes and brought an unprecedented degree of regulation and oversight to the laboratory.

The exposés had an especially critical impact on the leadership of the National Institutes of Health (NIH), by far the most important source of funds for clinical research, and the Food and Drug Administration (FDA), responsible for overseeing the testing and licensure of all new drugs. These agencies were exquisitely alert to congressional pressures: let public opinion be mobilized, and they might be hauled in to testify at hearings, criticized and embarrassed for failures to keep investigators in check, and left to suffer the consequences of budget cuts. Calculating in a most self-protective and painstaking manner the repercussions that would follow when public officials read articles about abuses in human experimentation and editorial writers questioned the wisdom of a continued trust in the individual researcher, they moved quickly to contain the crisis. Given the potential negative fallout, the price of inaction was unacceptably high. Thus, the fact that authority was centralized in bodies that were at once subordinate to Congress and superordinate to the research community assured that the scandals would alter practice. Indeed, this circumstance explains why the regulation of human experimentation came first and most extensively to the United States, rather than other industrialized countries.

To be sure, the leaders of the NIH and (to a lesser, but still important, degree) the FDA were integral to the medical research community. These were not outsiders or newcomers to clinical research, and they were not likely to adopt either far-reaching or consistently intrusive measures. Nevertheless, their need to act meant that this exposé would not capture headlines in today's newspaper and be forgotten tomorrow.

The NIH leaders initially concerned themselves with research ethics after the Kefauver hearings in 1962 disclosed that physicians were administering experimental drugs without informing patients. James

Shannon, then the head of the NIH, immediately requested Robert B. Livingston, the associate chief of the Division of Research Facilities and Resources, to investigate the "moral and ethical aspects of clinical investigation." Since the overwhelming sentiment in the Senate debate on the resolutions proposed by Kefauver and Javits was to leave research unfettered, the Livingston Report, delivered in November 1964, was under little external pressure to recommend a change in the laissez-faire policy. The authors of the report recognized that "there is no generally accepted professional code relating to the conduct of clinical research" and expressed "a mounting concern . . . over the possible repercussions of untoward events . . . [because] highly consequential risks are being taken by individuals and institutions as well as NIH." But they did not urge the adoption of stricter regulations. "There was strong resistance," recalled one of the participants, "on attempting to set forth any guidelines or restraints or policies in this area." The report's framers concluded that "whatever the NIH might do by way of designing a code or stipulating standards for acceptable clinical research would be likely to inhibit, delay, or distort the carrying out of clinical research," rendering any such efforts unacceptable.[1]

The Livingston Report was not to be the last word, for even before Beecher's article, disturbing incidents had continued to surface. The case that received the greatest publicity and most disturbed the NIH was Chester Southam's cancer research on senile and demented patients, begun in 1963. The attention was so great that within two years the research was the object not only of extensive press coverage but of a lawsuit and a disciplinary hearing for Southam before the New York State Board of Regents. Almost all the publicity was hostile, and none of it was lost on the NIH. "It made all of us aware," one official confessed, "of the inadequacy of our guidelines and procedures and it clearly brought to the fore the basic issue that in the setting in which the patient is involved in an experimental effort, the judgment of the investigator is not sufficient as a basis for reaching a conclusion concerning the ethical and moral set of questions in that relationship."[2]

Just as the ripple effects of Southam's research were being felt, Beecher's well-publicized 1965 lecture and then his 1966 *NEJM* article revealed that Southam's insensitivity to the ethics of experimentation was not idiosyncratic. Again, the NIH had to consider the implications of this publicity for its own functioning. At least one congressman asked NIH officials how they intended to respond to Beecher's charges, and the associate director for the extramural programs hastened to assure him that the findings "as might be expected have aroused considerable interest, alarm, and apprehension." Although "there are instances in the article which are either cited out of context, incomplete, or with certain mitigating circumstances omitted," still at NIH "constructive steps have already been taken to prevent such occurrences in research supported by the Public Health Service."[3]

However, a congressman's letter was only the most visible sign of NIH's vulnerability (or sensitivity) to political and legal pressure. Any Washington official who hoped to survive in office understood the need to react defensively—to have a policy prepared so that when criticism mounted, he or she would be able to say that yes, a problem had existed, but procedures were already in place to resolve it. The NIH director, James Shannon, readily conceded that one of his responsibilities, even if only a minor one, was "keeping the Government out of trouble." And his advisors concurred. It would be nothing less than suicidal to believe, as one of them put it, that "what a scientist does within his own institution is of no concern to the PHS." An ad hoc group appointed by Shannon to consider NIH policies reported back to him that if cases involving researchers' disregard of subjects' welfare came to court, the service "would look pretty bad by not having any system or any procedure whereby we could be even aware of whether there was a problem of this kind being created by the use of our funds."[4]

More than bureaucratic survival was at stake, though. The NIH response represented not just self-protection against potential legal and political repercussions but a reckoning with the substantive issues involved, an understanding of the causes behind the behavior of the individual researchers. By the mid-1960s it had become apparent to the NIH leadership that an incident like Chester Southam's protocol could be multiplied to twenty-two (to read Beecher) or to an even larger number by those familiar with the state of research at its own Clinical Center or other leading university and hospital laboratories. As a result of the exposés, the NIH leadership, as well as a number of individual researchers, also came to believe that a conflict of interest marked the interaction of investigator and subject: what was in the best interests of the one was not in the best interests of the other. The bedrock principle of medical ethics—that the physician acted only to promote the well-being of the patient—did not hold in the laboratory. (Later we will trace the implications of the discovery that this principle no longer held in the examining room either.) The doctor–patient relationship could no longer serve as the model for the investigator–subject relationship.

This conclusion moved Shannon and others at the NIH to alter its policies. Clinical research, they now recognized, "departs from the conventional patient–physician relationship, where the patient's good has been substituted for by the need to develop new knowledge, that the physician is no longer in the same relationship that he is in the conventional medical setting and indeed may not be in a position to develop a purely or a wholly objective assessment of the moral nature or the ethical nature of the act which he proposes to perform."[5] The researchers' aims, in other words, will distort their ethical judgments. The intrinsic nature of their quest renders them morally suspect. This postulate accepted, in February 1966 and then in revised form in July 1966, the NIH promulgated, through its parent body, the U.S. Public Health Service (PHS), guidelines covering all federally funded research involving human experimentation.

The regulators moved very carefully, aware that they were in unexplored and dangerous territory. "This policy," explained Dr. William Stewart, the surgeon general, "seeks to avoid the danger of direct Federal intervention, case by case, on the one hand, and the dangers inherent in decisions by an individual scientist on the other." The 1 July 1966 order decentralized the regulatory apparatus, assigning "responsibility to the institution receiving the grant for obtaining and keeping documentary evidence of informed patient consent." It then mandated "review of the judgment of the investigator by a committee of institutional associates not directly associated with the project"; and finally, it defined (albeit quite broadly) the standards that were to guide the committee: "This review must address itself to the rights and welfare of the individual, the methods used to obtain informed consent, and the risks and potential benefits of the investigation." As Stewart explained: "What we wanted was an assurance from [the grant-receiving institutions] that they had a mechanism set up that reviewed the potential benefit and risk of the investigation to be undertaken, and that reviewed the method that was used to obtain informed consent. And we thought that this should be done by somebody besides the investigator himself—a group. We thought this group might consist of a variety of people, and left it up to the institutions to decide." Stewart proudly stated: "We have resisted the temptation toward rigidity; for example, we have not prescribed the composition of the review groups nor tried to develop detailed procedures applicable to all situations. . . . Certainly this is not a perfect instrument. But . . . this action has introduced an important element of public policy review in the biomedical research process."[6]

Thus, for the first time and in direct response to the abuses of discretion, decisions that had traditionally been left to the individual conscience of physicians were brought under collective surveillance. Federal regulations, a compulsory system of peer review, assurances by universities and hospitals that they were monitoring the research, specific criteria that investigators had to satisfy, and a list of proscribed activities replaced the reliance on the researchers' goodwill and ethical sensibilities.

The new rules were neither as intrusive as some investigators feared nor as protective as some advocates preferred. At their core was the superintendence of the peer-review committee, known as the institutional review board (IRB), through which fellow researchers approved the investigator's procedures. With the creation of the IRB, clinical investigators could no longer decide unilaterally on the ethics of their research, but had to answer formally to colleagues operating under federal guidelines. Thus, the events in and around 1966 accomplished what the Nuremberg tribunal had not: to move medical experimentation into the public domain and to make apparent the consequences of leaving decisions about clinical research exclusively to the individual investigator.

For all the novelty of the response, policy changes designed and implemented by insiders had distinct limitations. For one, the NIH leadership did not at first insist on including in the collective decision-making process those who were outsiders to the world of research. The agency's 1966 policies still allowed scientists to review scientists to determine whether human subjects were adequately informed and protected. Given the NIH views on conflict of interest, the regulations did require that members of the review committee should have "no vested interest in the specific project involved." But they were vague about other criteria, stipulating that members should have "not only the scientific competence to comprehend the scientific content . . . but also other competencies pertinent to the judgments that need to be made." Accordingly, through the 1960s, most institutions restricted membership on the IRB to fellow investigators, and only a few included outsiders (most of whom were lawyers and clergymen) on the committee.

Second, and even more important, the NIH response focused more on the review process than the consent process. The agency did recognize the importance of the principle of consent, changing the title of its Clinical Center manual from *Group Consideration of Clinical Research Procedures* (1953) to *Group Consideration and Informed Consent in Clinical Research* (1967). And it did set forth guidelines for the researcher that cited the need to obtain "informed consent." But the NIH retained an investigator's skepticism about the ultimate value of the procedure, a position that was widely shared in the research community. As a Harvard colleague of Beecher's put it in responding to an early draft of his article: "Should informed consent be required? No! For the simple reason that it is not possible. Should any consent be required? Yes! Any teaching and research hospital must clearly identify itself as such . . . to the patient upon admission. . . . The fact that the patient is requesting admission to this hospital represents tacit consent. How do we interpret tacit consent? Not as a license but as a *trust*. This adds, not subtracts, responsibility."[7]

In keeping with this orientation, the internal memorandum enclosed with the new NIH Clinical Center manual read: "While there is general agreement that informed consent must be obtained, there is also the reservation that it is not possible to convey all the information to the subject or patient upon which he can make an intelligent decision. There is a strong feeling that the protection of the subject is best achieved by group consideration and peer judgment." Moreover, the NIH was not yet prepared or able to be very specific about what phrases like "informed consent" meant in practice. "Many of these key terms," conceded Eugene Confrey, the NIH director of research grants, "lack rigorous definition or are incompletely defined for purposes of general application." But the root of the difficulty was that NIH officials had trouble grasping the full implications of what it meant to obtain consent. The NIH publication explaining to "normal volunteers" at the Clinical Center that participation in the research was truly voluntary, declared: "You will be asked to sign a statement in which you indicate that you understand the project and agree to participate in it. If you find your assigned project to be intolerable, you may withdraw from it." Suggesting that the only grounds for withdrawal was the intolerability of the project was hardly the way to educate subjects to their freedom of choice.[8]

In effect, the NIH leadership was unwilling to abandon altogether the notion that doctors should protect patients and to substitute instead a thoroughgoing commitment to the idea of subjects protecting themselves. The 1966 guidelines were innovative, but only to a point. The NIH heads still looked to the professional to ensure the well-being of the layperson, and forced to reckon with the inadequacy of trusting to one professional, they opted to empower a group of professionals. The goal was to insure that harm was not done to the subjects, not to see that the subjects were given every opportunity and incentive to express their own wishes.[9]

FDA officials were also forced to grapple with the problems raised by human experimentation in clinical research. With a self-definition that included a commitment not only to sound scientific research (like the NIH) but to consumer protection as well, the FDA leadership did attempt to expand the prerogatives of the consumer—in this context, the human subject. Rather than emulate the NIH precedent and invigorate peer review, they looked to give new meaning and import to the process of consent.

In the immediate aftermath of the 1962 Kefauver hearings and the passage of the watered-down version of the Javits amendment, the FDA required investigators to obtain the consent of patients taking experimental drugs, but for the next several years, the precise nature of the obligation was unclear. By statute, investigators were not required to obtain consent when they found it "not feasible" or "not in the best interest of the subject"; and despite a number of efforts to have the FDA clarify the meaning of these terms (including an effort by Beecher), the agency steadfastly refused. Francis Kelsey, celebrated for holding back approval on thalidomide and now chief of the FDA Investigation Drug Branch, was prepared to say publicly that these clauses were meant to be applied narrowly for truly exceptional circumstances. But when Beecher, in 1965, asked the FDA's commissioner to confirm this position, he would only say: "The basic rule is that patient consent must be obtained except where a conscientious professional judgment is made that this is not feasible or is contrary to the best interest of the patient. It is my present opinion that it is not possible to go beyond this generalization at this time."[10]

In 1966, however, in the wake of the reactions set off by Beecher's article and the publicity given particularly to the cancer research of Chester Southam, the FDA shifted positions. On 30 August 1966, FDA officials issued a "Statement on Policy Concerning Consent for the Use of Investigational New Drugs on Humans," not only defining all the terms in the 1962 law but setting down what William Curran, one of the most astute students of NIH and FDA policies, described as "comprehensive rules regarding patient consent in clinical drug trials."

In the first instance, the FDA moved to close, albeit not eliminate, the loopholes. Distinguishing between therapeutic and nontherapeutic research (in accord with various international codes like the 1964 Helsinki Declaration and the arguments of critics like Beecher), it now prohibited all nontherapeutic research except where the subjects gave consent. When the research involved "patients under treatment" and had therapeutic potential, consent was to be obtained, except in what the FDA policymakers now frankly labeled the "exceptional cases," where consent was not feasible or in the patient's best interest. The FDA staff tried to define these terms more exactly. "Not feasible" meant that the doctor could not communicate with the patient (the example was a comatose patient) and "not in the best interest" meant that consent would "seriously affect the patient's disease status" (the example was the physician not wanting to divulge a diagnosis of cancer). In addition, the FDA, unlike the NIH, spelled out the meaning of *consent*. To give consent, the person had to have the ability to exercise choice and had to receive a "fair explanation" of the procedure, including an understanding of the experiment's purpose and duration, "all inconveniences and hazards reasonably to be expected," the nature of a controlled trial (and the possibility of going on a placebo), and any existing alternative forms of therapy available.[11]

The FDA regulations unquestionably represent a new stage in the balance of authority between researcher and subject. The blanket insistence on consent for all nontherapeutic research would have not only prohibited many of the World War II experiments but also eliminated most of the cases on Beecher's roll. The FDA's definitions of consent went well beyond the vague NIH stipulations, imparting real significance to the process. Nevertheless, ambiguities and irresolution remained. The FDA still confused research and treatment, and its clauses governing therapeutic investigations left a good deal of discretion to the doctor-researcher. Despite the insistence that consent was to be waived only in exceptional cases, the FDA allowed investigators to determine which cases these were. It was still up to them to determine the course of action for the incompetent patient or to decide when to withhold a diagnosis from the competent patient.

All these qualifications notwithstanding, the rules for human experimentation had changed, and the movement would continue and accelerate, with authority shifting from inside to outside the profession, from physicians to a very different group of actors. The NIH directors glimpsed this future. As they revised the agency's regulations, they predicted that the principles governing human experimentation (and, we may add, eventually all of medicine) were about to take new directions, the "consequence of increased attention to the problem by lawyers, physicians, psychologists, sociologists, and philosophers."[12]

Human experimentation did attract the critical attention of these professionals, almost all of whom rejected outright the utilitarian calculus adopted by the researchers. But the reasons for this rejection are not self-evident; indeed, it is easier to account for the investigators' pursuit of truth and fame than to understand why the others took so different an approach, why they did not accept the investigators' explanations and welcome the sacrifices made by a marginal, and by definition unprotesting, minority. But this was not the position adopted. Outsiders crossed over into medicine to correct what they perceived as wrongs, unwilling to accept the potential social benefit and trade off the individual interest. In short, they found harm where investigators perceived the opportunity for progress. Understanding the many reasons underlying this essential difference in outlook takes us through the rest of the book, for attitudes toward human experimentation were intertwined with attitudes toward physicians and hospitals—and then became inseparable from attitudes toward new medical procedures and technologies. Nevertheless, several points warrant immediate exploration.

First, the recognition by Beecher, as well as Shannon and others at NIH, that the traditional ethics of medicine no longer held in the laboratory and that a fundamental conflict of interest characterized the relationship between the researcher and the subject had an extraordinary impact on those outside of medicine. In fact, an appreciation of these very postulates brought philosophers, lawyers, and social scientists to a concern with medicine. Because the traditional precepts of medical ethics seemed inadequate to the problems posed by human experimentation, and because the hallowed maxims of "do no harm" and "act only in the interest of the patient," borne of a therapeutic context, did not appear to protect the subject in an experimental context, it became necessary to look to a different tradition and source for guiding principles. And this is precisely what the nonphysicians began to do, at first hesitantly and with apparent humility, later, in a more aggressive and confrontational style.

Two examples give the full flavor of the change. The topic of human experimentation initially brought to medicine Princeton University's professor Paul Ramsey, a philosopher who would exert a powerful influence over the development of the field of bioethics. In his own terms, Ramsey applied Christian ethics to contemporary issues, as evidenced in his previous books, *Christian Ethics and the Sit-In* and *War and the Christian Conscience: How Shall Modern War Be Conducted Justly?* Invited to lecture at the Yale Divinity School on medical ethics in 1968–69, he prepared for the assignment by spending a year at the Georgetown Medical School. As he later explained in *The Patient as Person*, the book that emerged from the lectures, the assignment was intimidating: "When first I had the temerity to undertake some study of ethical issues in medical practice, my resolve was to venture no comment at all—relevant or irrelevant—upon these matters until I informed myself concerning how physicians and medical investigators themselves discuss and analyze the decisions they face." He found their discussions "remarkable," convinced that no other profession "comes close to medicine in its concern to inculcate, transmit, and keep in constant repair its standards governing the conduct of its members."[13]

Nevertheless, Ramsey did not keep silent for very long, for he concluded that medicine could not be left to its own devices. Ethical problems in medicine, he declared, "are by no means technical problems on which only the expert (in this case the physician) can have an opinion," and his first case in point was human experimentation. Having read Beecher closely and having studied some of the protocols (particularly Krugman's hepatitis research), he was persuaded that the principle of the sanctity and dignity of human life was now under challenge. Raise this principle at a gathering of physicians, Ramsey observed, and one would be greeted by a counterprinciple: "It is immoral not to do research (or this experiment must be done despite its necessary deception of human beings)." His fear was that "the next step may be for someone to say that medical advancement is hampered because our 'society' makes an absolute of the inviolability of the individual. This raises the specter of a medical and scientific community freed from the shackles of that cultural norm, and proceeding on a basis of an ethos all its own."[14]

The force that drove medicine down this path was the investigators' thirst for more information, a thirst so overwhelming that it could violate the sanctity of the person. "I do not believe," insisted Ramsey, "that either the codes of medical ethics or the physicians who have undertaken to comment on them . . . will suffice to withstand the omnivorous appetite of scientific research . . . that has momentum and a life of its own."[15] In effect, Ramsey perceived, as others were starting to as well, an unavoidable conflict of interest. The goals of the researcher did not coincide with the well-being of the subject; human experimentation pitted the interests of society against the interests of the individual. In essence, the utilitarian calculus put every human (subject) at risk.

How was this threat to be countered? Ramsey had two general strategies. The first was to bring medicine directly into the public arena. We can no longer "go on assuming that what can be done has to be done or should be, without uncovering the ethical principles we mean to abide by. These questions are now completely in the public forum, no longer the province of scientific experts alone." Second, and more specifically, Ramsey embraced the idea of consent. It was to human experimentation what a system of checks and balances was to executive authority, that is, the necessary limitation on the exercise of power: "Man's capacity to become joint adventurers in a common cause makes the consensual relationship possible; man's propensity to overreach his joint adventurer even in a good cause makes consent necessary." Thus, Ramsey concluded: "The medical profession should no longer believe that the personal integrity of physicians alone is enough. . . . No man is good enough to experiment upon another without his consent."[16] In short, human subjects, not investigators, would have to define and protect their own interests.

These same concerns sparked the interest of other outsiders to medicine. In November 1967 and September 1968, *Daedalus* ran conferences devoted to the "Ethical Aspects of Experimentation with Human Subjects," the first time this broadly interdisciplinary publication had explored a medical matter in such depth.[17] Of the fifteen contributors to the issue that emerged from these meetings, six came from the health sciences (including Henry Beecher); the others represented a variety of specialties: five from law (including Guido Calabresi and Paul Freund) and one each from anthropology (Margaret Mead), sociology (Talcott Parsons), philosophy (Hans Jonas), and law and psychiatry (Jay Katz). Of course, some of these authors had already demonstrated a keen interest in bringing their disciplinary insights to medicine (most notably Talcott Parsons and Jay Katz). But most were just entering a field in which they would do outstanding work (Paul Freund, Guido Calabresi, and Hans Jonas, for example).

It was disconcerting to be among the first to cross over from one's home discipline to medicine; and it is doubtful, now that the route has been so well laid out, that anyone today would be as circumspect as Hans Jonas, a professor of philosophy at the New School for Social Research, was in describing his initiation. Reporting "a state of great humility," he declared: "When I was first asked to comment 'philosophically' on the subject of human experimentation, I had all the hesitation natural to a layman in the face of matters on which experts of the highest competence have had their say."[18] But he, like Ramsey, was convinced that the issues were intriguing and disturbing enough to require sustained philosophical analysis and, ultimately, new first principles.

Jonas's starting point was the inherent conflict between the noble purpose of gaining knowledge and the moral obligation to the subjects themselves. He, too, contrasted the social good with the personal good—or in the language of the laboratory, the need for an adequate sample size and the degradation implicit in making a person "a passive thing merely to be acted on," against the welfare of the individual. Rejecting the notion that society could command the subject's "sacrifice" under the terms of the social contract, and not completely satisfied with any method for resolving the conflict ("We have to live with the ambiguity, the treacherous impurity of everything human"), Jonas joined the ranks of those coming to rely primarily on the process of consent. Indeed, for him consent served not only as the justification of an individual's participation in an experiment but as a method for ranking those who should be asked to become research subjects. Those most capable of giving consent—the best educated with the greatest degree of choice—should be the first asked; hence, on Jonas's list, research scientists were at the top and prisoners at the bottom. He conceded that this principle of "descending order" might hamper experimentation and slow progress, but the danger to society from a disease was less than the danger of "the erosion of those moral values whose loss, possibly caused by too ruthless a pursuit of scientific progress, would make its most dazzling triumphs not worth having."[19] Thus, Jonas and Ramsey arrived at the same conclusion: the only escape, however incomplete, from the dilemmas in experimentation was through a revitalization of the principle of consent. Human subjects had to become their own protectors.

The approach drawn from philosophers' first principles fit neatly with the approach emerging from reformers' social principles. In this coincidence of vision one finds some of the reasons why, beginning in the 1960s, the public identified not with researchers and the triumphs they might bring forth from their laboratories (as had been true during the 1940s and 1950s), but with the subjects of the experiments and the harms they might suffer in the laboratory. The change in perspective mirrored a grander reorientation in social thought, one that now looked more to securing personal rights than communal goods, to enhancing the prerogatives of the individual, not the collective. The political culture of the 1960s fostered an extraordinary identification with the underdog and the minority, as evidenced by the fact that the tactics of the civil rights movement became the model for others to emulate. Just as these activists used a language of rights to counter discrimination, so too did advocates for women, children, gays, and students. It may not have been apparent or even correct to think that all of these groups actually constituted minorities (were women really a minority?) or in any conventional meaning of the term possessed rights (in what sense does a child have a right against a parent?). But those were quibbles that could not be allowed to interfere with the goal of reform. This same mind-set framed the experience of subjects in clinical research. As Beecher's protocols amply demonstrated, the subjects were drawn disproportionately from among the poor, the physically or mentally handicapped, the elderly, and the incarcerated. The result was an identification with the retarded and the senile in their vulnerability to exploitation, not with the investigators and the prospect for a vaccine against hepatitis or a cure for cancer.

This orientation fostered a distrust of constituted authorities and medical researchers became one group among many to feel the impact of the new skepticism toward the exercise of paternalism and the loss of trust in discretionary authority. "The list of those who have suffered this loss," I had occasion to write in the 1970s, "is as lengthy as it is revealing: college presidents and deans, high school principals and teachers, husbands and parents, psychiatrists, doctors, research scientists, and obviously, prison wardens, social workers, hospital superintendents, and mental hospital superintendents."[20] The momentum of change did not, however, merely consume one institution after another. *Research scientists* appeared on the list because of specific, powerful reasons for curbing the authority of the investigator—reasons that Beecher, Shannon, Ramsey, and Jonas, each in his own way, had supplied. The original purpose behind the grant of discretion, which had emerged in the Progressive Era, was that it would allow professionals, and others like parents and husbands, the opportunity to fulfill benevolent designs, to substitute their greater knowledge for that of their patients, students, children, or spouses. But now it seemed that discretion served self-interest—that deans acted in the best interests of the university, not its students; that husbands furthered their own needs, not those of their wives; that wardens looked to the needs of the prison, not the inmates. In this same fashion, investigators pursued their own goals—career advancement, discovery, prizes, and fame—while disregarding the risks to their subjects. It was a zero-sum game in or out of the laboratory. If the investigator was to win, the subject might well have to lose.

Moreover, the scandals and the way they were interpreted in terms of conflict of interest made it vital not only to import a language of rights into medicine but to bring formality and clearcut guidelines to procedures that had been casual and open-ended. In the realm of social welfare, it seemed best to define entitlements precisely rather than have the welfare mother trust to the discretion of the social worker; in treating juvenile delinquents, it seemed best to expand procedural protections instead of relying on the benevolence of a juvenile court judge or warden. And in this same spirit, in human experimentation it seemed best to establish an exacting review mechanism and a formal consent process rather than rely for protection on the conscience of the individual researcher. In sum, all these movements presumed a warfare between "them" and "us," in which self-serving motives were cloaked in the language of benevolence, and majorities took every occasion to exploit minorities. In such a combative world, one had to depend on rules, not sentiment, to secure fairness.

One last consideration helps tie all these movements together: the importance of events that converged in 1966 and signaled the heightened level of social conflict. This year witnessed the transformation of the civil rights movement from one that could dream, in Martin Luther King's eloquent words, about "a beautiful symphony of brotherhood" in which all of God's children joined hands to celebrate freedom, to one that designated "black power" as the only way to wrest control from an oppressive white ruling class. This year also witnessed the first defeat that the civil rights movement suffered in Congress, a defeat on a socially far-reaching question, relevant nationwide: open housing. And 1966 was the year that Beecher's *NEJM* article appeared and set off its many repercussions. Social change is too gradual a process to fit neatly onto a calendar (and social historians are prone to talk about generations and eras, not days and weeks), but 1966 has a special relevance to this story and makes connections among the various parts all the more secure.

CHAPTER 6

Bedside Ethics

However appropriate it appeared to restructure the relationship between medical researchers and human subjects, to reduce the discretionary authority of the investigator by expanding the formal authority of peers (through institutional review board oversight) and the role of the subjects themselves (through a new emphasis on informed consent), it was by no means obvious that such changes were relevant to the doctor–patient relationship. Although exposés had revealed the conflict of interest between investigators and subjects and undermined the sense of trust between them, the therapeutic encounter, at least on the face it, entailed none of these problems. The treating physician seemingly had no concern apart from the care and cure of the patient; even as NIH officials and other critics of research practices came to recognize that the bedrock principle of medical ethics—the doctor as advocate for his or her patients—did not fit with human experimentation, they did not doubt that it held in medicine itself. The physician was different from the researcher, Hans Jonas insisted: "He is not the agent of society, nor of the interests of medical science . . . or future sufferers from the same disease."[1] The doctor's only agenda was the patient's well-being.

In fact, physicians shared a powerful tradition of ethical discourse that went back to Hippocrates and continued through modern times. It was at once high-minded, generous, and even heroic, yet remarkably

101

insular and self-serving too. Physicians almost exclusively defined the problems and arrived at the resolutions, giving the deliberations a self-contained quality. Thus, any effort to bring a new set of rules to medicine, to introduce into the world of therapy the procedures that narrowed the prerogatives of the investigator, would bear a heavy burden of justification: it was one thing to regulate researchers, quite another to interfere with practicing doctors. Furthermore, any such effort was certain to provoke extraordinary resistance and hostility. Physicians, accustomed to making their own rules, were certain to find external intervention altogether unnecessary and frankly insulting. If medical ethics was to confront other traditions in ethics, whether religious or more systematically philosophical, the meeting was likely to be adversarial. Medical ethics was not lay ethics—or "bioethics," to use the more popular and current label.

From the classical age onward, the most distinguishing characteristic of medical ethics was the extent to which it was monopolized by practicing physicians, not by formal philosophers, with the minor qualification that sometimes, as in the case of a Maimonides, one person fit both categories. Physicians typically wrote the texts and, no less important, read them. As late as the 1950s, the noted psychiatrist Karl Menninger aptly commented: "With the one stellar exception of Catholic moralists, there is a strange blind spot about the ethics of health and medicine in almost all ethical literature. Volume after volume in general ethics and in religious treatises on morality will cover almost every conceivable phase of personal and social ethics *except medicine and health*." And one of the first contemporary philosophers to break with this tradition, Joseph Fletcher, agreed with Menninger that "it is a matter for wonder that the philosophers have had so little to say about the physician and his medical arts."[2]

Medical ethics as conceptualized and written by physicians had a very practical bent, concerned not as much with discerning first principles as with formulating maxims for practice. Predictably, too, the definition of what constituted an ethical problem and the choice of solutions reflected the vantage point of the doctor, not the patient—for example, what the physicians' rights and responsibilities were and how they should behave toward patients and, no less important, colleagues.

To many contemporary readers, these tracts seem most remarkable for elevating medical etiquette over medical ethics, for moving ever so nimbly from high-minded injunctions—do no harm—to professionally self-serving propositions—do not slander a fellow doctor or pay social visits to his patients or contradict him in front of his patients. In this literature, coveting a colleague's patients appeared a more serious breach than coveting his wife. But the distinction between etiquette and ethics hardly mattered to the tracts' authors or to the audience of practicing physicians. These were not exercises in philosophical discourse but manuals for practitioners who were intent on doing equally well by their patients and their practice.

Although etiquette dominated, it would be a mistake to dismiss all the tracts as business manuals on the theme of how to win patients and influence colleagues. The writings in medical ethics spelled out a series of obligations for physicians that required them to act not only responsibly but virtuously, to ignore self-interest in the pursuit of the patient's welfare. To limit the examples to the United States, Benjamin Rush, the celebrated Philadelphia physician and signer of the Declaration of Independence, in 1801 delivered a series of lectures on the "vices and virtues" of the physician in which he set down the most rigorous standards for physician behavior. The virtuous physician was abstemious, even ascetic: "The nature of his profession renders the theatre, the turf, the chase, and even a convivial table in a sickly season, improper places of relaxation to him. . . . Many lives have been lost, by the want of punctual and regular attention to the varying symptoms of diseases; but still more have been sacrificed by the criminal preference, which has been given by physicians to ease, convivial company, or public amusements and pursuits, to the care of their patients."[3] (Perhaps here one finds the roots of a tradition of physician isolation; however, Rush was anything but isolated from his society.) Moreover, Rush's ideal physician was not pecuniary minded; recognizing an ongoing obligation to the poor, he would never refuse to treat patients because of poverty, or exploit their vulnerability. Indeed, the virtuous physician was heroic: should a plague strike a community, the physician was obliged to stay and treat the ill, even at the risk of death.

A century later, Dr. Richard Cabot, a professor at the Harvard Medical School, both expanded the range of issues that belonged to medical ethics (such as fee splitting) and gave unconventional answers to conventional questions (favoring the use of birth control through contraception and always telling patients the truth). Hence, physician-dominated medical ethics was much more than a low-minded enter-prise, although it did often lack intellectual rigor. The presumption was that students learned ethics not in the classroom but on the wards by emulating their teachers, by having senior attending physicians serve as role models for their juniors. "I know of no medical school in which professional ethics is now systematically taught," Cabot wrote in the mid-1920s, and the situation remained essentially unchanged through the 1950s.[4]

Just how confident physicians were about the integrity of medical ethics, and how jealously they kept it as their own special preserve, is demonstrated by the pronouncements of the American Medical Asso-ciation (AMA). In the 1930s, for example, the AMA appealed to a timeless and physician-dominated medical ethics to justify its opposi-tion to a variety of proposed policies, including national health insur-ance, group practice, and physician advertising. "Medical economics," declared the AMA policymakers, "has always rested fundamentally on medical ethics," whose principles were universal, not varying by time (ancient or modern) or place (Europe or the United States) or type of government (monarchy or republic). "Such continuous persistence through so wide a diversity of environments," they argued, "seems to prove that judged by the 'survival test,' medical ethics has demon-strated its essential social soundness." The reason for this astonishing record was that the ethic was based on empirical experience: "Each new rule or custom was tested in actual practice" and then judged in terms of how well it supported the "close personal relationship of the sick person and his trained medical adviser," and how well it "pro-moted the health of patients, as measured by morbidity and mortality statistics." In this way, AMA leaders explained, "ethics thus becomes an integral part of the practice of medicine. Anything that aids in the fight on disease is 'good'; whatever delays recovery or injures health is 'bad.' " And with a confidence that tipped over into arrogance, they concluded: "This development and treatment of medical ethics gains much greater significance when compared with the development of ethics in society as a whole." Unlike ethics in general, where one school of thought did battle with another, medical ethics had been spared "metaphysical or philosophic controversies."

All this added up to a dogged insistence that medical ethics should be left entirely to medicine, which also meant that health policy should be left entirely to medicine. For example, since "the close personal relationship of the sick person and his trained medical adviser" was an essential element in the ethic, public interference with medicine through health insurance or through the sponsorship of group practice was wrong. Indeed, any effort by outsiders to rewrite or violate these centuries-old precepts would both subvert sound medical practice and, even more drastically, subvert the social order, for "ethical rules and customs are among the most important of the stabilizing elements in society."[5] In sum, medical ethics belonged to doctors, and outsiders had no right to intrude.

These claims did not go entirely uncontested. Catholic theologians, for example, had their own vigorous tradition of analyzing medical ethics, although the impact of their analyses and recommendations was restricted to those within the Catholic fold. Publications like the *Linacre Quarterly* were replete with articles applying Catholic dogma to medical questions. For example, a number of Catholic ethicists debated whether it was permissible, in the event of a tubal pregnancy, to remove the fetus—in effect, killing it—in order to save the mother's life, or whether one had to leave the fetus in place, despite the fact that a failure to intervene would cause the death of the mother and the fetus as well. (Most commentators opted for intervention, distinguishing between direct and indirect harm; death to the fetus was morally acceptable, provided it was the indirect result of treating the tubal defect.)[6] The Catholic tradition in medical ethics was actually powerful enough to inspire critics of its own. The journalist Paul Blanshard, for example, wrote a blistering attack on the authority that Catholic priests ostensibly exercised over Catholic doctors and nurses in their professional lives. But whatever its internal strength, the Catholic example exerted little influence over medicine more generally and did not inspire non-Catholics to make medical ethics a central intellectual concern.[7]

One of the first efforts to break the physician monopoly and explore issues of medical ethics was Joseph Fletcher's 1954 book, *Morals and Medicine*. Fletcher's route into this field, like Paul Ramsey's later, was through Protestant religious ethics, not formal academic philosophy. Fletcher's aim, however, was not to apply religiously based doctrines to medical practice, but to analyze, very self-consciously, ethical issues "from the patient's point of view." He took his guiding premise from outside of medicine, insisting that individuals, in order to act as responsible moral beings, had to have the freedom and the knowledge to make choices; otherwise, he contended, "we are not responsible; we are not moral agents or personal beings." Brought into medicine, this principle meant that patients kept ignorant and rendered passive by their doctor were not moral agents but puppets in a puppet show, "and there is no moral quality in a Punch and Judy show."[8] Hence, Fletcher argued that physicians were obligated to tell patients the truth about a diagnosis and condition, not in order to satisfy a professional medical creed or legal requirement, but because patients had to be able to exercise choice.

This same assumption guided Fletcher's positions in the area of reproduction and led him to a fundamental disagreement with Catholic doctrines. In his view, contraception, artificial insemination, and sterilization were not "unnatural acts" but procedures that enhanced individual choice. Contraception "gives patients a means whereby they may become persons and not merely bodies." Artificial insemination was a method that kept the accidents of nature (sterility) from overruling "human self-determination." Fletcher also wanted to leave decisions about sterilization to the individual because "moral responsibility requires such choices to be personal decisions rather than natural necessities." He even approved of active euthanasia, since the alternative, "to prolong life uselessly, while the personal qualities of freedom, knowledge, self-possession and control, and responsibility are sacrificed is to attack the moral status of a person."[9]

Although the subject matter that Fletcher explored was relatively traditional—the ethics of reproduction and euthanasia had a long history in Catholic literature—his approach was not. Fletcher moved the discussion away from the privileges of the physicians or the requirements of religious creeds to the prerogatives of the patient, and in 1954 such a formulation was highly original. Perhaps too original, for his work did not immediately stimulate a different kind of dialogue in medical ethics. For another decade at least, the book remained an odd contribution, not, as it now appears, the beginnings of a new departure. To bring outsiders into medical decision making, to have philosophers take a place at the bedside, in effect to substitute bioethics for medical ethics would require far more than one man adopting a new approach. It would demand nothing less than a revolution in public attitudes toward medical practitioners and medical institutions, a revolution marked by a decline in trust in the doctor, and, concomitantly, in the relevance, the fairness, and the wisdom of beside ethics.

Such a revolution in attitudes is precisely what occurred between 1966 and 1976. The new rules for the laboratory permeated the examining room, circumscribing the discretionary authority of the individual physician. The doctor–patient relationship was molded on the form of the researcher–subject; in therapy, as in experimentation, formal and informal mechanisms of control and a new language of patients' rights assumed unprecedented importance. The change at first affected not so much the context of medical practice, such as licensure requirements or reimbursement schedules (that would come later), but the content of medical practice—treatment decisions made at the bedside for a particular patient. Jonas's image of the doctor alone in the examining room with the patient (and with God) gave way to the image of an examining room with hospital committee members, lawyers, bioethicists, and accountants virtually crowding out the doctor.

From the vantage point of the 1950s, the transformation would have appeared startling and unexpected. In the 1950s, after all, therapeutics had assumed unprecedented efficacy, eliminating the most deadly and crippling infectious diseases (before AIDS, one would have said all deadly infectious diseases), including polio and tuberculosis, and making notable advances against such chronic diseases as cancer and heart disease. Given this remarkable progress, one might have anticipated a golden age of doctor–patient relationships. And even the fact that other professions in the 1960s were being challenged by expressions of individual rights might not have weakened the strong bond of trust that had existed between doctors and patients. But that was not to be the case. To paraphrase the title of a 1970s collection of essays on health care, medicine was doing better, but patients were feeling worse.

Physicians themselves, as would be expected, were acutely sensitive to these changes. A few of them, as we shall see, helped inspire the movement, serving as guides in introducing outsiders to the new issues; in fact, the transformation in the ruling of medicine probably would not have progressed so rapidly or thoroughly without their assistance. But the majority, expressing themselves in the editorial columns of medical publications and from witness chairs in congressional hearings, displayed a barely disguised disdain and hostility. They inveighed against the new regulatory schemes and the empowerment of lay bodies and boards, and when they suffered defeat, took the losses badly.

How are we to understand this decline of trust, this sense that the physician, like the researcher, does not share a common interest with the patient? Why did the language of rights and the politics of a rights movement enter health care, challenging the exercise of medical discretion? Why were the traditions of medical ethics not seen as sufficient to the doctor–patient relationship? As with any broad change, the causes are multiple. The precipitous rise in physicians' income in the post-1945 period, particularly in the post–Medicare period, helped foster a belief that doctors had become more concerned with their pocketbooks than their patients. The enactment of Medicare and Medicaid instigated some of the first systematic efforts to measure quality of care, and these measurements revealed such substantial variations in physician practices (most notably, in the frequency of surgery) as to suggest that greed and ignorance were more endemic in the profession than had been imagined. In light of these findings, critics then began to analyze the weaknesses in licensure requirements and to look even more closely at the failure of the profession to discipline errant members.[10] However important these elements were in undermining a sense of trust between doctor and patient, a still more fundamental consideration first widened the breach. In the post–World War II period, a social process that had been under way for some time reached its culmination: the doctor turned into a stranger, and the hospital became a strange institution. Doctors became a group apart from their patients and from their society as well, encapsulated in a very isolated and isolating universe. The familiarity that had once characterized the doctor–patient relationship gave way to distance, making the interactions between the two far more official than intimate. By the same token, the links that had tied doctors to their communities—whether through club life, economic investments, or civic activities—were replaced by professional isolation and exclusivity. Finally, the bonds of neighborhood and ethnicity that had once made a hospital a familiar place for its patients were practically severed, giving to the institution an alien and frightening atmosphere. In sum, a three fold break occurred that severed the bonds between doctor and patient, doctor and community, and hospital and patient and community.

This enlarged social distance in large part explains why new rules and new players came into medicine and why bioethics came to replace medical ethics. Physicians who were strangers could not be trusted to exercise discretion over weighty matters of life and death; hence, a growing contingent insisted that the norms about sharing information change so that physicians would be compelled to tell patients the truth, no matter how grim the diagnosis. Physicians could not be left to decide unilaterally about terminating or withdrawing treatment; hence, a growing contingent insisted that a practice of making pencil marks on nursing charts should be replaced with a formal code that required the explicit approval of the patient and consultations among physicians. Indeed, suspicion toward physicians ran so high that the practice began of relying on third parties, the clinical bioethicist or hospital ethics committees, to protect and strengthen the patient's role in decision making.

It is not romanticizing the past practice of medicine to observe that in the pre–World War II period, physicians were more closely connected both to their patients and their community.[11] So broad a generalization inevitably does an injustice to the diversity of social class and region, but during the late nineteenth and early twentieth centuries, practically all aspects of health care worked to strengthen the ties between the medical and lay worlds. Whatever suspicion the public had toward the medical profession and its institutions (which was especially acute before 1910) did not foment a distrust of one's own physician or hospital. The exercise of medical discretion seemed less a conspiracy to maintain professional hegemony over the patient than a confident expression of beneficence, that is, the physician being willing and able to spare the patient the burden of choice or the direct confrontation with death.

When contemporary observers, like Jay Katz, a professor of psychiatry and law at Yale, portray the traditional doctor–patient relationship as "silent," their angle of vision is too narrow. Katz, for example, bases his characterization almost exclusively on normative statements, the prescriptions set down by codes of ethics or commencement-day speakers, that physicians not divulge a grim diagnosis.[12] But a wider view of the historical record amply demonstrates that doctors could be silent with their patients about a diagnosis precisely because they had not been silent with them over the years. The interactions at a time of medical crisis built on a prior history. The element of trust was strong enough to legitimate medical paternalism.

The physicians' incentives to maintain close links with patients came not so much from an abstract commitment to a principle of good doctoring but from the exigencies of maintaining a day-to-day practice. A physician had few ways of attracting or keeping patients except by establishing personal ties with them and their neighbors. Doctors might occasionally be able to rest on their credentials or expertise. By the 1920s and 1930s a medical degree from Johns Hopkins or the Columbia College of Physicians and Surgeons carried weight, and some physicians had mastered a procedure (such as thoracic surgery) that most others had not. But given the limited number of diagnostic tools (of which reading an electrocardiogram or X ray was probably the most demanding) and therapeutic interventions available, physicians had difficulties distinguishing themselves from each other on purely professional grounds.[13]

In fact, professional criteria were of such limited relevance that a huge body of medical writing warned laypeople against quackery. Undoubtedly, some of this effort was self-serving and promotional, motivated as much by professional envy as patient well-being. But some of it was genuinely altruistic, presuming with good reason that an absence of professional credentials made patients susceptible to the blandishments of charlatans. However well-intentioned, the cautionary advice tended to be negative and dispiriting: do not trust those who promise cures—those who, in effect, tell patients what they most want to hear.

On the more positive side, the medical and popular writings emphasized the primacy of personal compatibility: Choose a physician as you would choose a friend. When it fell to the renowned physician Oliver Wendell Holmes to address the graduating class of the Bellevue

Medical School in 1871, he spent most of his talk instructing them on how to get along with their patients: Be prompt in keeping appointments; never let your face mirror the gravity of the disease; resort to such stock favorites as, "You have a 'spinal irritation,'" if you wanted to disguise a diagnosis; and never forget that "we had one physician in our city whose smile was commonly reckoned as being worth five thousand dollars a year to him." Holmes also set down the principles by which patients should select their doctors, making his lead one: "Choose a man who is personally agreeable, for a daily visit from an intelligent, amiable, pleasant, sympathetic person will cost you no more than one from a sloven or a boor."[14] And all this advice, of course, came from the professor of anatomy at Harvard who ranked among the earliest physicians to appreciate the value of clinical trials to test efficacy of treatments. Some sixty years later a Yale professor of medicine comfortably reiterated the same advice: In choosing a physician, the prospective patient should engage the doctor in conversation; "if he spoke well on general matters the chances were that he was also intelligent in his practice."[15] This type of advice, of course, had the unintended effect of making it all the more difficult to distinguish quackery from professional medicine. As one historian of medicine has put it, "We can hardly overestimate the importance of the psychological aspects of the medical art, but it is true that psychological needs could also be largely satisfied by quacks."[16]

Patients were likely to follow such subjective and personal judgments, allowing similarities in religion, ethnic group, and socioeconomic background to guide their choice. In an era when major eastern and midwestern cities were divided into ghetto enclaves, immigrants tended to select their doctors along ethnic and religious lines. Catholics turned to Catholic doctors, Jews to Jewish doctors—a fact that, incidentally, provided incentives for members of each group to become doctors. These patterns are borne out not only by anecdotal evidence (would that some archives included the papers of neighborhood doctors along with those of the medical pioneers), but, as we shall soon see, by the structure and functioning of sectarian hospitals.

By the same token, the well-to-do were likely to use the services of equally well-to-do doctors. And rural residents were generally served medically (when they were served at all) by someone with some sympathy or at least understanding of their way of life.[17] Indeed, there was nothing unreasonable or naïve about these choices and strategies. Probably the most important attribute of physicians was their own character and the nature of their relationships with patients. In selecting a doctor, personal style, education, religion, and family background were criteria as useful as any.

Strengthening these tendencies and reflecting their importance was the fact that the great majority of doctor–patient encounters took place in the patient's home, not in an office or a hospital. One survey of 8,758 families (in eighteen states) from 1928 to 1931 reported an average of 526 physician-care visits per 1,000 people, and 294 (or 56 percent) of them involved one or more house calls.[18] In other words, more than half of patients who saw a doctor, saw him in their own home. Another survey of the period, examining physician practice patterns, revealed that a little over one-third of all their contacts with patients came through house calls, again demonstrating the centrality of the home in medical encounters.[19]

Although one cannot be certain of all the psychological and social implications of house calls, and descriptions are usually so sentimental as to arouse skepticism, on these occasions doctors were likely to gain greater insight into the patient's needs, and patients may well have become more trusting of doctors. Francis Peabody, a professor of medicine at Harvard in the 1920s, was being more than romantic in noting: "When the general practitioner goes into the home of a patient, he may know the whole background of the family life from past experience; but even when he comes as a stranger he has every opportunity to find out what manner of man his patient is, and what kind of circumstances makes his life. . . . What is spoken of as a 'clinical picture' is not just a photograph of a sick man in bed; it is an impressionistic painting of the patient surrounded by his home, his work, his relations, his friends, his joys, sorrows, hopes, and fears."[20] Or as one son recalled about a day when he accompanied his physician-father on rounds: "We spent the rest of the afternoon climbing up and down stairs and in and out of his patients' houses. I can remember being impressed by the consistently warm welcomes he received. Always he was offered tea, cakes or cookies by people anxious to hear what he had to say and grateful for his presence. And my father—he seemed to know everyone's friends and relatives. He was full of reminiscences which he and his patients shared. Every visit was an occasion for warm conversation in addition to the medical treatments. I can remember feeling proud of him, envious ('how come we didn't know him this way?'), and very tired."[21]

A recurring image in physicians' autobiographical accounts is the ride through town on the way to pay a house call. Lewis Thomas has straightforwardly described the frequency of these trips: "My father spent his hours on the road. In the early morning he made rounds at the local hospital. . . . Later in the morning, and through the afternoon, he made his house calls."[22] Others have embellished the rides with allusions to a royal tour: "The family physician, dressed in his frock coat and silk hat, driving a beautiful pair of dapple gray horses, came majestically down the avenue, when it seemed as if the whole neighborhood ceased activity to pay homage to the honored gentleman and his procession; he was their advisor, counselor and friend. . . . His human understanding seemed to draw him so near to the heart of the family."[23]

Some commentators invoke the image of Norman Rockwell–like general practitioners making house calls as the pretext for celebrating the golden age of the past when patients trusted doctors and neither lawyers nor government officials were around to pester them. But others take the image as a departure point for historical debunking: "In the United States by the early 1900s," insists one historian, "it appeared that general practice was moribund if not dead. While the role of the family doctor as advisor and counsellor was idealized . . . the archetypical family physician . . . had largely disappeared in 1915. Out-patient departments of city hospitals provided general services for the indigent masses. The American middle class was already going directly to specialists."[24] But the obituary is premature, certainly for the middle class and even for many among the poor.

It is true that through the 1930s, specialization was on the increase, and outgoing presidents of local medical societies frequently delivered valedictories on "The Passing of the Family Doctor." Prominent medical educators and prestigious national commissions also complained that the specialist was changing medicine for the worse. "In the trend toward specialism," Francis Peabody insisted, "the pendulum is swinging too far."[25] So too, in 1932 the authors of the *Report of the Commission on Medical Education*, appointed by the Association of American Medical Colleges, found that "specialism has developed beyond the actual needs in the larger community. . . . There is great need of a wider appreciation on the part of the public as well as the profession of the important function of non-specialized practice."[26]

Yet, despite the complaints, specialization was far from overtaking general practice. A 1928-to-1931 survey of health care delivery reported that 81 percent of patient visits still were to general practitioners; only a minority of encounters (19 percent) occurred with specialists. The proportion of specialists to general physicians also remained relatively low; as late as 1940, the overwhelming majority (some 70 percent) of physicians were in general practice.[27] Moreover, specialization in its initial appearance was not equivalent to specialization later. Of all medical specialists, 30 percent were in pediatrics or obstetrics-gynecology, and another 40 percent, in surgery.[28] If by the hegemony of the specialist one means physicians with great technical competence in one special area whose patients overwhelmingly come through referral from another physician and for one particular procedure, then the specialist was not at the center of American medicine before World War II. Neither pediatricians nor obstetricians-gynecologists fit this pattern, and the social consequences of the separation of surgery from general medicine can be (and undoubtedly were) grossly exaggerated.

To be sure, these changes did take away patient dollars from general practitioners—the pediatrician captured the young patient, the ob-gyn practitioners the female patient, and the surgeons the operative cases— and many of the complaints undoubtedly were inspired by this fact. As the outgoing president of the Michigan State Medical Society lamented in 1930: "I know of but one condition for which the family doctor has no competition, and that is making the emergency night call." Otherwise, "he is apologetically informed that father was injured at the factory recently and of course the factory doctor took care of him, that Sammy recently had his tonsils out by a tonsillectomist, and that when daughter contracted pneumonia of course they wanted the best and therefore employed an internist, and mother's last baby was delivered by her obstetrician."[29] But the general practitioner was still alive and well, and the specialists were hardly such devotees of research or masters of arcane procedures as to be removed from sustained contact with individual patients.

Surveys of particular communities in the pre–World War II period demonstrate the staying power of the family physician. In his survey of *The Health of Regionville*, for example, sociologist Earl Koos soon learned that physicians were well-integrated and prestigious in the community; one informant put Doctor X high on the list of the most influential townspeople and explained: "He's one of the best-educated men in town, and makes good money—drives a good car, belongs to the Rotary, and so forth." Koos also discovered that 80 percent of his class 1 households ("the successful people of Regionville") and 70 percent of the class 2 ones ("the wage-earners") had a family doctor. When he asked families how they chose their doctor, they most often cited a general reputation in the community (people speaking well of the doctor), a recommendation of a friend or relative, or a long history of treatment by the doctor. A considerable number of respondents also remarked that their choice reflected the fact that they "had come to know the doctor socially." Although Koos regretted the fact that social criteria outweighed expertise in guiding the choices ("It is perhaps a sad commentary . . . that more sensitive criteria were not available, or at least not employed, in the selection of the professional person"), his data made clear how outside the mainstream his own predilections were.[30]

The lower classes certainly experienced a different kind of medical care, but even here a significant degree of familiarity between doctors and patients existed. The poor were neither so completely dependent on public services (the inpatient beds or the outpatient dispensaries of municipal hospitals) nor so thoroughly distanced from private practitioners as has often been assumed. It is true that those deep in poverty almost always ended up in a hospital-almshouse or its clinic. (The especially "worthy" cases or "interesting" cases would make it onto the wards of a voluntary or university hospital.) But poverty was typically a transitory, rather than a fixed and permanent, state. The poor moved back and forth across the line, with their exact position at a given time fixed by the condition of the local economy, the health of the breadwinner, and the number in the household who were working.

And it was their exact position at a time of illness that helped determine the type of medical care they received.

The most precise account of this process comes from a 1938 study by Gladys Swackhamer of 365 lower-class families (81 percent had incomes under $2,000 a year) living in three New York neighborhoods, the lower East Side (heavily Jewish and Italian), the Chelsea district (polyglot, composed of east Europeans, Greeks, and others), and East Harlem (predominately Italian, with some east Europeans). Half of the families relied on both private and public medical resources, close to 30 percent used only public, and 20 percent used only private. The pattern was not complicated. If the money was at hand, the family would often choose a fee-for-service practitioner, not a clinic or agency physician, to treat the acute case that did not respond to family remedies or to the treatment recommended by the local druggist. On the other hand, should the acute case turn chronic or a chronic condition develop (including pregnancy), the patient was likely to seek care at a clinic. But if clinic treatment proved ineffective and the ailment became more bothersome or interfered with an ability to work, then the patient might return to a private doctor. Accordingly, Mr. and Mrs. K took their sick baby to the baby health clinic, but when improvement was slow in coming, they turned to a nearby private physician recommended by friends. Meanwhile, Mrs. K became pregnant and went for prenatal care to a nearby public maternity hospital; but when she became ill during her pregnancy, she went to Mr. K's family doctor, who had treated him since childhood.[31]

This does not mean that the poor had a stable relationship with a physician and could, when asked, name a family physician. Although more than two-thirds of these families had seen a private practitioner over the past twelve months, only one-third reported having a family doctor. In fact, this finding of the Swackhamer study generated the most commentary; the *New York Times*, for example, ran several stories lamenting the disappearance of the family doctor.[32] But the results of the study were more complex than this: First, one-third of a lower-class population did name a family doctor. Second, even though most of the poor had no ongoing relationship with one doctor, they were remarkably consistent in choosing a neighborhood doctor and relying on friends for referrals. When asked how they came to select their private physicians, 58 percent of the families answered that they followed the recommendations of relatives or friends; another 8 percent cited the physical proximity of the physician; and 7 percent, a personal tie to the physician (through business, religion, or language). Thus the majority of the poor did not have *a* doctor, but they had doctors who were integral to their communities.

To view these findings from the physician's perspective, neighborhood reputation counted most in terms of maintaining a following. The critical elements in building a practice were not degrees, specialty certification, hospital affiliation, or special skills. To attract and hold patients, physicians had to be sensitive, caring, able to listen, committed, and responsive to crises—not because they were saintly, but because the marketplace required it. The incentives put a premium on intimacy, and involvement with the community. In a very real sense it paid to listen to patients, so that they would not only come back but also send their friends and relatives.

The pace of medical practice also strengthened the personal ties between physician and patient. The number and power of diagnostic tools were so limited that the physician had to rely essentially on the case history. The patient's report of symptoms, the way the pain moved along the arm or the frequency of a stomach upset, were often the best guides the doctor had to the problem. One reason why medical educators and leaders worried so much about the disappearance of the family physician was because in the absence of diagnostic technologies, they put a premium on knowing the patient's constitution and family history. Information on what illnesses the patient had previously experienced—or those that the patient's parents or siblings had experienced—were vital clues to diagnosing the patient's current ailment. As Holmes explained in his *Medical Essays*: "The young man knows his patient, but the old man knows his patient's family, dead and alive, up and down for generations. He can tell beforehand what diseases their unborn children will be subject to, what they will die of if they live long enough."[33] So too, the novelist George Eliot has a character remark in *Janet's Repentance* that "it's no trifle at her time of life to part with a doctor who knows her constitution."[34] And well into the 1930s physicians continued to insist that "the family medical adviser with his knowledge of personal habits, familial tendencies and environmental conditions" would understand the "special meaning" of the symptoms of fatigue, impaired appetite, cough, dizziness, and headaches.[35]

In all, a personal knowledge of the patient had a diagnostic and therapeutic importance in medicine that is almost impossible to appreciate today. The knowledge was so complete that as two students of doctor-patient relations have observed, office records "were rarely kept, being considered unnecessary by the solo practitioner who knew, and had no trouble remembering the patient, family and their illnesses without taking notes."[36] These circumstances also help to explain why there were so few voices even in the 1920s or 1930s stressing the need to humanize medical care. Medical care was essentially composed of the human touch, and there was no need for educators or critics to promote the obvious.

Physicians were also more closely connected to their community and well integrated into the fabric of social life. One of the more suggestive indicators of this relationship may be found in literary depictions of physicians. Without minimizing the variety of descriptions in late nineteenth- and early twentieth-century texts—in some the doctor is demonic; in others, incompetent—it is notable that the narratives give physicians many roles distinct from that of professional healer.[37] Doctors can be neighbors, lovers, and friends—they come to tea and stay to flirt. They move quite freely outside the hospital setting and without a white coat or stethoscope. In other words, physicians did not inhabit a world unto themselves.

The most compelling sketch of a late nineteenth-century physician is Lydgate in George Eliot's *Middlemarch*, and although the novel is English, Eliot's portrayal was not idiosyncratic to her side of the Atlantic. The fact of Lydgate being a doctor was essential to the narrative; but he is a fully drawn character, found more often in the drawing room than in his fever hospital. Eliot frequently remarked on the low state of medicine and medical practices, which was certainly as true in the United States as in England. But Lydgate takes his profession seriously, vehemently objecting when his wife, Rosamond, wishes that he had chosen a calling that commanded more respect: " 'It is the grandest profession in the world, Rosamond,' said Lydgate gravely. 'And to say that you love me without loving the medical man in me, is the same sort of thing as to say that you like eating a peach but don't like its flavour.' " The novel, however, focuses on Lydgate the person, not the doctor. Rosamond is initially attracted to him not because of his profession but because of his relatively high birth, a fact "which distinguished him from all Middlemarch admirers, and presented marriage as a prospect of rising in rank and . . . [having] nothing to do with vulgar people." And his failings have to do with his "arrogant conceit," which is displayed far more often toward his fellow practitioners than toward his patients, and in the "commonness . . . [of] the complexion of his prejudices. . . . That distinction of mind which belonged to his intellectual ardor did not penetrate his feeling and judgment about furniture, or women, or the desirability of its being known (without his telling) that he was better born than other country surgeons."[38] In short, his virtues were those of his profession at its best (his intellectual ardor), and his faults were those of ordinary people (boring prejudices)—and such an ordering of virtue and vice, as we shall see, will not often be found in the post–1945 literature.

What was true of Eliot's Lydgate held for Anton Chekhov's Dr. Astrov in _Uncle Vanya_. "I've worked too hard," he explains in his first appearance on stage: "I'm on my feet from morning to night, I don't know what rest is. . . . During all the time you've known me, I haven't had a single free day. . . . In the third week of Lent, I went to Malitskoye, there was an epidemic . . . typhus . . . In the huts people lay on the floor in rows. . . . Filth, stench, smoke . . . I was on the move all day, didn't sit down or have a morsel of food, and when I got home they still wouldn't let me rest." But it is Astrov the misguided lover, not the doctor, who is at the core of the plot. He rejects the advances of the woman who loves him, and he proceeds to make a fool of himself in pursuit of one who does not. Over the course of the events, Astrov becomes more and more pathetic, and the strengths that remain relate to his doctoring: "Just think what sort of life that doctor has! . . . Impassable mud on the roads, frosts, snowstorms, vast distances, uncouth, primitive people, poverty and disease all around him—it would be hard for a man working and struggling day after day in such an atmosphere to keep himself sober and pure." His weaknesses are those of a man forced to live his life in what he describes as a suffocating, insipid, and vulgar atmosphere, who becomes fascinated with the idle

rich and is brought to ruin by them. His closing lines to Elena An-
dreyevna, his temptress, capture this duality and tension well: " 'You
came here with your husband, and every one of us who had been
working, bustling about trying to create something, had to drop his
work and occupy himself with nothing but you and your husband's
gout the entire summer. Both of you—he and you—have infected
us with your idleness. I was infatuated with you, and have done nothing for a whole month; meanwhile people have been sick. . . . I'm
convinced that if you had stayed, the devastation would have been
enormous.' ''[39]

   In the end, both Lydgate and Astrov are fully developed characters—
doctors and lovers; indeed, better doctors than lovers—which is what
gives *Middlemarch* and *Uncle Vanya* their story lines. These physicians
are altogether part of the social life of their communities, in no way
isolated or cut off. The narrative takes place in the drawing room, not
in the hospital; the exchanges are between friends and lovers, not between doctor and patient. That the men are doctors is not incidental
to the works, but this fact does not overwhelm or determine their every
response.

   By the 1930s this dictum was losing some of its strength. The conflict
at the center of one of that decade's most popular dramas about physicians, Sidney Kingsley's *Doctors in White*, went to this very point.
Laura, the would-be wife of the young doctor George Ferguson, pleads
with him to have a life outside of medicine: "The important man,
George, is the man who knows how to live," something her physician-
father and Ferguson's mentor apparently never learned. "They have no
outside interests at all. They're flat—they're colorless. They're not
men—they're caricatures!" Ferguson, however, rejects her plea and the
romance breaks up. This kind of scenario, however, was unusual in
literary or dramatic depictions of physicians. At least before the 1950s,
doctors were more generally portrayed as individuals, not as caricatures
of single-minded professionals.[40]

   Undoubtedly the most widely read book on American medicine in
the pre–World War II period was Sinclair Lewis's *Arrowsmith*. The
hero, Dr. Martin Arrowsmith, does give up everything, including wife
and children, to flee to the Vermont woods and pursue his career. But
this act represented the single-mindedness of the researcher, not of the

practicing physician; Arrowsmith was rejecting an overbearing scientific establishment, what Lewis's guide in these matters, Paul de Kruif, called the "barrack spirit." The earlier chapters of the novel celebrate the country family doctor, De Kruif's "splendid old type of general practitioner," who was assuredly not detached from the life of the community.[41]

Reading a very different kind of text, the autobiographies of pre–World War II American doctors, also demonstrates how little distance separated doctor, patient, and community. Although physician autobiographies began appearing in the nineteenth century, a whole spate were published in the 1920s and 1930s, inspired by the same impulse: to set down an experience that seemed destined to disappear, that is, being a family doctor. Sensing that medicine was on the brink of change, these physicians wanted to preserve a record of the demands, limitations, and rewards of their profession, as reflected in such titles as *The Horse and Buggy Doctor* and *Castor Oil and Quinine*. As one writer explained, his family persuaded him to write his autobiography because "there should be a record of the old country doctor by one of the species." Another wrote: "I have been a family doctor for over thirty years. . . . My story might be called a 'case history' in defense of the family doctor. . . . The family doctor is indispensible to the community and the nation."[42]

Given such goals, the genre does not make for very interesting reading. The autobiographies are anecdotal, the stories seem trivial, and the sorts of questions one would have wanted these doctors to address (such as how they coped with therapeutic helplessness) are missing. Instead, we read about the woman who did not admit to being pregnant but who in fact was; or about the family that called doctors out at night, always exaggerated their illnesses, and never paid their bills; or about how a doctor rode through a storm (or blizzard or hurricane) to deliver a baby or mend a leg or minister to a feverish child. But the triviality is precisely the point: being a family doctor meant to work on this scale of things, to be involved with obscure people and minor events. These are not tales of heroic interventions or brilliant solutions to puzzling symptoms, but of physicians whose professional lives were intimately connected with their neighbors and community. Their visions were local; they thought small, and their victories and

losses had less to do with the power of medications and more to
do with the fit of personalities. They took pride in being doctors
who were "capable of instantaneous automatic adjustment to every
shade of human nature," rather than masters of diagnosis, treatment,
or surgery.

If Lydgate and Astrov frequented the drawing rooms of the better
sort, their American counterparts frequented the club rooms of their
communities and mixed regularly with the local elite. Dr. Frederick
Loomis's memoir of his 1920s and 1930s obstetrics practice, *Consultation Room*, described the traditional Wednesday at the country club:
"The Locker rooms are filled with the bankers and the lawyers and the
doctors and the brokers." In Loomis's "locker alley" were some of his
"closest friends," including the president of the bank and a leading
lawyer. "Each week, I looked forward eagerly to my association with
these and other men at the club. My days and nights were necessarily
spent with women—sick ones—and, much as I like my work, it is a
pleasant contrast to step into another world, the world of men."[43]
Indeed, doctors may well have been in the locker rooms as much for
business as for pleasure. At a time when social relationships were essential to building and maintaining a practice, physicians, no matter
how skilled or well trained, could not dare to adopt a posture of aloof-
ness. "A physician is judged by the company he keeps," Dr. D. W.
Cathell advised young practitioners (in a book so aptly entitled *The
Physician Himself and What He Should Add to His Scientific Acquirements*).
"Avoid associating with those who are 'under a cloud,' or are notori-
ously deficient, or whose hopes and ambitions are blighted. Let your
associations be as far as possible with professional brethren and other
people of genuine worth."[44]

The intimate and familiar manner in which doctor and patient interacted casts in a very different light some traditional physician practices toward patients, especially on the matter of truth telling. Although
physicians undoubtedly differed in the degree to which they shared
information with patients or sought their permission before carrying
out procedures (some historians would have physicians sharing this
responsibility in the early nineteenth century, whereas others date it to
the 1970s), there is no question but that the ethic of medicine, from
Hippocrates onward, was to have physicians keep bad news to them-

selves—to be the purveyors of hope, not doom. Oliver Wendell Holmes echoed this traditional wisdom when he counseled those about to enter the profession: "Your patient has no more right to all the truth you know than he has to all the medicine in your saddlebags. . . . He should get only just so much as is good for him. . . . It is a terrible thing to take away hope, every earthly hope, from a fellow creature."[45]

Behind this advice, however, was a confidence that the physician could measure out just what degree of information was good for the patient. This medical tradition was borne not only of paternalism and the relative emptiness of the doctors' saddlebags, but of a confidence that doctors were capable of substituting their judgment for that of their patients, able to spare them pain because they intuited their patients' wishes. Because they knew their patients' families "dead and alive, up and down for generations," Holmes concluded, physicians knew not only what the patients would die of if they lived long enough, but also "whether they had better live at all or remain unrealized possibilities, as belonging to a stock not worth being perpetuated."[46] Since they shared their patients' religious or class or ethnic perspective, since they had been in their patients' homes and spent time with them over the course of various illnesses, physicians were comfortable making decisions on behalf of the patients.

Well into the twentieth century, patients entering a hospital did not confront a strange or alienating environment. For one, they often entered their own ethnic institutions, and to be a patient at a St. Vincent's or a Beth Israel, a Mt. Sinai or a Sisters of Mercy, was to be in familiar surroundings at a time of crisis. By 1930, for example, there were some 640 Catholic hospitals in the United States (one-seventh of all nongovernmental hospitals), and the Catholic Hospital Association (CHA) took pride in the fact that "there was available one bed . . . for every 231.2 of the Catholic population," compared to a ratio double that for the general population.[47] In New York City from 1925 to 1945, 60 percent of the fifty-eight general hospitals had religious sponsorship (most of them Catholic or Jewish); moving westward (where one might have imagined the ethnic impact to be lower), Cincinnati in 1925 had nine general hospitals, of which four were sponsored by

Protestant groups (chiefly Methodists), two by Catholics, and one by Jews. That year, 308 Catholic patients in Cincinnati had to enter a hospital, and 165 of them (54 percent) chose one of the three Catholic hospitals; so too, 54 of the 71 Jewish patients (76 percent) entered the Jewish hospital. (Among Protestants, the figures were lower, for those in the majority did not experience the same incentives.) To be sure, Catholic and Jewish hospitals served more than Catholic and Jewish patients—the CHA estimated that 49 percent of its patients were non-Catholic—and not every member of an ethnic or religious group patronized the group's own hospitals. But a majority of Catholics did use the group's hospitals, and the figures may even have been slightly higher among Jews.[48]

There were many reasons why religious and ethnic communities built and frequented their own hospitals. They were, for example, self-consciously offering a gift to American society, paying tribute and demonstrating allegiance to American values. Immediate self-interest operated as well. For minorities, each hospital represented a place in which the group's members could learn and practice medicine, and in an era when prejudice against Jewish and Catholic applicants to medical schools and residency programs at major hospitals was widespread, this opportunity was critical. The sectarian hospital, then, was an investment in professional careers for those who might otherwise be excluded from medicine, which meant, of course, that in these hospitals the sick were most likely to be treated by fellow ethnics or coreligionists, that patients and doctors would share language, traditions, and values.

The mission of the sectarian hospitals also strengthened the bonds of trust between patient and institution. In explaining what differentiated Catholic hospitals from other hospitals, staff members emphasized meeting the human, as well as medical, needs of their patients. Their regard for the patient's spiritual welfare prompted them to look beyond the mere treatment of disease to a more general well-being. Only on their wards would nursing sisters comfort patients and make certain that priests would always be available to give extreme unction. Only on their walls would patients find the crucifix along with paintings that expressed "the deepest Catholic piety." As one Catholic physician explained, it was not enough to prescribe a medication and

ignore the person; the patient could not be effectively treated "as though
he were nothing but a 'curiously developed lump of matter.' " Or as
another Catholic clergyman insisted, "The sweet influence of religion
has ever been the means of dispelling the nervous gloom of the patient,
so dangerous to his physical recovery."[49]

This same orientation pervaded Jewish institutions. Beth Israel Hospital, for example, was founded in 1900 on New York's lower East
Side, first, to meet "the great necessity of having a hospital convenient
to the crowded tenement district of this part of the city; second, to
have a hospital that should be conducted on strictly orthodox principles
in its kitchen as well as in other respects."[50] Only in a Jewish hospital
would the patient be certain to find kosher food on his tray and be
able to join a group in daily prayer. And only in a Jewish hospital
would a Yiddish-speaking patient be assured that in a time of grave
illness the doctor would know the right language and phrases with
which to provide comfort.

Many of the attributes of the sectarian hospitals reappeared in the
numerous small voluntary and proprietary hospitals that served local
communities. The typical community hospital had less than 100 beds
and was likely to be class and race specific, that is, serving the well-to-
do in well-to-do neighborhoods, and the lower classes in lower-class
neighborhoods. Whatever social inequalities were fostered, such arrangements helped make the institutions familiar and comfortable to
their patients, and accordingly, patients sought them out. In 1933, for
example, 89 percent of the patients in hospitals in the borough of
Queens were from Queens, and 88 percent of all patients in Brooklyn's
hospitals were Brooklyn residents. (The figure for the Bronx was 85
percent and for Staten Island, 98 percent; only in Manhattan did the
percentage drop to 62 percent.) Moreover, community hospitals were
generally staffed by neighborhood doctors—attending privileges were
not difficult to obtain—making them more a part of the local community than the scientific community.[51]

With homogeneity and intimacy such major considerations, the idea
of a "surplus bed" did not carry the meaning that it now has. Hospital
and state administrators were alert to occupancy rates, but their degree
of anxiety was not great. Over the 1920s and 1930s the larger voluntary general hospitals typically had occupancy rates of 60 percent of

capacity, about 10 percent below the standard proposed in the health policy literature of the time. But the fact that voluntary hospitals did not attain the standard caused no alarm. In part, this attitude reflected an absence of pressure from third-party payers—federal bureaucrats did not insist that hospital administrators become more efficient in using beds. But the complacency also testified to a definition of the hospital bed as a resource that should be open in advance of need, as opposed to always in use. The CHA was more proud of the number of beds it had available to meet unexpected need than it was concerned about a relatively low occupancy rate (57.5 percent), precisely because a Catholic who suddenly required a bed should have a bed lest he or she end up in another denomination's institution. Hospital beds were not interchangeable: a Protestant hospital bed was not suitable for a Catholic or a Jew; a bed 100 miles away was not suitable for a neighbor.[52]

The longer length of patient stays also reduced the strangeness of the institution. In the 1920s the average stay (excluding newborns) in general hospitals was a little over eleven days in private hospitals, and when patients remained in a hospital for weeks rather than days, a patient subculture flourished. Patients became guides for each other, most dramatically, perhaps, in chronic-care facilities, but in acute-care hospitals as well. Their conversations served effectively to introduce and explicate the hospital to newcomers—all the more effectively when the conversations were between fellow ethnics or members of the same social class and neighborhood. The longer stays also gave physicians greater opportunities to talk with patients, and although the evidence is largely anecdotal, they may well have done so.[53]

In sum, the doctor and patient occupied the same social space. The critical element in their relationship was not silence but a shared outlook. Under these circumstances, the degree of mutual trust was great enough to keep strangers away from the bedside, and to give bedside ethics standing not only with the profession but with the lay public.

CHAPTER 7

The Doctor as Stranger

PRACTICALLY every development in medicine in the post–World War II period distanced the physician and the hospital from the patient and the community, disrupting personal connections and severing bonds of trust. Whatever the index—whether ties of friendship, religion, ethnicity, or intellectual activity—the results highlight a sharp division between the lay world and the medical world. By the 1960s the two had moved so far apart that one could have asked a lay audience about the last time they spoke to a physician and had their clothes on, and they would have been unable to remember an occasion. By the same token, if one had asked physicians about their social contacts outside the profession, they would have been hard pressed to come up with examples. The separation from the hospital has become so extreme that columnist Meg Greenfield, in a 1986 commentary entitled "The Land of the Hospital," announced that she had "just come back from a foreign place worth reporting on . . . a universe, really of its own," where she felt like "a tourist in an unfathomable, dangerous land."[1] In a spate of recent medical self-help books writers have advised patients to prepare to enter a hospital as though they were going on a trek in Nepal—take food and organize family and friends to provide necessary help. It has even been suggested that patients hang up school diplomas and pictures of their children to make certain that the chieftains of this exotic place know that they are valued persons in the outside world.

Some results of such changes are well recognized and endlessly discussed. One staple of both family magazines and medical journals is the complaint that physicians have lost their ability to relate to patients, that they have neither the desire nor the time to communicate with them. But however familiar some aspects of this subject may be, it is important to analyze the transformation closely, for not all of its causes and, even more important, not all of its implications have been recognized.

To read some of the critiques, one would think the problem is mostly a matter of educating medical students by emphasizing communication skills (so doctors learn better how to interview and how to listen) and incorporating the humanities into the curriculum (on the theory that studying the classics will increase empathy). But however worthwhile these efforts, a reliance on the education of the future practitioner as the vehicle for change minimizes the structural barriers to recasting the doctor–patient relationship. The organization and delivery of medical care almost guarantees that at a time of crisis patients will be treated by strangers in a strange environment. This circumstance has transformed many patients' behavior, encouraging a style closer to that of a wary consumer than a grateful supplicant. Moreover, this distancing helps explain why a cadre of outsiders felt compelled to enter the medical arena and promote a commitment to a more formal and collective type of medical decision making, including regulatory guidelines and committee oversight.

The first and most obvious of the structural changes that distanced patients from doctors in the post-1945 decades was the disappearance of the house call. By the early 1960s, home visits represented less than one percent of doctor–patient contacts.[2] Surprisingly, the demise of the house call is a relatively unexplored phenomenon, but it reflects a combination of professional and technological considerations. By bringing the patient to the office and hospital, physicians increased their own efficiency and incomes, enabling them to examine many more patients in much less time. The change also served to give patients quicker access to medical technologies (at first, X-ray and electrocardiogram machines; later, computerized scanners and magnetic imagers). But whatever the reason, the effect was to remove patients from familiar surroundings and deprive the doctor of a firsthand knowledge of the patients' environment. In both symbolic and real terms, doctors and patients moved apart.

This distance was further enlarged as medical specialization and subspecialization transformed the profession in the post–World War II years. The fears of the 1930s became the realities of the 1950s and 1960s; only 20 percent of physicians now identified themselves as general practitioners, and occasional efforts to increase the pool through training programs in community medicine or family medicine showed few results. Not only were doctors now trained so intensely in the functioning of a particular organ or system that they might well lose sight of the patient's presence, but specialization meant that patients and doctors were not likely to have met before the onset of the illness, let alone to have developed a relationship. Unable to predict which organ would become the site of disease, patients had no way of anticipating whether they would require the services of a cardiologist or neurologist, and thus had no way of knowing the physician across the desk in a time of crisis. Even those with a primary physician could not be certain that the doctor would be able to follow them into the hospital; since admitting privileges to tertiary-care medical centers were often very restricted, the odds were that as the stakes in illness mounted and decisions became more critical, the patient was more likely to be in a strange setting surrounded by strangers.[3]

As specialization took hold, both the hospital and the patient also gave unprecedented weight to merit in the selection of a physician. Although an "old boy" network survived in some settings or specialties, medicine has come astonishingly close to being a meritocracy. In few other fields is sheer talent as likely to be rewarded with prestigious appointments. In most contexts, of course, such a finding would be cause for celebration, but here one must take note of an altogether unintended but significant consequence: rules of merit can foster anonymity. Doctors who gain their positions through merit might or might not share their patient's religious persuasion, ethnic identity, or social values. The triumph of the most qualified has helped make the doctor into a stranger.

After the 1950s, even sectarian hospitals no longer relied on such criteria as religion or ethnicity to select most of the house staff and senior physicians. Put another way, choice by merit accelerated the process by which the ethnic hospital lost its special relationship to its patients. It became increasingly difficult to define what was Presbyterian about Presbyterian Hospital or Jewish about Mt. Sinai Hospital, and the answer could not be found in the characteristics of either the patients or the attending physicians. (Catholic hospitals have withstood this trend to a degree, but they barely resemble their predecessors of the 1930s, which were dominated by the nursing sisters.) The trustees of Montefiore Hospital in New York, for example, celebrated the hospital's 100th anniversary in 1985 by amending its charter and eliminating the provision that a majority of its board had to be Jewish. Although the revision paid homage to the scientific ideal of universalism, it also reflected the decline of the ethnic character of the hospital. The few management tactics that attempt to keep some traditions alive—chaplains going around the wards or the opportunity to order kosher food—while not trivial, hardly reduce the impersonal atmosphere of the hospital. The ethnic hospital survives in name only. It is now in all senses a public space, with the same personal ties to its patients that a busy midtown hotel has to its guests.[4]

By the same token, demographic trends in major urban areas have disrupted the ties between patients and hospitals. Many of the voluntary hospitals, when first founded, served the residents of their immediate neighborhood. But then many residents moved to the suburbs, and few, if any, of the original constituents for the hospital remained to use its services. They were replaced by groups with very different backgrounds, identifications, and languages. If, for example, they were Hispanic, they often found the hospital even more mysterious because the staff spoke only English.

In much the same way, the hospital as a neighborhood institution almost disappeared. In New York City, for example, between 1963 and 1978, thirty-five hospitals closed; and they were, typically, smaller facilities that served a special section of the population. As the authors of one report concluded: "The communities for which these institutions had been established—generally comprising either the educated and affluent or immigrants of a single particular ethnic group—had vanished in a massive turnover of population."[5] The same process has affected smaller communities. Since the 1970s many rural and small-town hospitals have closed, reflecting mounting costs, inefficiencies of size, and patients' preference for hospitals staffed by specialists and equipped with advanced technologies.[6] The trade-off, of course, is that seriously ill patients must travel to a distant regional hospital to be cared for by strangers.

Not only the anonymity of the doctor and the hospital but the new style of medical practice have made it nearly impossible to maintain a personal and intimate link between the patient and the health care providers. Even if doctor and patient had common backgrounds or values, they might never discover it, for the pace and rhythm of contemporary medical practice erect extraordinary barriers between them. As the seriousness of the illness mounts, and the patient is more likely to be in a hospital than a physician's office, the time available to doctors to spend with one particular patient declines. Neither house staff nor attending physicians can linger at the bedside, not because they are uncaring or poorly trained, but because the external pressures to move on to the next case are overwhelming. Compared with the pre–World War II period, the patient population in major medical centers has become more seriously ill. This increased severity of disease reflects a shortened length of patient stay—usually achieved by curtailing the period of in-hospital recuperation and recovery—and a closer scrutiny over patient admissions to make certain that they really need a hospital bed. Whether the driving force is the need to cut costs or to spare the patient days in so alien an environment or to reduce the likelihood of iatrogenic complications, the result has been to transform the practice of hospital medicine.

On the wards, doctors typically scramble from crisis to crisis. No sooner do they stabilize a patient and get her on the road to recovery, than she is discharged and the next acutely ill patient takes the bed. House staff, who actually do most of the scrambling, often devise ingenious strategies to keep a recuperating patient in bed, not as a favor to the patient but as a way of reducing their workload. But ploys, like lining up an additional test, do not work for very long, for as clever as house staff might be, hospital administrators are not far behind. So physicians soon are again performing intake exams, diagnosing symptoms, devising a treatment plan, and responding to emergencies, knowing that the moment they rescue one patient, the cycle will inevitably begin again.

If doctors do not as a rule linger around the bedside, it is also because the methods of diagnosis and treatment require both frequent and split-second interventions. Take, for example, the pace of cardiac care. By the late 1960s the entire treatment pattern had changed: Patients underwent a battery of exceptionally intrusive and time-consuming diagnostic tests, including the insertion of an arterial catheter in order to measure blood pressure, with the continuing need to check the line to make certain no infection developed. New drug therapies required scrupulous monitoring, typically, checking the blood pressure every fifteen minutes and then adjusting the dosage. Thus, the opportunity for the physician to develop or sustain a relationship with the patient has become one of the casualties of a more powerful medical arsenal.

Furthermore, pausing by the bedside has come closer to being, diagnostically speaking, an indulgence, for the patient is frequently far less interesting and less revealing about his symptoms than the technology. In the 1930s, conversation with patients was inseparable from diagnosis and treatment, and thus it was not necessary to emphasize the need to talk with them. Three decades later such conversations were add-ons—something physicians ought to do as a moral, not medical, obligation. Not surprisingly, as the pressure of time mounted and the limits of energy were reached, such conversations were among the first things to drop away.

All the while, of course, the hospital had become the prime, almost exclusive, setting for treating serious illness, bringing with it isolation from family and friends which hospital policies only exacerbated. The most compelling critique of this change came from Dr. Elisabeth Kübler-Ross, one of the first physicians to make dying her specialty. "I remember as a child the death of a farmer," she wrote in her 1969 bestseller, *On Death and Dying*. "He asked simply to die at home, a wish that was granted without questioning. He called in his children, arranged his affairs and asked his friends to visit him once more, to bid good-bye to them." By contrast, we now "don't allow children to visit their dying parents in the hospitals," and the patient himself undergoes a kind of torture: "He may cry for rest, peace and dignity, but he will get infusions, transfusions, a heart machine, or tracheostomy." The loneliest, and cruelest, setting was the intensive care unit. Kübler-Ross recounts the frustration and agony of an elderly man allowed only a five-minute visit every hour with his desperately ill wife in the ICU. "Was that the way he was to say good-bye to his wife of almost fifty years?" Kübler-Ross well understood that "there are administrative rules and laws" and "too many visitors in such a unit would be intolerable—if not for the patients, maybe for the sensitive equipment?" But surely, some way had to be found to reduce the distance between hospital, patient, and family.[7]

However important these structural considerations, they are not the totality of the story. To understand the separation of the medical and nonmedical worlds, one must also reckon with changes in the patterns of recruitment to medicine and training in medicine in the post–World War II period. For here too lie elements that have promoted the insularity of physicians and their separation from the nonmedical world. In very dramatic fashion these changes undermined the patient's confidence in the exercise of physician discretion. It made sense in an earlier era to trust to the wisdom of the doctor, knowing that his decisions would be informed not only by his greater experience—he had been there many times before—but by the ethics of the community, which he too shared. But in the postwar decades this confidence eroded. The doctors' decisions, like the researchers', seemed likely to reflect their own or their subspecialty's idiosyncratic judgments.

The process that encapsulates physicians in their own universe begins surprisingly early in their lives. A study in the 1950s of six successive classes of medical students at the University of Pennsylvania revealed that just over half the students were already considering a medical career by the time they were thirteen; if their fathers were physicians, the percentage climbed to three-quarters.[8] High school administrators and faculty (to say nothing of classmates) had little difficulty identifying which students would enter medicine. Frank Boyden, for many years the headmaster at Deerfield Academy, was convinced "that medicine stands out among all careers as being the one that schoolboys select early and with a manifest clarity of preference." And physician autobiographies confirm his point. "I cannot remember a time in my youth," recalled one doctor, "when I did not want to be a doctor."[9]

As applicants to college and as entering freshmen, the premeds identified themselves quickly—far more quickly, for example, than law students. In one comparative study, 44 percent of medical students had their minds made up about their careers before entering college; among the law students the figure was 15 percent. By the beginning of their junior year, three-quarters of those who would go on to medical school had decided on their careers, compared to one-third of law students. (Medical students, one observer quipped, decide to go to medical school just about when they get out of diapers, whereas law students decide the week before the semester begins.)[10] In the classroom, premeds stand as a group apart, already following a different work routine; three times as many premedical as prelaw students (49 percent as against 18 percent) reported finding a "great deal" of competition in college.[11] So if medical schools required a particular course (say, basic chemistry), many colleges offered a variant for nonpremed students (like chemistry for poets), who were reluctant to compete with the premeds. The premed student, noted one graduate, "narrows his horizons, intensifies his efforts in physics, chemistry, and biology and limits the amount of his general cultural baggage during precisely the three or four years that offer the last chance of a liberal education."[12]

Once in medical school, most medical students face time demands—to say nothing of the substance of the curriculum—that further separate them from their peers. By comparison to law, business, or graduate school in the arts and sciences, the daily class schedule and the academic terms are very long; and the medical campus is often distant from the other parts of the university, so even those inclined to mix with other graduate students are unable to do so. The isolation only increases during the years of residency and fellowship training. Time not spent on the wards is usually spent catching up on sleep. Thus, when physicians earn the requisite degrees and pass the national and specialty board exams, they have spent some fifteen years since high school on the training track, most of this time, segregated in a medical world.

• • •

The stuff of medicine is also isolating. To deal on a daily basis with injury, pain, disfigurement, and death is to be set apart from others. Modern society has constructed exceptionally sturdy boundaries around illness, confining it to the hospital and making it the nearly exclusive preserve of the medical profession. In effect, the hospital does for illness what the insane asylum intended to do for mental illness: enclose it in its own special territory. To be sure, this process is not new, but it has surely accelerated over the last several decades. The two great rites of passage, birth and death, have both moved into the hospital, the first by the 1920s, the second by the 1950s. The isolation of disease is certainly not complete, however. Epidemics, whether Legionnaires' disease or AIDS, rivet public attention; chronic illness is more likely to be treated in the community; and bookstore owners devote more space than ever before to self-help books explaining everything one wants to know about heart disease, diabetes, and cancer. Nevertheless, serious disease is not the substance of everyday discourse, and in more ways than might be at first recognized, this phenomenon cuts doctors off from others.

Physicians' shoptalk is not so much boring as it is filled with tales that would strike outsiders as tragic and gruesome, stories that no one else would want to hear around a dinner table, or for that matter, anywhere else. Let one personal experience clarify the point. No sooner did I join a medical school faculty than I met with the chairman and chief of service of various clinical departments (pediatrics, medicine, and so on) to explore what interest each department might have in social medicine. The sessions were informal, but much of these first conversations turned on "interesting cases," which typically involved descriptions of devastating illnesses. As each chairman told his tale, I recalled how my grandparents, whenever they heard about a case of severe disease, would chant some ritual incantation to protect their family from experiencing such a calamity. At first I thought these stories were an initiation ritual—was a historian trained to do archival work up to the stuff of medicine? But I slowly learned that this was not a rite of passage but a sharing of anecdotes and gossip; they assumed that because I was part of the faculty, I, too, would be fascinated by the shoptalk. Then, in turn, when friends asked about these meetings, I would share the stories; but as I watched their faces get tense and drawn, I learned to put aside the question and change the subject. The substance of medicine, I was learning, was easiest talked about with medical people, not because of its technical or dry qualities, but because of its scariness in exposing the frailty of human beings and the dimensions of suffering.

Recent accounts by medical school graduates of their initiation into medicine reiterate this experience. Melvin Konner's description of *Becoming a Doctor* after a career in anthropology opens with compelling images of a journey "no less exotic . . . [or] devoid of drama and palpable danger" than fieldwork. More relevant still is his emphasis on the violent aspects of medicine. The first case he relates is about Madeline, a trauma victim, who has multiple stab wounds to the chest. In order to insert a tube and facilitate her breathing, the resident anesthetized an area between two ribs under her shoulder blade. Telling the others "matter of factly" to hold down the now naked, "writhing and yelling" woman, he inserted a scalpel deep into the chest wall; and "Madeline practically leaped off the stretcher when the blade went in, screaming and writhing deliriously."[13] In effect, Konner chooses to introduce the layperson to medicine through a scene that violates ordinary conventions, describing acts that in another context would be defined as torture, and in any context, as gruesome.

Whether the isolation of physicians is self-imposed or socially imposed, the results are apparent in a variety of contexts. Physicians are notable for their lack of political involvement, particularly given their high status and incomes. Because the American Medical Association has been so vocal a lobby, one tends to forget just how removed most doctors are from politics. Questionnaires distributed to the 1959 and 1963 Harvard Medical School classes, for example, revealed that only 4 to 6 percent of the students intended to be politically active.[14] That they, and other physicians, meant what they said is evident if one looks at the number of physicians in high office or active at the state and municipal levels—probably less than 100 if one excludes agencies dealing directly with matters of health or research policy.

In fact, medical practice seems to leave very little room for any other activity. Physicians report an average workweek of fifty-four hours, not including time spent reading professional journals or educational activities. Almost 30 percent spend over sixty hours a week at work, roughly 8:00 A.M. to 6:00 P.M., six days a week. Their hobbies are remarkably few, and their range of interests narrow. One sample of physicians reported spending less than three hours a week in cultural activities and less than four hours a week on family outings.[15]

This life-style helps explain why studies of physicians' family life take titles like Lane Gerber's *Married to Their Careers*. And professional norms reaffirm this outlook, expecting that medicine will not merely dominate but monopolize the practitioner's life, to the exclusion of both family and community. For example, in an address to colleagues, the president of the American College of Cardiology declared that "television, vacations, country clubs, automobiles, household gadgets, travel, movies, races, cards, house hunting, fishing, swimming, concerts, politics, civic committees, and night clubs" all are "distractions . . . [that] leave little time for medicine. . . . To the master cardiologists, the study of cardiology is the only pleasure." That his statement was not ironic or idiosyncratic is evident in the values that medical house staff everywhere are expected to adopt. As one first-year pediatric resident put it: "One of the things you learn from all the work and all the time put in at school and then the hospital is that you can't be very involved with other kinds of interests. Oh you can dabble a little, but that's all. . . . It's as if a person can't be a good doctor and a good wife or mother at the same time." And such an attitude inevitably drove doctor and patient further apart. In the words of another resident: "Sometimes all this emphasis on working constantly seems to lead to a kind of bitterness . . . toward those in society. . . . It is like all of those people are outsiders. They are really not like us. They really don't understand the kind of hours and pressures and all of the other things that happen."[16]

The validity of the lament that doctors and patients inhabit very different worlds is confirmed as well by recent popular literature. The social distance between doctor and patient finds an interesting confirmation in the disappearance of physicians from the pages of modern literature, or more precisely, their disappearance as individuals without a white coat on. The immediate post–World War II novels and stories frequently depicted doctors in hospitals and in examining rooms, but seldom in other contexts. Painters, professors, writers, lawyers, basketball players, sportswriters, soft-drink salespeople, business tycoons, journalists, farmers, and carpenters all have served as heroes or heroines, lovers, or dinner guests. But rarely doctors. A few exceptions aside, writers did not—and for the most part still do not—casually bring a doctor onto their pages. The days when the suitors could be physicians, as in *Middlemarch* or *Uncle Vanya*, have passed, apparently because the physician requires too much introduction and demands too much of a spotlight (as though the reader would ask, Why is a doctor at this party?). The physician is too distant from the writer's imagination, too alien from both the writer's and the readers' world, to fit comfortably in the dining room or the bedroom.

Sometimes, if illness or hospitalization is not integral to the story, a character who becomes a doctor disappears altogether. A 1984 novel by Alice Adams, *Superior Women*, purports to trace the lives of five Radcliffe women from college days through middle age. Actually, it traces only four of them: the fifth, Janet Marr—Jewish, aggressive, and least integrated into the circle—decides to go to medical school, and with that, drops out of the book. Another of the group, Megan Greene, meets up with a young doctor she had known as an undergraduate (the common ploy authors use to bring a doctor into the plot). The two "discuss his work at Columbia-Presbyterian. He tells her a couple of grizzly medical jokes. Of his colleagues there he says, 'A really great bunch of guys.' . . . Their conversation is in fact so sketchy, so impersonal that for a moment Megan crazily wonders if he is really sure who she is." We, in turn, may wonder why connecting a doctor to the rest of humanity seems beyond the reach of the author.[17]

Nathan Zuckerman, on the other hand, in Philip Roth's novel *The Anatomy Lesson* fantasizes about becoming a doctor as a way of alleviating the pains of body and soul. By good fortune, his college roommate, Bobby Freytag, is a physician on the faculty of the University of Chicago (how else would Zuckerman know a doctor personally?). Zuckerman turns to him for advice, only to hear, of course, that forty-year-olds should forget about going to medical school. But Zuckerman does not give up easily. He visits Freytag and envies him, as his German name promises, his freedom, that is, the freedom to become wholly immersed in one's work. " '*This is life. With real teeth in it,*' exclaims Zuckerman." No holds are barred: "What the doctor wanted to know the patient told him. Nobody's secret a scandal or a disgrace—everything revealed and everything at stake. And always the enemy was wicked and real." And just how wicked emerges in the patients' diseases: a woman whose face has been half eaten away by cancer, and another who must have her larynx removed. "Another catastrophe—every moment, behind every wall, *right next door*, the worst ordeals that anyone could imagine, pain that was ruthless and inescapably real, crying and suffering truly worthy of all a man's defiance." Zuckerman thrives on it all.

Yet, the practice of medicine emerges as too exotic, too apart from the life that others lead. To read *The Anatomy Lesson* is to learn why most laypeople are content to let doctors take care of disease. The hospital is fantastic, filled with unlimited material for the novelist (or for that matter, the anthropologist), but not a place anyone else would want to frequent. And not coincidentally, neither Bobby nor any of the other physicians come alive except with their white coats on. The interns struck Zuckerman as "artless, innocent children. It was as though, leaving the platform with their medical-school diplomas, they'd taken a wrong turn and fallen back headlong into the second grade." All we learn of Bobby is that he is divorced and has a disobedient son and a grief-stricken, almost crazed father. Of Bobby's colleagues, we meet only one, and he, an emergency room doctor named Walsh, lacks the right stuff to fight disease "day after day . . . over the long haul." "You've got to watch them die without falling apart," he observes. "I can't do that."[18] To be a doctor, then, is to pursue an all-encompassing and worthy calling, but those who respond to it remain shadowy. Medicine is heroic but its knights obscure.

If not obscure, then disconnected. Dr. Solomon, the orthopedic surgeon in C. E. Poverman's 1981 novel, *Solomon's Daughter*, cannot relate to either of his children, Rose or Nick. Medicine is apparently the right profession for a writer to assign to a father who is deeply caring but incapable of reaching out. Nick, as his psychiatrist explains to Solomon, is one of those children "who have given up trying to reach anyone because they feel it won't do any good. They feel they can't make themselves understood or get any real response." Rose, after a wretched marriage, nearly kills herself in an automobile accident and is left severely damaged mentally and physically. Solomon does all he can for her, including performing a futile operation, but she is beyond the reach of either his talents or his love. Dr. Solomon is responsible and caring, but intimacy in his relationships goes beyond his ability—which may well represent the contemporary view of the physician.[19]

The most favorable depiction of a physician in popular literature takes as its hero a doctor of the 1920s and 1930s with a very odd practice. Dr. Wilbur Larch, in John Irving's *Cider House Rules*, is founder and superintendent of the St. Cloud orphanage in Maine, and his practice consists of delivering wanted babies and aborting—illegally—unwanted ones. Larch is by contrast all that a modern doctor is not, bearing even less resemblance to his successors than Mr. Chips would to a grant-driven researcher in a high-powered university. There is nothing conventional—or contemporary—about Larch. He loves his orphans, particularly Homer Wells, and does all in his power to give them a real home; he is equally passionate about the wisdom and ethics of not bringing more orphans into this world. He is not in office or hospital practice but in charge of an asylum; and he is an ether addict. When he selects Homer Wells to be his successor, he trains him as an apprentice (forget about medical schools) and designs an elaborate fraud to get Wells certified as a doctor and appointed as his successor. Larch's purpose in all this is to make certain that love, and not a rigid adherence to rules, will guide Homer's actions and his institution. Thus, when we finally have a doctor as the hero, he is unreal, a throwback to an earlier time—not someone who unites all that is so conflicted in modern medicine, but someone who represents all that modern medicine appears to have lost. Larch is an appealing, even captivating, character but in all ways irrelevant.[20]

Medicine has never lacked critics. As the historian John Burnham noted in a 1982 article aptly entitled "American Medicine's Golden Age: What Happened to It?" there is a venerable tradition of denigrating doctors that stretches from Aristophanes to Molière, and on to Ivan Illich.[21] But as a sense of doctors as strangers and hospitals as strange places permeated American society, the thrust of the critique changed, and so did the implications for public policy.

From the 1930s through the 1950s, most of the attacks on medicine were inspired by shortcomings in the system of health care delivery, particularly because medical care was often beyond the reach of the poor and increasingly placed a heavy financial burden on the middle class, especially the elderly. To critics, like journalist Richard Carter, problems began with the fact that the AMA was a powerful trade lobby and the doctor, a rapacious businessman. The opening pages of his 1958 book, *The Doctor Business*, tell about an accident in which a young boy fell into a well; after volunteers worked unstintingly for twenty-four hours to dig him out, his parents took him to a local doctor, who proceeded to bill $1,500 for his services. A public outcry followed (one U.S. senator spoke of "the outrage in my soul"), and even the AMA disassociated itself ("Not one doctor in a thousand would have charged a fee"). Pointing to this story, Carter criticized the "fee-based relations" between doctor and patient, concluding that "without presuming to tell a single M.D. how to care for a single appendix, the public can upgrade medicine from the bazaar."[22]

This type of faultfinding persisted well into the 1960s. In *The Troubled Calling*, another journalist, Selig Greenberg, described the doctor's position in terms of "the clash between the priestly nature of his vocation and the economic considerations of his career." Wondering why "such a profound discontent and unease hang over the American medical scene at the very time of medicine's greatest triumphs," Greenberg concluded that the public's hostility rested, perhaps unfairly, on an image of the doctor in his Cadillac and his wife in a mink coat. "Medicine has infinitely more to give people than they are actually getting . . . numerous health care needs remain unmet in the richest country in the world. . . . The profession's clinging to a grossly outdated concept of rugged individualism has a great deal to do with the prevailing climate of unrest."[23]

A very different critique characterized the late 1960s and 1970s, inspired not by economics but by distance and distrust, not by considerations of cost but of sentiment. To be sure, even earlier there had been numerous complaints about the unfeeling specialist or busy doctor, but they had never before reached the pitch of these protests or served as the basis for new organizations. The distinctions between the two sources of discontent emerged in the formation of the Society for Health and Human Values. They appeared even more vividly in the approach of the women's rights movement, a movement that at once fed on and reinforced a sense of separation—the doctor as stranger, indeed as male stranger.

The origins of the Society for Health and Human Values, as reconstructed by Daniel Fox, were in the early 1960s, when a small group of clergy concerned with medical ministries constituted themselves as the Committee on Medical Education and Theology. The issues that most worried them were "depersonalization," the "centrality of mechanical biology," and the "teaching of mechanistic medicine." Their goal was somehow to counter these trends through changes in medical education. Although ad hoc, unfunded, and imprecise in its aims, the committee signaled the emergence of a new concern. In 1968, the group expanded, becoming more secular than religious; it changed its name to the Committee on Health and Human Values, and its ranks came to include such physicians as Edmund Pellegrino, who had a sophisticated and abiding interest in these issues.

Not surprisingly, in light of its goals, the committee, at its 1968 meeting, addressed the specific problems emerging in human experimentation and it soon received a grant to examine how academic institutions reviewed such research. But even more central to its mission was the establishment of an institute that would "identify explicitly the human values that are lacking or inadequately represented in the study and practice of medicine and to begin to remedy this deficit." This formulation, in Fox's view, represented a kind of "doctor-bashing"; a tone of adversariness was apparent, as it would be in the introduction of bioethics. But in a larger framework, the committee was attempting to reintegrate medicine's values with societal values, to use the humanities to reduce the insularity and isolation of the medical world. Its methods and strategies were too nebulous to boast of any rapid accomplishments, but its program testified to both the growing recognition of the severity of the problem and the sources of energy that would be devoted to resolving it.[24]

Using a very different language and approach, the new feminism challenged social practices in the physician's office. They redefined doctor-patient relationships that had once seemed natural and appropriate (the good patient as compliant) as part of a larger male design to keep women powerless, and at the same time, as part of a professional design to keep all laypeople powerless. Feminist scholars and advocates denounced both the inherited politics of gender and the politics of the professions, so that the issue of men dominating women was inseparable from doctors dominating patients. Medicine, in fact, was a sitting target, first, because its ranks were almost exclusively male, and at least in obstetrics and gynecology, all the patients were female. Second, the medical establishment had been expansive in its reach, medicalizing phenomena that had once been outside the doctor's ken, capturing for its own professional territory the area of reproduction, childbirth, and sexuality. To the feminists and their supporters (like Illich), these matters ought to have remained in the lay world, particularly with the women in that world.

Feminist scholars explored the history of medicine not to celebrate great discoveries or to trace the scientific progress of the profession but to analyze the dynamics by which male doctors had excluded women and enlarged their own domain. The articles and books were passionate, even bitter, as they described physicians' opposition to women's education (on the grounds that their frail bodies could not tolerate the strain), the exclusion of women from medical schools (on the assumption that they were not sufficiently dedicated to or temperamentally suited for medicine), and the insistence that women's proper place was in the private sphere (in the belief that anatomy dictated destiny, that God had fashioned a uterus and then built the woman around it). Feminist researchers then went on to explore more generally the medicalization of American society. When doctors expelled midwives from the delivery room, or when doctors replaced women as the authors of popular child-rearing tracts, the change spoke to a reduced role not only for women but for all laypeople. When male doctors discriminated against women physicians, they were minimizing the role of sympathy against science in the profession, and thereby encouraging an impersonal and distant style of medical practice.

Feminists presented these same points to a wider public in such bestselling books as *Our Bodies, Ourselves*, originally published in 1971. Their primary target was gynecologists, but the onslaught extended to all (male) doctors, and the prescriptions were not gender specific. Take, for example, its summary paragraph on doctors: "The image and myth of the doctor as humanitarian, which has been so assiduously sold to the American public for the last fifty years, is out of date. If there ever were such doctors, they are mostly all gone now. . . . Most men in practice today most closely resemble the American businessman: repressed, compulsive, and more interested in money (and the disease process) than in people." Ascribing most of the blame to medical education and medical recruitment, the authors of *Our Bodies, Ourselves* complained that "medical students are usually very carefully selected by men who are attempting to reproduce themselves, and usually succeed. After four years of training they have almost invariably become . . . even more detached and mechanistic than they were to start with. As a group they are also more immature emotionally and sexually than their peers or the rest of the population. . . . Most doctors finishing their training are in late adolescence, psychologically speaking." The concluding advice to women—really, to all patients—followed logically on the critique: "We want you to be more alert to your responsibility in the relationship, just as you would in any other adult relationship where you are purchasing services."[25] The rules for patients had changed: docile obedience was to give way to wary consumerism. Thus, if kept waiting, a patient should take her business elsewhere; if denied information, she should find another source. The adage "never trust a stranger" now expanded to "never trust a doctor."

One final piece of evidence confirms just how widely shared this judgment was becoming in the post-1965 period, namely, the mounting sense of crisis around malpractice litigation. The apparent increase in litigation (record-keeping methods varied so greatly from state to state that firm conclusions on actual increases were difficult to reach) spurred a 1969 congressional study (chaired by Connecticut's Senator Abraham Ribicoff) of what role the federal government might play in resolving the problem. Then, two years later, President Richard Nixon appointed a HEW commission to study the causes and issue recommendations, and the AMA also organized a survey. Although these various committees noted that American society was becoming more litigious generally, they agreed that one critical element in the rise of malpractice suits was the breakdown of the doctor–patient relationship. The overwhelming majority of suits were filed against specialists, not general practitioners, because here the distance between physician and patient was greatest. Thus, it was experts in malpractice law, not consumer activists, who counseled doctors: "When the physician–patient rapport remains at a high level of trust and confidence, most patients will ride out a bad result, but when that rapport is inadequate in the beginning or is permitted to deteriorate in route, a suit is likely to follow."[26] Not only were patients distrustful of strangers, they were ready to sue them.

No one document better illustrates how new social attitudes and practices redefined both the concept of the good patient and the obligations of health care professionals and institutions than the Patient Bill of Rights, promulgated first by the Joint Commission on the Accreditation of Hospitals (JCAH) in 1970 and formally adopted by the American Hospital Association (AHA) in 1973. The initial inspiration for the document came, fittingly enough, from the National Welfare Rights Organization (NWRO). Dedicated to bringing a rights orientation into areas dominated by concepts of charity and worthiness, its leaders devoted most of their energy to making relief and welfare policies responsive to a concept of entitlement. But the NWRO also focused on other institutions that affected the lives of the poor, including public schools, and most important in our context, voluntary and public hospitals. Recognizing that the hospital system was essentially two-track, with the poor typically consigned to twelve-bed wards, treated by medical students and house staff, and, apparently, disproportionately experimented on by investigators, the NWRO attempted to impose a rights model on hospitals. In 1970, it presented a list of twenty-six proposals to the JCAH, and after negotiations, the JCAH incorporated a number of them into the preamble to that group's "Accreditation Manual." This preamble was the only document composed by health care professionals that *Our Bodies, Ourselves* reprinted and credited.[27]

As befit its origins with the NWRO, the preamble first addressed issues that particularly affected the poor. First, "no person should be denied impartial access to treatment . . . on the basis of . . . race, color, creed, national origin, or the nature of the source of payment." In this same spirit, all patients had a right to privacy, including the right not to be interviewed without their consent by "representatives of agencies not connected with the hospital," that is, welfare agencies. A patient's right to privacy also meant a respect for "the privacy of his body," and so, regardless of source of payment, the patient should be examined "shield[ed] . . . from the views of others" and should be made a part of clinical training programs (for medical students) only voluntarily. These points made, the preamble framers then addressed concerns that affected all patients, whatever their social or economic status. The process of defining rights moved across tracks, from concerns more relevant to the poor to concerns relevant to everyone. Thus, the document continued: "The patient has the right to receive . . . adequate information concerning the nature and extent of his medical problem, the planned course of treatment, and prognosis." In brief, all patients had the right to be told the truth about their medical condition.

The preamble served as the basis for the 1972 Patient Bill of Rights, adopted by the AHA after a three-year discussion by a committee that included not only the trustees of the association but four outsiders representing consumer organizations. The first of the twelve points in this bill of rights was a general statement of the right to "considerate and respectful care," and then the document addressed the most central concern, patient consent. It enlarged on the JCAH standard for truth telling by insisting that explanations be given in ways that "the patient can reasonably be expected to understand," and spelled out, in language reminiscent of the FDA stipulations, the requirements for obtaining consent both in treatment and experimentation. Its remaining points emphasized the patient's right to privacy and to a "reasonable" degree of continuity of care.

To be sure, the document disappointed a number of patients' rights activists.[28] They were quick to note that rights would not be achieved when they were handed down from on high by the medical establishment. Willard Gaylin, a psychiatrist who at that moment was helping to organize the Hastings Institute of Society, Ethics and the Life Sciences, charged that the process amounted to "the thief lecturing his victim on self-protection."[29] Others observed that none of these documents (or the variants on them that particular hospitals adopted) included any procedures for enforcement or for levying penalties, and still others criticized them because the stipulations on truth telling allowed a major exception: when doctors believed that bad news would be harmful to the patient, they were to convey it to the family. Indeed, the provisions on consent generally appeared to be self-serving restatements of legal precedents intended to reduce the frequency of patient dissatisfaction with physicians, and thereby, the frequency of malpractice suits.[30]

But these objections notwithstanding, the preamble and bill of rights had both symbolic and real importance, affecting attitudes and practices of both doctors and patients. The position on truth telling, for example, at once acknowledged the need for physicians to follow a new standard and promoted its realization. When the 1960s began, almost all physicians (90 percent in one study) reported that their "usual policy" was not to tell patients about a finding of cancer. By the close of the 1970s, an equal percentage reported that they usually did tell patients such a diagnosis.[31] Practice may not have always conformed to stated principles, but there is no doubt that, given traditional mores, a small revolution had been effected.

Thus the Patient Bill of Rights reflected the new ideological orientation that was making the concept of rights so powerful throughout American society. Leading national professional organizations, responding to external pressures, were now adopting the language and concepts of rights to delineate medical obligations. Behind the transformation lay, first, the recognition that the social distancing of doctor from patient and hospital from community rendered obsolete inherited maxims and practices. But to understand this reorientation fully, we must continue our story, for the transformation in medical decision making also reflected a series of developments taking place in medicine itself. We must return again to the 1960s, this time to examine the impact of the extraordinary innovations in the science and practice of organ transplantation.

CHAPTER 8

Life Through Death

THE scandals in human experimentation and the broader, but no less potent, sense of the doctor as stranger first introduced new players and new rules to the once insular field of medicine. But however important these initial changes, they were only the opening forays. In the 1960s, medical procedures and technologies, especially in the area of organ transplantation, posed questions that appeared to some physicians—and to even more nonphysicians—to go beyond the fundamental principles of medical ethics or the expertise of the doctor and to require societal intervention. One advance after another framed questions that seemed to demand resolution in the public arena, not the doctor's office. Put another way, these issues combined to take medical ethics (and, to a degree, medical decision making) out of the hands of the doctor and empower a new group of lay participants.

No sooner does one mention medical procedures and technologies than a cloud of clichés threatens to descend on the subject. By now it is common for television documentaries or talk-debate shows to open with the observation that medical technology has forced agonizing choices upon us, that technology has created hard questions for which there are no right answers. But shrouded within this mist are a series of critical developments that should be highlighted. For one, it was not medical technology alone that was responsible for the change but the fact that the technology appeared at a special time, when Americans' long-lived romance with machines was weakening, indeed, when Americans' trust in physicians was weakening. For another, the technology came in special ways that were neither inevitable nor predictable, challenging the inherited precepts of medical ethics not only by an initial scarcity but by compelling doctors to make unusual trade-offs and choices. As we shall soon see, the fact that organ transplantation was the test case (as against, say, artificial organ replacement) engendered a whole series of novel dilemmas. For still another, despite the lament that there are no right answers, the more critical point is that an entirely new group of people, whether in government, the law, or the academy, were ready to pose the questions and even attempt to answer them. Finally, these developments provoked a fascinating split within medicine itself. Some doctors followed Beecher's example, alerting outsiders as well as insiders to the problems at hand. Others, the larger contingent by far, complained bitterly about the efforts to trespass on their domain, attempting by one or another strategy to rebuild their fences. For the most part, the effort was futile, but it did lend a combative tone to the entire enterprise.

The first of the technological developments that called into question the sovereignty of physicians over medical ethics and decision making involved kidney dialysis, one of the earliest and most successful of life-saving interventions. The question that the dialysis machines posed was perfectly framed to rivet both professional and lay attention. In formal terms, How was access to the technology to be determined? In its more popular version, Who gave out the seats in the only lifeboat? The answer was, not necessarily the ship's captain.

The issue captured nationwide attention in 1962, courtesy of an extraordinary piece of reporting by Shana Alexander in *Life* magazine. Two years earlier, Dr. Belding Scribner of the University of Washington Medical School in Seattle had made the breakthrough that transformed kidney dialysis from a short-term to a long-term treatment. Techniques had existed since World War II to treat an acute episode of kidney failure; William Kolff, in the Netherlands under German occupation, had devised a way to filter a patient's blood through a cellophane tubing, thereby cleansing it of impurities. The difficulty was that in order to undertake the process, a surgeon had to cut into an artery and vein to divert the flow of blood through the cleansing filter and then back to the body again—and sooner, rather than later, the patient exhausted available blood vessels. In the case of a traumatic and temporary injury to the kidneys, this mode of dialysis could tide a patient over until the organ recovered. But if the problem was chronic kidney failure, the process was useless.

In 1960, Dr. Scribner designed a permanent indwelling shunt that allowed the patient to be connected to the dialysis machine, plugged in as it were, in a matter of minutes and without a new surgical procedure. Now patients with chronic end-stage kidney disease could be kept alive with the machine performing the function of the kidneys. But the machines were in very short supply, with far fewer available than the number of patients who could benefit from them. Thus arose the decision Alexander explored in her article: who would live and who would die.

To answer the question about allocation of this scarce resource, the Seattle physicians asked the county medical society to appoint a lay committee of seven "quite ordinary people" to determine "life or death." Alexander sat in on their meetings and described their procedures and responses. The physicians at the hospital initially screened out all kidney patients not medically or psychiatrically suited for the procedure. They also made some "rather arbitrary decisions," such as ruling out children and anyone over forty-five years of age; even so, the number of claimants was still too high. The committee itself decided to limit access to residents of the state of Washington on the dubious grounds that state tax dollars had supported the research, but four candidates still remained for each place. So to select the fortunate patients, the committee relied heavily on family considerations, giving preference to heads of households with a wife and children to support. It also attempted to weigh the contribution each of the candidates would make to the community—If we give you life, what will you do for us?—invoking criteria of a conventional middle-class sort: church membership, scout work, and the like.

As fascinating as it is to reconstruct how the Seattle committee did its job, the most critical feature for our purposes is that a group of physicians, in unprecedented fashion, turned over to a lay committee life-or-death decisions prospectively and on a case-by-case basis. A prerogative that had once been the exclusive preserve of the doctor was delegated to community representatives. Why did the physicians make this extraordinary grant of power? In part, a lay committee would protect the doctors from political fallout, from charges of doing each other favors (as when the wife of a fellow physician fell ill and needed dialysis) or from abusing their authority. In part, too, a lay committee seemed preferable to a lottery or to a first-come, first-served rule. In this sense, the committee was a symbolic representation of the hope (or faith?) that a scarce resource could be distributed without abdicating all ethical responsibility, that life and death were not arbitrary, that the "good" people should first be spared suffering. The committee's assignment was daunting, but the alternative of a random process, of letting chance rule, seemed worse.

Most important, physicians turned to a lay committee because they realized that the traditional medical ethic of each doctor doing everything possible to enhance the well-being of the particular patient could not operate in these circumstances. It was apparent to the physicians that the decision was unresolvable if each advocated the well-being of an individual patient and urged that he or she be given access to the machine. Hence, it seemed preferable to empower a lay committee rather than compel doctors to abdicate their responsibilities. Rather than have physicians give first allegiance to the functioning of the system as a whole, the Seattle group turned to outsiders for help.

In making this choice, the committee transmitted a message, as Alexander accurately noted: the "acceptance of the principle that all segments of society, not just the medical fraternity, should share the burden of choice as to which patients to treat and which to let die. Otherwise society would be forcing the doctors alone to play God."[1] No matter how idiosyncratic the dialysis experience, the inevitable conclusion to be drawn from it was that experts in kidney functioning were not experts in judging the comparative value of lives. The result was that a once exclusive prerogative of the doctor was becoming socialized. A lay committee—by physicians' invitation, to be sure—had entered the examining room.

Even with this innovation, the Seattle experience did not sit well with Americans. That anyone, whether doctors or a group of laypeople, should be playing God was unseemly—and all the more so as word got out on how such committees reached their decisions. There was a patent unfairness to preferring the married over the single, the employed over the unemployed, or churchgoers over nonchurchgoers; it seemed positively un-American to reward conformists over nonconformists—or as the authors of a highly critical law review article remarked, for the Pacific Northwest to be so inhospitable toward a Henry David Thoreau with kidney trouble. Thus, the Seattle experience taught a second lesson: committees, whatever their makeup, would not necessarily resolve difficult choices. One might well need to construct principles or guidelines to make certain that medical decision making represented more than the accumulated prejudices of a handful of people, whether their training was medical or not.*

As with dialysis, physicians found the principles of traditional medical ethics inadequate to cope with the innovations in transplantation. The problems that the new techniques of kidney transplantation posed about maiming the healthy, allocating scarce resources, and defining death led a core of physicians again to bring outsiders into medicine's territory.

Although the thought of transplanting a major organ from one person or animal to another has ancient roots, and sporadic attempts to carry it out had occurred in the nineteenth and early twentieth centuries, not until the late 1940s did the procedure become more than a fantasy. The first experiments were with the kidney, for this organ was paired (making donation possible without the donor incurring great risk), and the surgical techniques were relatively simple (in contrast, for example, to transplanting a liver). The chief barrier to success was the immune system, which reacted to the new organ as though it were a foreign body and tried to reject it. In 1954 surgeons at Boston's Peter Bent Brigham Hospital successfully transplanted a kidney from one identical twin to another, thereby demonstrating that when im-

---

*A third lesson emerged from the experience, one worth noting briefly because of its staying power and controversial character: problems of scarce medical resources can be resolved by money. Congress eventually underwrote the costs of care for all patients with end-stage kidney disease, the first time a specific patient group received open-ended funding; and with funds available, the proliferation of dialysis machines and centers followed quickly. But as we shall see, not all allocation decisions are resolvable in this fashion, and it is debatable whether the federal budget will support such programs again.

munological responses were minimized (because of the twin's genetic similarity), the procedure was feasible. But the lifesaving feat did not point the way to controlling rejection in cases where recipients and donors were unrelated.

Investigators experimented with a number of procedures to reduce the immune response without leaving the body helpless to fight off infections. After initial failures (including the use of massive doses of X rays), they identified several chemotherapeutic agents that inhibited rejection without completely crippling the body's ability to combat disease. The number of kidney transplants then rose, and so did the success rates. In 1963 and 1964, a total of 222 kidney transplants were performed, and about half of the recipients were alive one year after the operation. Patients who received kidneys from relatives had the best chance of success (12-month survival rates for 4 out of 5 identical twins, 31 out of 45 siblings, but only 9 of 29 unrelated donors, which was about the same success ratio for those receiving kidneys from cadavers). Still, everyone recognized that more sophisticated chemical agents would soon make the procedure even more effective.[2]

In its experimental phase, kidney transplantation, particularly involving cadaver organs, raised ethical issues relatively easy to resolve. Although the death rates for the first recipients were high (most dying within a few months after the procedure), the surgeons persisted, and no one faulted them, for all the patients were on the verge of death and had no alternatives—dialysis for chronic patients was still in the future. In the 1960s, even unusual variations in transplantation research did not create significant controversy. When Dr. Keith Reemtsma, then at Tulane, put a chimpanzee kidney into a patient dying of kidney disease, there were practically no public protests and only a few raised eyebrows at the NIH. So too, Thomas Starzl, then a surgeon at the University of Colorado Medical School, solicited kidney donations from prison inmates for transplantation; when a few physicians, informally, took him to task, Starzl stopped the practice. Had kidney transplantation had to undergo scrutiny only as an experiment, it would have fitted neatly under the emerging codes governing research.[3]

As transplantation moved from experiment to therapy, however, a whole series of novel questions had to be addressed. Once again, as with dialysis, the bedrock principle of medical ethics—namely, physicians as the uncompromising advocates for their patients—did not resolve the questions at hand. A physician determined to give his or her patient the best of care faced a series of dilemmas once transplantation became a treatment option.

These dilemmas were laid out with special clarity at a three-day conference in 1966, under the auspices of the CIBA Foundation, which explored "Ethics in Medical Progress, With Special Reference to Transplantation." The conference attendees were almost all physicians, except for one lawyer and one minister; in 1966 a medical conference on ethics was still largely an internal affair. But a recognition of the limits of traditional medical ethics did prompt the participants to call for wider counsel from those who had not before played a role in medical decision making. Michael Woodruff, a transplant surgeon at the University of Edinburgh and the organizer of the conference, made this point in his opening remarks: "This symposium was planned because of the growing realization that progress in medicine brings in its train ethical problems which are the concern not only of practicing doctors but of the whole community, and which are unlikely to be solved without intensive study of an interdisciplinary kind."[4]

The first of the ethical problems that Woodruff identified was that transplant surgeons would be removing a healthy organ from a would-be donor, and such an operation might well constitute maiming a patient, a purposeful infliction of harm. Whatever the benefit to the recipient, the removal of a kidney posed an immediate danger to the donor (the anesthesia itself, to say nothing of the surgery, carried a low but real risk), as well as a long-term one—for the remaining kidney might become diseased. Some of the physicians responded that donating a kidney was the same as dashing into a burning building to rescue a trapped child; but the contention was quickly rebutted, because the would-be rescuer, unlike the kidney donor, was not directly harming himself. His aim was to bring out the child and have both of them escape—any ensuing injury would be an indirect and unintended result of his action. But in transplantation, the injury was inseparable from the act, the essence of the donation itself.[5] Woodruff wondered whether the ethical dilemma was resolved in light of the fact that the risks of living with only one kidney were low. But others countered that a maiming was no less a maiming if the injury inflicted was relatively minor. Besides, whatever the risks, medical ethics would seem to preclude a physician from carrying out such a procedure. "As physicians motivated and educated to make sick people well, we make a basic qualitative shift in our aims when we risk the health of a well person, no matter how pure our motives."[6]

The fact that the donor consented to the procedure did not obviate the difficulties. The scandals around human experimentation made all the conference participants acutely aware of the need for donor consent, but they were not convinced that the consent could be truly voluntary. Did a twin who was asked to give one of her kidneys to her dying sister make a noncoerced choice? Was she truly free to say no? And what about taking a kidney from a minor? Could a parent agree to the donation on behalf of the child? (Physicians at the Brigham hospital had already faced this dilemma and had requested and received court approval for the donation.)[7] Until now, physicians had been confident that a patient's consent to a therapeutic intervention was little more than a technicality, for doctors would not perform a procedure against the patient's best interest. But in transplantation, the premise did not hold. In strictly medical terms, losing a healthy kidney could not advance the patient's well-being.

Second, as the CIBA participants recognized, this new form of therapy, like dialysis before it, posed in stark and unavoidable terms the problem of triage, of allocating scarce resources among a pool of would-be beneficiaries. Rationing was certainly not new to medicine, and it was widely recognized both within and outside the profession that not all who required services received them. But the rationing that went on was covert, unacknowledged, and most important, external to the doctor's office. If the poor did not receive the same care as the rich, it was not the physician who made the choice or necessarily had any firsthand awareness of the problem. (Indeed, many physicians insisted, justifiably, that they reduced their fees for low-income patients and contributed their fair share of charity work.) Transplantation, however, placed the problem of rationing directly into the doctors' hands. Now physicians, not some impersonal social force or government agency, would have to select the patient who would receive the benefit of life-saving medical technology, and neither they nor anyone else had much experience in making such choices. Even triage under battlefield conditions was of little relevance. Physicians there passed over the hopeless case or the minor one so as to treat those who would most benefit from medical intervention; transplantation (and dialysis, as well) forced a choice among *all* those who would most benefit from intervention. Moreover, the physician who remained a staunch advocate for his or her patient rendered any choice among patients impossible, and the result was a stalemate. Forceful advocacy, in other words, did not solve the dilemma but exacerbated it.

Finally, the CIBA conference addressed an issue that transplantation framed in a most dramatic way: the definition of death. The issue needed to be confronted in order to increase the efficacy of the transplant procedure; if physicians continued to mark death by the stoppage of the heart, they maximized the potential for damage, for kidneys deprived of blood even for a short time deteriorated. As we shall see, the need to define death also arose from causes independent of transplantation, namely, the new artificial respirators. "Many people," noted Woodruff, "are now maintained in a sort of twilight state by the use of machines which do the work of their lung or their heart while they are completely unconscious. . . . Many of these people will never resume an independent existence away from the machines, but they can't stay on the machines for ever and ever. . . . One has to decide therefore when to switch off the machines."[8] But the decision was still more complex in transplantation. In the case of general organ failure, physicians at the bedside reached a decision that they believed represented the wishes of the patient. The transplant surgeon, however, appeared to be in a conflicted situation—possibly more concerned about the well-being of the organ recipient than the potential organ donor. In short, transplantation put the physician in the position of having to confront not only the difficult question of when life is over, but the even more excruciating question of when life is over for one patient when another may benefit.

The transformation that began with kidney dialysis and transplantation accelerated dramatically with heart transplantation. Not only did the medical marvels of this procedure capture the public's imagination in a way that no postwar innovation had, but so did its ethical and social implications. After heart transplantation, there was no keeping medical ethics or medical decision making exclusively a physician's prerogative.

With ample justification, 1968 was labeled the "year of the heart transplant." The first operation was performed by South Africa's Dr. Christiaan Barnard in December 1967. Although the recipient, Louis Washkansky, lived only eighteen days, Barnard immediately took his place alongside Charles Lindbergh, John Glenn, and other pioneering heroes. Within a short time a number of American surgeons, including Adrian Kantrowitz and Norman Shumway, performed transplants. In fact, the initial enthusiasm for the procedure was so overwhelming that in 1968, surgeons performed 108 transplants and in November alone, 26 transplants.

Francis Moore, a professor of surgery at Harvard and Peter Bent Brigham Hospital and an exceptionally articulate and socially aware physician, immediately recognized the implications of heart transplantation for medical ethics. In the early 1960s Moore had written at length and with insight about the ethics of kidney transplants. (His 1965 book, *Give and Take*, remains one of the best histories of kidney transplantations.)[9] Now, in the late 1960s, he was convinced that heart transplantation gave an unprecedented popularity, even panache, to the field. And like a climber who learns that others—and amateurs at that—have discovered his favorite route, Moore fretted about the impact that outsiders might have. Heart transplantation, he noted, "has brought a new set of ideas and perplexities to the general public. A surprising number of eminent people, who appear to be surprised, shocked, and startled into public statements by heart transplants, have actually been silent, apathetic, and as uninvolved as distant spectators during the extremely critical years of kidney transplantation in the United States." Moore trusted that they would study this earlier experience, especially what he and others had said about it, for otherwise, "listeners and readers must likewise be sentenced to a long series of statements by newcomers as they gradually become aware of the problems that others have faced and solved for many years."[10]

Moore's expectation that newcomers would respect and appreciate that doctors had been there first was fanciful. Heart transplantation did raise many of the same questions as kidney transplantation, but the fact that it was now hearts meant that concerns about conflict of interest, the definition of death, and allocation of the scarce organs commanded wider attention and made it seem more obvious that the questions were too fraught with social and political consequences to allow doctors to monopolize the discussion. From 1968 to 1970 the ranks of those ready to influence medical decision making increased dramatically, and the popular press, academic journals, and the *Congressional Record* all reflected the change.

Again, it was not a medical procedure or technology that was the decisive consideration but the widespread sense that older rules of medicine no longer were sufficient to guide decisions. Heart transplantation made it apparent that an ethic of advocating for one's patient and doing no harm were not sufficient to the task of knowing when to terminate care for one patient so another might live. One Oregon physician, writing in the *Journal of the American Medical Association,* declared that "the people, law, and medicine must come into some comfortable and realistic rapprochement on the moral, ethical, legal, humanistic, and economic aspects of this problem," precisely because transplantation involves the interests of "two individuals, the donor and the recipient."[11] Another physician, a neurosurgeon, went even further, urging in a *New England Journal of Medicine* article that his colleagues do the almost unthinkable, that is, adopt the mind-set of lawyers in order to resolve what appeared "at least on the surface to be a conflict of interest." Attorneys "can remain the best of friends . . . and yet fight each other relentlessly in the courtroom on their respective client's behalf." In this spirit, physicians should take sides, one protecting his patient's welfare (the potential donor) even as his colleague (representing the recipient) clamored for the organ. "This state of mind," he conceded, "is foreign to the physician's make-up, since he has always worked with his colleagues for a common cause." But transplantation compelled physicians to recognize "a conflict of interest, acknowledge its existence," and adopt a new outlook.[12]

Those outside, as well as inside, medicine fully appreciated the strains that transplantation placed on the conventional doctor–patient relationship. Even as the popular press devoted pages to Barnard's first transplant, it pondered the potential for conflict of interest. "Can I ever be certain," *Newsweek* reported one woman as saying, "that doctors would do everything possible to save my life if I had a nasty accident or a terrible disease, that they would not be influenced by what I could contribute to another person?"[13] In effect, heart transplantation helped to equate the physician with the researcher and the patient with the subject. No one—neither doctor nor patient—could be confident that the patient's best interest would be the sole or even central concern. The doctor at the bedside might be thinking about benefits to humanity—by perfecting the heart transplant procedure— or about benefits to the patient in the next room who needed a new heart, but not necessarily about the desperate patient before him.

Heart transplantation also required exquisite calculations on allocating scarce medical resources, a predicament that encouraged lay involvement in medical decision making. Questions of allocations obviously had a social component: Was it in the public interest to devote enormous resources to a procedure that would benefit only a handful of individuals? And whatever the answer, it was evident to many observers that the profession would have to be far more open and sharing about the decision. "The public has acquired the right to be informed of our activities," declared Dr. Rene Menguy, chairman of the department of surgery at the University of Chicago School of Medicine. "There is no place in our own society for taxation without representation, and for the simple reason that the American public has supported our efforts . . . it has acquired the right to be informed of our activities. Whether we like it or not the transplantation of a human heart, like a space launch at Cape Kennedy, now belongs to the public domain."[14] For heart transplantation to flourish, the legislature had to be allowed into the examining room.

Finally, whatever ambiguities about the definition of death could be skirted with kidney transplantation or with mechanical respirators had to be confronted directly when the heart was the organ at issue.[15] Even as late as 1968, neither the use of cadaver kidney transplants nor the dependence on mechanical respirators was sufficient to make brain death a public issue. To be sure, the number of patients using artificial breathing devices in intensive care units had increased, and so had those in a kind of limbo between life and death—not alive, because they were in a coma and incapable of breathing of their own; but not dead, because their heart and lungs, albeit with mechanical assistance, continued to function. But the question of what should be done was not yet of general concern (and would not be until 1976, when Karen Ann Quinlan's parents asked to have her removed from a respirator). The issue remained relatively obscure because doctors, inside the closed world of the intensive care units, turned off the machines when they believed the patient's death was imminent and irreversible. "Very few hospitals," reported a committee of neurologists in 1969, "had any regulations on the matter of discontinuing the mechanical aids to respiration and circulation. No one has encountered any medicolegal difficulties. Very few have sought legal opinions."[16] The intensive care units were a private domain, whatever the formal definition of death, and doctors exercised their discretion.

Heart transplantation, however, a far more public act, forced a clear-cut consideration of the validity of a brain-death standard. Once doctors transplanted a beating heart from donor to recipient—and the feat was celebrated in the media—the need to redefine death was readily apparent. The heart to be transplanted, remarked one noted surgeon, "should be removed and implanted in the recipient patient as close as possible to the moment when death of the donor can be established. This fact makes transplantation surgery more dramatic, and gives rise to much more emotional thinking and discussion than any other field of surgery has done."[17]

The first systematic effort at redefinition took place at Harvard, for reasons that return us to Henry Beecher. His concern for the ethics of experimentation had prompted Harvard to establish a Standing Committee on Human Studies, in essence a research review committee, with Beecher as its chairman. Since Beecher was an anesthesiologist, he had daily experience with respirators and intensive care units, and his surgeon colleagues at the Massachusetts General Hospital, especially Dr. Joseph Murray, had led the way in kidney transplantation. (Murray later won the Nobel Prize in Medicine for his work in this area.) All these elements encouraged him in October 1967 to suggest to Robert Ebert, the dean of the Harvard Medical School, that the Committee on Human Studies broaden its concerns to redefine death: "Both Dr. Murray and I think the time has come for a further consideration of the definition of death. Every major hospital has patients stacked up waiting for suitable donors."[18] Ebert thought the idea a good one, but it took Barnard's transplant feat to have him appoint such a committee. "With its pioneering interest in organ transplantation," Ebert told prospective committee members, "I believe the faculty of the Harvard Medical School is better equipped to elucidate this area than any other single group."[19]

The committee, which became known as the Harvard Brain Death Committee, deliberated from January through August 1968, and its final report, published in *JAMA*, represents an important transition in the history of who shall rule medicine.[20] On the one hand, the committee was sensitive to many of the legal and ethical implications of its assignment, taking the still unusual step of including among its members nonphysicians. Not only were all the appropriate medical specialties represented—medicine, anesthesiology, and neurosurgery (for its work with electroencephalographic [EEG] machines), but so was law, in the person of health law professor William Curran. Beecher also asked Professor George Williams of the Harvard Divinity School to join the committee, but Williams suggested instead "not a church historian who instinctively looks to the past, but rather a professional ethicist," someone "primarily oriented to the present and the future." Williams recommended his colleague Ralph Potter, who had already written on abortion and "whose special ethical field right now is the problem of the just war in the atomic age."[21] Beecher followed his advice and the committee had both a lawyer and a philosopher. At the same time, the committee's approach remained traditional in the sense that its members supported prerogatives for medicine that were in the process of being challenged, attempting, unsuccessfully, to make the definition of death a strictly medical concern. In the end, the Harvard report did not so much resolve the questions around brain death as propel them into the public domain.

The committee worked smoothly and quickly. Its members agreed from the outset that irreversible coma should be "a new criterion for death," and without much difficulty they defined the procedures that should establish the condition: two flat EEG readings from a patient not on barbiturates who displayed no reflex activity. The committee was quick, indeed too quick, to presume a broad social consensus on the desirability of a brain-death definition. The members concluded that at a time when "the improvements in resuscitative and support measures . . . [produce] an individual whose heart continues to beat but whose brain is irreversibly damaged," everyone was likely to agree that new criteria for terminating treatment were desirable. "The burden is great on patients who suffer permanent loss of intellect, on their families, on the hospitals, and on those in need of hospital beds already occupied by these comatose patients." Surely what was best for society—like making hospital beds more available—was best for the individual. The committee was also very concerned with transplant patients. "An issue of secondary but by no means minor importance," read the introduction to an early draft of the report, "is that with increased experience and knowledge and development in transplantation, there is great need for tissues and organs of, among others, the patient whose cerebrum has been hopelessly destroyed in order to restore those who are salvageable."[22]

Finally, the committee insisted that defining the concept of death and formally pronouncing death were the exclusive privilege of doctors: "The patient's condition can be determined only by a physician. When the patient is hopelessly damaged as defined above, the family and all colleagues who have participated in major decisions concerning the patient, and all nurses involved, should be so informed. Death is to be declared and *then* the respirator turned off. The decision to do this and the responsibility for it are to be taken by the physician-in-charge, in consultation with one or more physicians who have been directly involved in the case. It is unsound and undesirable to force the family to make the decision." The committee gave short shrift to potential religious objections and even to the role of law. "If this [brain death] position is adopted by the medical community," the members declared, "it can form the basis for change in the current legal concept of death. No statutory change in the law should be necessary since the law treats this question essentially as one of fact to be determined by physicians."[23] In effect, the committee presumed that because a doctor pronounced a particular patient to be dead, therefore doctors automatically were the ones who should define the standard of death.

The Harvard Brain Death Committee had many supporters among doctors. Medical journals endorsed its recommendations both because its case for brain death was well substantiated and they shared its readiness to maintain physician authority.[24] As one *JAMA* editorial noted: "In the resolution of whatever differences there are between medical and legal definitions of death, it seems clear that physicians rather than barristers must be the ones to establish the rules. . . . Lawyers and judges are not biologists, nor are they often 'in at the death.' They would doubtless be glad to follow the leader."[25]

And yet, the Harvard committee members sensed that the group's effort to control the definition of death might not succeed. The report did, after all, urge the physician in charge of the patient to consult with other colleagues—something not ordinarily required in pronouncing death—because it might be helpful in "providing an important degree of protection against later questions which might be raised." The committee also recognized that the patient's family might want to have a say in the decision to discontinue the respirator and firmly advised that "it is unsound and undesirable to force the family to make the decision." But even this formulation suggested a more complicated reality than the committee would admit. If the physician was first to pronounce the patient dead and then to turn off the machine, then the family's intervention was not merely unsound but absurd. To debate the role of the family was to recognize on some level that a finding of brain death involved more than strictly medical criteria; no matter what the committee said, this pronouncement of death was not like all other pronouncements of death. The committee might well wish to assert its authority, but the family, like the bar and the pulpit, would not necessarily abdicate responsibility.

Hence, the Harvard report immediately sparked criticism and opposition. A number of medical colleagues took Beecher himself to task, arguing that his eagerness to facilitate transplantation violated the very maxims he had set forth to govern human experimentation, namely, that worthwhile ends do not justify unethical means. When Ebert had reviewed an early draft, he counseled Beecher to modify the introductory language on transplantation. "The connotation of this statement is unfortunate, for it suggests that you wish to redefine death in order to make viable organs more readily available to persons requiring transplants. Immediately the reader thinks how this principle might be abused. . . . Would it not be better to state the problem, and indicate that obsolete criteria for the definition of death can lead to controversy in obtaining organs for transplantation?"[26] Beecher and the rest of the committee agreed, and adopted more guarded language: "The decision to declare the person dead, and then to turn off the respirator [should] be made by physicians not involved in any later effort to transplant organs or tissue from the deceased individual. This is advisable in order to avoid any appearance of self-interest by the physicians involved."[27] But even so, the suspicion remained that brain death was a tactic that would sacrifice the well-being of some patients for that of others.

Still more controversial outside of the profession was the committee's readiness to have physicians unilaterally define the moment of death. Just how problematic the position was is apparent from the extensive media coverage of the issue; if this had simply been a doctor's prerogative, one would not have seen articles on "When Is Death?" become commonplace in magazines like *Reader's Digest* and "thanatology" become a headline word in *Time*.[28] And at least some physicians found this attention altogether proper. A lengthy editorial in the *Annals of Internal Medicine*, entitled "When Do We Let the Patient Die?" declared: "The public is becoming much more aware and wants to know, and indeed should know, about these problems; after all, they not only are the final arbiters of the moral standards operative in our society— they are the patients."[29]

The brain-death issue galvanized more than a diffuse public discussion. Particular groups, especially religious ones, insisted on having their say. The Harvard committee blurred facts (this patient is dead) and values (this is the proper definition of death), but others scrupulously maintained the distinction. Thus, one Protestant ethicist argued that only religious leaders could "dispel our myths about life and death"; and if he was ready in this instance to put religion at the service of medicine "by disspiritualizing the heart from its poetic and romantic mythicization and shattering the superstition which surrounds the life–death threshold," the price that medicine had to pay in return was to abandon "the 'hands-off' attitude that seeks to guard the autonomy of the medical profession to deal in an isolated fashion with the great social ethical issues."[30] By the same token, Orthodox Jewish spokesmen objected to the definition because their tenets made the heart, not the brain, the seat of life. Catholic leaders feared that the state, following the physicians' lead, would soon be passing other legislation about life and death—here it involved the comatose; next it might affect the fetus. In response to such sentiments, hospitals began to hold joint clergy–physician meetings on brain death, recognizing that the question of when a person is dead "not only concerns physicians, but philosophers, theologians, moralists, lawmakers, judges, in fact—everyone."[31]

Heart transplantation brought into the public domain not only issues about medical resources and definitions of life and death, but the ability of medicine to keep its own house in order. Too much of a circus atmosphere surrounded the first transplant procedures, and physicians seemed to be more intent on celebrity status than on advancing the welfare of their patients. "There has never been anything like it in medical annals," Dr. Irvine Page, president of the American Heart Association, told a specially convened National Congress on Medical Ethics of the AMA. The frantic hunt for publicity among surgeons, with Barnard as the leading case in point; the instant reporting of results to the press; the neglect in presenting findings to scientific publications; and the readiness to ignore considerations of patient privacy and confidentiality all led Page to conclude, "I fear the public has gotten a view of medicine which will further downgrade its intellectual and compassionate aspects."[32]

Moreover, observers inside and outside medicine were convinced that surgeons had joined a "me-too brigade." Heart transplantation was moving too rapidly, and the outcomes did not justify the frequency of the procedure. The mortality rates were very high (only 9 of the first 100 patients given a heart were still alive as of June 1969),[33] and the major cause of failure, the body's rejection of the organ, was not well understood. In January 1968 the readers of the *New York Times* learned from medical correspondent Howard Rusk of an "international epidemic of cardiac transplants," which made it "practically impossible . . . for the average television viewer to get out of the operating room or the cardiac clinic." Worse yet, he continued, neither the viewer nor the surgeon belonged there, for "the technological advances and surgical techniques have completely outstripped the basic immunological knowledge needed to prevent rejection."[34] A few months later, the Board of Medicine of the National Academy of Sciences declared that heart transplantation should be considered an experimental procedure, "a scientific exploration of the unknown," and urged that only inter-disciplinary teams under rigorous research protocols—not simply tech-nically proficient surgeons—should do the procedure and publish "systematic observation," not press releases.[35] Then in June 1968, ed-itors of the leading British medical journal, *Lancet*, insisted that "too much was attempted too soon." Furthermore, they contended, "the story of the past months . . . is not one that the profession round the world can look upon with ease. It was not only the too-ready-acclamation in the papers, on television. . . . Surgical skill and ambi-tion clearly ran some way ahead of the advice about the control of rejection and infection that immunologists and pathologists could con-fidently give."[36] By the winter of 1968, what might well be called a moratorium set in. Never officially acknowledged as such, the mora-torium represented an almost complete about-face, with the number of transplants dropping sharply for almost all of the teams (with the ex-ception of Norman Shumway's exemplary group at Stanford).

All these pronouncements and decisions were reported blow by blow in the popular press, and in Washington as well. As sociologists Renee Fox and Judy Swazey noted at the time, "Debates about the pros and cons of cardiac transplantation have taken place as much on the pages of daily newspapers as within the medical profession."[37] *Time, News-week*, and the *Nation* followed the story carefully, frequently running their accounts under such headlines as "WERE TRANSPLANTS PREMA-TURE?" and "TOO MUCH, TOO FAST?" They reported on the National Academy of Sciences resolution, the negative remarks of Page, the call by a group of physicians for a transplant moratorium, and a conference of "physicians, lawyers and theologians . . . to discuss the legal, ethical and practical aspects of transplants." They also kept a box score: *Time* noted in December 1968, the one-year anniversary, that among recip-ients "another death is being reported almost daily."[38]

That the events around transplantation swelled the ranks of outsiders ready to look over the physician's shoulder was apparent to the pro-fession, who reacted very defensively. Whatever their views toward transplantation, physicians wanted to keep medical decisions in med-ical hands. Their pleas and comments reveal just how powerful the antipathy was to laypeople telling physicians what to do. As critical as Irvine Page was of the transplant circus, he was equally apprehensive about the "plethora of committees, task forces, and the like discussing transplantation. It would be surprising if they discovered anything new." Page worried, too, about a reliance on legislation to solve such problems as defining death or deciding just how long the life of a desperately ill patient must be prolonged: "There is a grave error in equating the amount of health legislation passed, the good of the patient, and the ethical behavior of the physician! . . . We must not overdo a good thing as may happen as legislation begins to replace conscience. The physician cannot dispose of his responsibility by abdication."[39] Writing in *JAMA*, Dr. Lyman Brewer also lamented the "carnival atmosphere around the performance of a surgical operation," and he fully appreciated that the procedure raised many ethical questions, particularly which patients should receive the "seldom available transplant." Nevertheless, he insisted: "This is a problem that should be solved by clinicians and not lay groups. . . . The medical profession control circumstances under which cardiac transplants are performed. Rigid laws passed by the legislature, rules laid down by legal and clerical boards or other groups, might becloud rather than clear the atmosphere. . . . The sine qua non of the practice of medicine is the integrity of the physician and the surgeon in treating the patient. Without it, filling-in of forms and reports to comply with rigid rules and to justify the operative procedure is meaningless."[40]

To Brewer, as to Page, rules and laws were inevitably rigid, futile, and detrimental to the doctor–patient relationship. No matter how inadequate the profession's initial response to transplantation, outside intervention would only make matters worse. Or as Dr. Michael DeBakey, who would soon take his place among the ranks of transplant surgeons, put it: "The moral, ethical, legal, and psychologic implications of human cardiac transplantation will undoubtedly be more far-reaching than anticipated from the present brief experience. . . . Should medical scientists abrogate their responsibility to their patients and to society to resolve such issues when they arise, they can expect restrictions to be prescribed from without."[41] Which, of course, is precisely what came to pass.

CHAPTER 9

Commissioning Ethics

IN 1968, the U.S. Congress joined the growing ranks of those interested in medical ethics and decision making. The controversies moved from professional journals and conferences into Washington committee rooms, and despite the opposition and delaying tactics of physicians, in 1973 Congress created a national commission charged with recommending policies for human experimentation, and then in 1978 appointed a successor commission to examine almost every pressing issue in medical ethics. The commission idea was first fueled by the controversy surrounding heart transplantation; it then gathered momentum from a more general concern with new medical technologies, and finally became a reality in the wake of recurring scandals in human experimentation. In each instance, whether the case at hand was cardiac surgery or innovations in genetics and behavior modification, outsiders came to believe that the medical profession was incapable of self-regulation. As a result, the transformation we have been tracing became all the more anchored. As late as 1966, physicians had a monopoly over medical ethics; less than a decade later, laypeople, dominating a national commission, were setting the ethical standards. Medical decision making had become everybody's business.

In February 1968, three months after Christiaan Barnard's surgical feat, Walter Mondale, then a senator from Minnesota, introduced a bill to establish a Commission on Health Science and Society to assess and report on the ethical, legal, social, and political implications of biomedical advances. Mondale was struck by the novel questions that transplantation raised and the limited relevance of traditional medical ethics. As he explained in opening the subcommittee hearing on his resolution: "The scientific breakthroughs of the last few months were current highlights in a dazzling half century of truly unprecedented advance in the medical and biological sciences. . . . These advances and others yet to come raised grave and fundamental ethical and legal questions for our society—who shall live and who shall die; how long shall life be preserved and how shall it be altered; who shall make decisions; how shall society be prepared." Mondale urged the establishment of a national commission to serve as a forum in which not only doctors and biomedical researchers but lay representatives would explore these issues together. "Some professional must understand that society has a stake in what he is doing, and that society must know not only what he is doing, but the implications of his efforts." Oklahoma's Senator Fred Harris, who chaired the subcommittee and carried a populist's distrust of the expert, shared Mondale's concerns. "These matters," he declared, "ought to be talked about in the open by people from various backgrounds with various viewpoints—theological as well as medical, legal as well as sociological and psychological."[1]

To many physicians and investigators, particularly those working on the frontiers of their disciplines, the prospect of a federally sponsored national commission was, to understate the point, dismaying. Even those who did not object to bringing a few representatives from law or philosophy onto medicine's turf, to have them join a physician-dominated committee, thought it exceptionally meddlesome to have Congress organize a Commission on Health Science and Society, allot a few places on it to doctors, make the majority laypeople, and then have the group frame recommendations binding the profession. Given the size of the NIH research budget, Mondale was able to persuade some physicians to testify (albeit without great enthusiasm) in favor of such a commission. But much more impressive was the unbending opposition to the proposal. In 1968 the leaders of medicine fought doggedly to maintain their authority over all medical matters, in the process educating Mondale and others to the fact that whatever influence outsiders would exert would have to be wrested away from the profession.

The hearings opened with lukewarm endorsements from the first witnesses, who, fittingly enough, were all transplant surgeons—John Najarian, Adrian Kantrowitz, and later, Norman Shumway. They enthusiastically told the subcommittee to increase federal investments in research, and only then went on to allow, in vague terms, that the ethical and social questions surrounding transplantation made a commission appropriate. "I think no longer must that portion of our society cloak itself in an aura of mystique about medicine," conceded Najarian. "For a long time I think justifiably we had to. We worked more or less by a pinch of this, a pinch of that, and so as a result it was just as well to remain some sort of pseudo deity. . . . But today . . . we have accumulated scientific knowledge to the point that we stand on firm ground." He believed that a commission would do well to standardize a definition of brain death; but, he warned, it had to be very careful not to disrupt the mainstream work of science or interfere with the ongoing research at the leading institutions: "As far as the general ethical questions are concerned, I think . . . if these transplant operations are carried out in the university atmosphere, you are in the milieu here I think of the best social conscience you can have." University medical schools and hospitals, he noted, were already establishing their own review committees "and should be left to these devices, and . . . not be imposed [on] by the Federal Government. . . . However . . . if these operations are to be performed outside of teaching centers . . . then there may be some external needs for imposing certain restrictions."[2] In other words, a commission might well be needed to superintend the minor league players, but it had little relevance to the major leaguers. Norman Shumway, for his part, grudgingly allowed that "transplantation of the heart, fortunately or unfortunately, cannot be done without public notice and public support. . . . We are at the threshold of a wondrous new era in medicine, and doctors will need help to realize fully its potential."[3] But the priorities should be clear: the commission should assist physicians, not coerce them.

The qualifications and hesitations disappeared when laypeople or an unusual physician like Beecher testified. To them it seemed self-evident that in some fashion or another, public input had to shape the direction of medicine. Beecher's testimony in support of a commission drew on the lessons he had learned in human experimentation: Laypeople must bring their own ethical rules to medicine because "science is not the highest value under which all other orders of values have to be subordinated. . . . Science must be inserted into the order of values."[4] The Reverend Kenneth Vaux from the Institute of Religion at the Texas Medical Center shared these convictions, making his point by quoting J. Robert Oppenheimer's aphorism: "What is technically sweet, though irresistible, is not necessarily good." Everett Mendelsohn, a historian of science at Harvard who had served on its brain-death committee, staked out the commission's territory by distinguishing, as others had begun to do, the technical component in health care from the social component: "On this social component, the physician's judgment . . . is no more informed than that of the layman, or the social scientist whose view is based on his other knowledge of the social needs that a society may have."[5] And Jerald Braver, the dean of the University of Chicago Divinity School, happily anticipated that the commission would help ensure that "research in the health sciences not be conducted as if it is divorced from society and totally independent or autonomous."[6] In sum, to all these witnesses it was time to bring new rules to medicine.[7]

However strong this presumption appeared to Mondale and his supporters, it was far from accepted truth among many of the leading medical practitioners and researchers. The one witness who most vigorously contradicted their claims was Christiaan Barnard. His opposition was unqualified, almost nasty, perhaps reflecting the fact that he came from a country in which the doctor's authority was still unchallenged, or that he was not dependent on Congress or NIH for his funding. Barnard testified on Friday afternoon, March 8, just three months after his first transplant, and the media attention was ample proof of how thoroughly transplantation had captured the public imagination. ("May I say to you," Mondale noted, "this is . . . an indication of your significance in modern society—when you consider how crowded this room is with press and television at five o'clock on a Friday afternoon in Washington.") Such pleasantries brought the Senator little in return. Barnard led off with a brief description of the transplantation at Capetown and then immediately declared his all-out opposition to a public and nonmedical commission. To Mondale's intention of creating something more than a hospital-based committee of doctors, Barnard responded, "I must say that I think you are seeing ghosts where there are no ghosts. If I am in competition with my colleagues of this country, which I am not . . . then I would welcome such a commission, because it would put the doctors [in the United States] . . . so far behind me, and hamper the group of doctors so much that I will go so far ahead that they will never catch up with me."[8]

Mondale and his committee colleagues tried to get Barnard to concede that physicians did require guidance on some questions, but Barnard would not yield an inch: "It has been said," he observed, "that we now need a new definition for death . . . and we should have other people to tell us when we should say a patient is dead. I do not see why this is necessary. Doctors are called in every day in hospitals to certify that a patient is dead. . . . That doctor is often a very junior doctor—an intern—and he comes, he examines the patient, and establishes that the patient is dead. . . . In the case of a transplant of an organ, this decision is made by an expert team of doctors. . . . So why do we have to have new definitions for death, or commissions to tell us when we should say that a patient is dead. We as doctors have done that for many, many years." As for help in allocating a scarce resource: "This decision should be made by the doctors—because they have made the same decision in the past." He was asked, Since surgeons everywhere have waiting lists for operations, how do they determine who goes to the top of the list? "By deciding which patient needs it most," he replied.[9] When pushed by Connecticut's Senator Abraham Ribicoff on whether he truly believed that "doctors only should decide among the multiplicity of patients," Barnard responded: "A lot of these problems that you are seeing today, and a lot of people are mentioning today, these problems the doctors have had to handle for many years. These are not new problems. You cannot tell me one single new problem in our heart transplantation that we have not had for many years." When Ribicoff countered that for a physician to decide who lived and who died was new, and that it was debatable whether doctors should make that determination alone, Barnard answered: "I do not think the public is qualified to make the decision. . . . You cannot have control over these things. You must leave it in the people's hands who are capable of doing it."[10]

Reluctant to have this celebrity so unequivocally oppose his proposal, Mondale took a turn: "We have the ethical questions of when is a person dead, who gives the vital organ to whom, who decides when there are many who will die, but only a few can be saved. . . . Don't you believe that these issues could be profitably studied by a sophisticated and responsible commission composed of the finest men in the medical fields, health administrators, responsible theologians, attorneys and other persons?" Barnard gave an unqualified no: "Senator, by wanting to set up a commission, you must have one of two reasons. Either you are seeing new problems, or you are not satisfied with the way the doctors have handled the problems in the past. That is the only reason you can ask for a new commission." Mondale ended the questioning, and Barnard left with his opposition unqualified: "If we [in South Africa] could have done this without a commission to control and to give us guidance—do you feel it is necessary in this country to have some commission to guide your doctors and your scientists? I feel that if you do this, it will be an insult to your doctors and what is more, it would put progress back a lot."[11]

Considering that a Senate subcommittee usually enjoys broad latitude in inviting testimony, the depth of the opposition to the commission indicates just how hostile medical opinion was. Mondale was effusive in introducing Dr. Owen Wangensteen, who from 1930 to 1967 directed the department of surgery at the University of Minnesota Hospital; however, Dr. Wangensteen was anything but effusive about the commission. The thought that theologians might pronounce on medical questions raised for him the specter of Puritan ministers thundering against the practice of smallpox vaccination. Wangensteen's greatest fear was not that ethical questions would be ignored but that medical innovators would be "manacled by well-intentioned but meddlesome intruders." He told the committee, "I would urge you with all the strength I can muster, to leave this subject to conscionable people in the profession who are struggling valiantly to advance medicine."[12] Mondale, ever persistent, asked, "Don't you think there are non-doctors, persons not in the medical profession, who could bring to this problem useful insights, or do you think it ought to be left exclusively to the medical profession?" To which Wangensteen replied: "The fellow who holds the apple can peel it best. . . . If you are thinking of theologians, lawyers, philosophers, and others to give some direction here . . . I cannot see how they could help. I would leave these decisions to the responsible people doing the work."[13]

This was also the position that Jesse Edwards, the president of the American Heart Association, defended. The public was too emotional to be involved in this type of inquiry, and a commission, he feared, might prematurely restrict transplant surgery. The Heart Association leadership was sensitive to the need to draw up guidelines and included on the organization's committee a number of nonphysicians. But for Congress to enter this field and empower a lay body to superintend medicine would bring disastrous results. Concluded Edwards: "The one thing we would want to avoid would be getting into a technical situation which would make it easy for restrictive legislation."[14]

However unyielding the opposition, Mondale and his supporters were convinced that this battle had to be fought and won. As they surveyed the territory, transplantation was only the lead issue, at the top of a burgeoning list of concerns whose resolution appeared to them to require more than the insights of physicians. Indeed, many of the developments that worried them seemed to have less to do with doctoring (in the old-fashioned sense) and much more to do with machines and research. It was not the physician at the bedside but the technician at the dial and the investigator at the bench that appeared, at least to those outside medicine, to demand new players setting down new rules.

Hence, the Mondale hearings moved from transplantation to two other innovations—genetic engineering and behavior control, where the breakthroughs were yet to come, but the potential social and ethical consequences already seemed scary. Transplantation, after all, remained a procedure whose sole purpose was to benefit the patient, and considerations of equity drove the debate. Genetic engineering and behavior control, whatever their therapeutic potential, raised apocalyptic visions of George Orwell's *1984*, with political misuse and social control of the most egregious sort. "The transplantation of human organs," explained Mondale, "already has raised such serious public questions as who shall live and who shall die. But coming techniques of genetic intervention and behavior control will bring profound moral, legal, ethical, and social questions for a society which one day will have the power to shape the bodies and minds of its citizens."[15]

Nevertheless, the geneticists and the psychiatrists who testified were as antagonistic to the idea of a commission as the surgeons. Again, what seemed apparent and beyond dispute to the senators was irrelevant or even mischievous to these witnesses. Mondale's remarks were studded with references to "the terror of a brave new world" and "the terror of nuclear holocaust." But the researchers were certain that all this was fantasy, and government's primary obligation was to fund their research and stay out of the way.

Just how far apart the two sides were emerged in the testimony of Dr. Arthur Kornberg, winner of the 1959 Nobel Prize for his work in the biochemistry of DNA. Kornberg, in his own terms, had synthesized a DNA copy of a simple virus with six genes, and the replication had the full genetic activity of natural DNA. To laypeople, however, Kornberg had "created life in a test tube." He recognized that the media preferred to use an attention-grabbing word like *creation*, as opposed to *synthesis*, and that people were startled to learn not only that "genetics or heredity was simply chemistry" but also that genetic engineering was now a "prospect." And Kornberg could appreciate that "this prospect fascinates people. It also frightens them and I can understand why it does." But for the foreseeable future, the difficulty, he believed, was "not too much but too little knowledge. I see no ethical or moral problems that are different in kind or quantity that face us today with this new knowledge of genes and gene action." Kornberg desperately wanted Congress to devote the resources necessary "to exploit the opportunities to expand our knowledge," but beyond that, it should not intervene.

The Mondale committee, however, was not so complacent. Senator Ribicoff immediately asked, "Do you see this work of yours leading to the creation of a master race?" "Oh no," responded Kornberg. "This is so very remote." "What about the legal and ethical questions that do arise from genetics," Ribicoff continued. "Who makes the decision of who uses it, with what people?" Kornberg found the question sophomoric. "I really do not have the capacity to answer some of the questions that are not well-defined and still so distant. I have learned from experience it is more meaningful for me to focus on problems that confront me directly. What confronts us is a great opportunity to exploit openings . . . for understanding the chemical basis of the human organism." Ribicoff, still dissatisfied, persisted. "Is science amoral? Does science concern itself with the ethical, social and human consequences of its acts and its achievements? . . . At what stage does the scientist become concerned with the good as well as just the success of the work that he is doing?" Kornberg had little more to add: "I can only repeat that many of the dire consequences of genetic research are still remote."[16]

Mondale brought the questioning back to the commission. Addressing both Kornberg and fellow geneticist Joshua Lederberg (who had also testified), Mondale noted that both had demonstrated a "great interest" in reviewing their "financial problems—but a great reluctance for review of the social problems that might flow from the research." Continued Mondale, "I find your reluctance to take that second step . . . to be a little bit mystifying." Kornberg impatiently explained that this was the first time he had ever testified before Congress and that it was "an arena for which, as scientists, we are not trained, and for which we have no natural affinity." Indeed, it was not just a matter of taste but of priorities, and in lines that Mondale would not forget, Kornberg declared: "There are absolutely no scientific rewards, no enlargement of scientific skills that accrue from involvement in public issues. . . . The biochemist who deals with molecules cannot afford any time away from them. Today I am not in the laboratory. I do not know what is going on at the bench. Tomorrow I will be less able to cope with the identity and behavior of molecules. . . . If the research worker were to become a public figure, it would destroy him as a scientist." A commission would only serve to thwart or distract the scientist, and all to the aim of tilting at windmills. "This concern [over] our creating little men in test tubes, and a super race, is really not so relevant today."[17]

The commission proposal fared somewhat better when the committee turned to the last of its major concerns, behavior control. The committee learned from Dr. Seymour Ketty, a professor of psychiatry at Harvard Medical School, about the advances in biochemistry and physiology of the brain that were bringing a new dimension to the study of behavior and emotions. Ketty reported that electrodes placed in the brain of animals could stimulate rage or aggression, and "when similar techniques have been applied to man during neurosurgical operations, reports have been obtained of . . . recollections of the past, blocking of thought, as well as emotional changes such as anxiety, fear, friendliness or happiness."[18] David Krech, a professor of psychology at the University of California at Berkeley, told the committee about drugs that seem to be able to improve the memories and problem-solving abilities of laboratory animals. The senators took this information as one more item that belonged on the commission's agenda. The group would have to explore the implications of an ability to manipulate behavior by techniques that would alter moods or heighten intellectual capacities; they would even have to consider whether it would be possible to put a pill into a reservoir and turn an entire community into . . . political slaves? supermen? great thinkers? working drones?

Ketty, like the other investigators, thought the concerns—and the commission enterprise—premature at best. If the Orwellian fantasy was to be realized, it would arrive through a political, not a scientific, route: "Manipulation of the brain by any of the biological techniques which could be developed in the foreseeable future would involve such drastic invasions of privacy, integrity, and the inalienable rights of the individual that in their application behavioral control would already have been achieved even if the electrodes carried no current and the pill were a placebo." Krech, on the other hand, was far more enthusiastic about the commission: "Neither the medicine man nor scientist is better equipped to deal with the question of ethics and values and social good . . . than is any other thoughtful and concerned man. The brain researcher . . . has neither the requisite wisdom nor experience nor knowledge to say to society: 'Don't worry your unscientific heads about this; I will save society (from me!).' " It was to Krech, not Ketty, that Mondale remarked, "I am most appreciative for this very fine testimony."[19]

Mondale's 1968 proposal to establish a National Commission on Health Science and Society did not win immediate passage for a variety of reasons. For one, the Nixon administration was unwilling to support the creation of a forum that would give liberals like Mondale, Harris, and Ribicoff the opportunity to play farsighted policy analysts, or for that matter, to create a forum that would rival the executive department's own committees and review structures in the Department of Health, Education and Welfare. For another, the proposal itself was much too broadly drawn, and no one could precisely define its assignment. Was this commission to review and make recommendations on all of transplantation, genetics, behavior modification, and human experimentation and do so in a one-year period? Several witnesses also suggested that the most pressing problem facing American medicine was not the implications of future technologies but the immediate problem of getting minorities access to current technologies. (The report of the Kerner Commission had just been released, and its image of America as two nations—one rich, the other poor—highlighted the inequities in health care delivery. Whites had a life of expectancy of 71 years; nonwhites, 64 years. Whites had an infant mortality rate of 16 deaths per 1,000 births; nonwhites, 25 deaths.)[20] Mondale recognized the need to examine access to medical care, and he suggested that the commission would take on this task as well, thereby making its mandate even more impossible to fulfill.

The most important cause of initial failure, however, was that Mondale had not anticipated the depth of the opposition. What he defined as a "measly little study commission," physicians and researchers defined as a major battle in the war to rule medicine. Looking back, Mondale was frankly bitter about their opposition: "All we have said is, 'Let's have a public study commission.' . . . But the reaction has been fantastic. In 1968, they bootlegged Christiaan Barnard down here to tell us why this would put South Africa ahead of the United States in medical science. He said, 'You will have a politician in every surgical room.' The major portion of the American public bought what he said. . . . They got Doctor Kornberg in here, who is a great scientist, and what did he say? . . . The biochemist who deals with molecules cannot afford any time away from them. . . . In other words, he asked us, 'Why are you wasting my time here?' . . . I sense an almost psychopathic objection to the public process, a fear that if the public gets involved, it is going to be anti-science, going to be hostile and unsupportive." Mondale concluded: "I have a feeling that medicine does not want to explain its case partly because they went through the period [of the 1950s] . . . in a preferred status, like the FBI. I think we are at a point now where American medicine has to explain itself.''[21]

The roots of the divide went much deeper than a 1950s mind-set, though. The gap between a Mondale on the one side and a Kornberg on the other was well nigh unbridgeable. Starting from diametrically opposed premises, they reached contradictory conclusions, talking past each other, without the slightest appreciation of the alternative position. And in this separation one finds yet another impetus to the movement to bring new rules to medicine, and another reason for its eventual success.

The controversy did not come down in any simple sense to a dispute over technologies. Christiaan Barnard did have a point when he argued that the technologies did not pose social or ethical challenges; physicians had been trusted before to make difficult decisions, and public policy willing, they could be trusted again. But a number of outsiders found this response unacceptable, in part, for the reasons we have already explored—the scandals in human experimentation, the social distancing of the physician, and the inadequacies of traditional medical ethics. The Mondale hearings, however, added still another consideration: the feats made possible by medical technologies had transferred medicine from the category of the helping profession to the category of engineering. The image of the physician that ran through the testimony was not of a person holding the patient's hand at the bedside but of someone turning the machine's dials in an intensive care unit. The focus of the hearings was not the doctor–patient relationship—no one made a single reference to this subject or to allied ones like truth telling—or the mounting cost of medical care—no one mentioned the percentage of the GNP going to health care. Rather, the primary concern was with the potential misuse of the technology—framed by the assortment of anxieties and ambivalent feelings that technology raised in other, nonmedical settings. It was somewhat paradoxical, and not a little unfair, but just as medicine became technological, the medical establishment brought upon itself all the distrust that technology in the late 1960s and 1970s generated. Just when doctors and investigators could promise "better living through chemistry," the slogan had become suspect, even the object of derision.

Thus, those who wished to circumscribe the autonomy of the medical profession gained strength not because medical technology in some inevitable way demanded it, but because social definitions of technology demanded it. There was nothing automatic or inevitable about the presumption that when a respirator ventilated a patient, a federal commission was needed to explore the ethics of medicine, or that an ethics committee or a philosopher had to be present on the hospital floor. Rather, because a machine ventilated the patient, outsiders thought such interventions legitimate and necessary.

Keenly aware of these attitudes, Mondale often commented during the hearings that "this society is in a constant race to keep up with advancing technologies, understand them, and see that they are put to constructive use. We have been too late, too secret, and too superficial in too many cases. One of the results is the terror of automation-produced unemployment. Another is the terror of nuclear holocaust. . . . Our experience with the atom teaches us that we must look closely at the implications of what we do." It seemed to him self-evident that "when a scientist unravels a technique for engineering future generations [note "engineering," not "curing" or "helping," future generations], that is not a matter solely for the scientist's interest. It fundamentally . . . affects mankind—perhaps in a more searching sense than the atomic bomb."[22] Fred Harris took his cautionary text on technology from the environment: "Wouldn't it have been far wiser of us to have thought about the consequences of detergents long before we put them on the market, and messed up all our streams with the effluent?"[23] By the same token, "the highway planners were . . . moving that traffic, it is true, but they forget about the people." It would not be the experts, the insiders, who would make cities "more liveable, more rewarding," but outsiders.[24] And in this same fashion, Abraham Ribicoff likened medical technology to nuclear technology: Would doctors Kornberg, Lederberg, and Barnard later have doubts and be "soul-searching" about the wisdom of their research like those scientists "who were involved in the creation of the atomic bomb and hydrogen bomb? . . . I have been personally struck by the traumatic effect that the consequences of atomic research and atomic bombs, and hydrogen bombs, have had upon so many pure scientists, brilliant scientists, who worked in this field. And you get the feeling that many of them felt that when they see the consequences of their discoveries maybe they wish they were a plumber or a truck driver." Ribicoff came away from the hearings convinced that "society does have a concern with the great breakthroughs that are taking place." He concluded, "I think it is well that people worry about them now instead of both scientists and society in general waking up with a guilty conscience 20 years after the event."[25]

However obvious and persuasive the analogies seemed to Mondale, Harris, and Ribicoff, they seemed irrelevant and misleading to the physicians and researchers who testified. What outsiders defined as technological, they saw as therapeutic; they were not engineers but doctors, and to inhibit their enterprise was to set back the development of life-saving interventions for desperately ill patients. Heart surgeon Adrian Kantrowitz told the committee that although others puzzled over "the question of whether experimental heart surgery contains ethical, moral, social, legal, economic, and political problems of a quality or magnitude ever before encountered," he sorted through them easily. "The ethics of heart transplantation . . . are, first of all, the ethics of medicine, the ethics of reverence for human life. . . . The ethical problem can be summarized in a few words: can the patient survive by any other known means? . . . The process is no different from . . . deciding whether a patient is an appropriate candidate for some new drug. Will anything else probably help the patient?"[26] One did not need a commission—or a committee of philosophers, lawyers, and clergymen—to answer such questions.

Those in genetics and psychiatry were no less confident about the therapeutic character of their work. They would not be second-guessing themselves twenty years later, for they were creating agents of cure, not of destruction. They were not in the business of genetic *engineering* or behavior *control* but of treatment, and once the general public grasped the distinction, its anxiety would be reduced and it would stop peering over doctors' shoulders. Thus, when Senator Ribicoff asked Arthur Kornberg whether his research might promote a master race, Kornberg responded that his aim was "to relieve a good deal of suffering and distress . . . correcting well-known diseases that plague people." As for a master race, he replied, "I would like to be part of 'a master race' relieved of some of the scourges that have plagued people for centuries."[27] If Kornberg preferred staying in his laboratory to appearing at a hearing in Washington, it was not only because he found testifying uncongenial but because he thought the questions miscast.

Once again, as in the case of human experimentation, insiders and outsiders had contradictory perspectives. To the one view, technology was threatening to outdistance social values, and laypeople had to join with scientists—knowledgeable, but not wise—to ponder the implications of their research. In light of the history of technology in the twentieth century, surely this was a most necessary and reasonable proposal. But to the other view, the public was, once again, misconstruing the work of the physician-scientist. At best, a national commission would take the researchers away from their laboratories for a number of days; at worst, it would tie investigators' hands and retard scientific progress. Thus, each side found its own propositions axiomatic, and its opponents perverse for resisting the obvious merits of the arguments.

Although Walter Mondale's hopes for a commission fell through in 1968, he did not abandon the idea. In 1969, Senator Harris's Subcommittee on Government Research was dissolved, and Mondale failed to become chairman of the Subcommittee on Health.[28] In 1971 and then again in 1973, he reintroduced the resolutions, finally reaping victory in 1974, with the creation of the National Commission for the Protection of Human Subjects of Biomedical and Behavioral Research. What accounts for both the persistence and the accomplishment? Why did the initial stalemate give way to the creation of a commission that, even if it was not as powerful as its first supporters would have preferred, assuredly gave a new weight and legitimacy to the role of outsiders in medicine?

First, there is no discounting Mondale's disgust with the 1968 testimony and the attitude of medicine's representatives. The hostility of Christiaan Barnard and Arthur Kornberg not only provoked his anger but reinforced his sense that researchers could not be trusted to keep their house in order. Moreover, support for a national commission broadened from 1968 to 1973 as scandals recurred in human experimentation, each one eroding the degree of trust between investigators and the public. Undoubtedly, the most disturbing incident was the Tuskegee research of the U.S. Public Health Service (PHS). From the mid-1930s into the early 1970s, its investigators had been visiting Macon County, Alabama, to examine, but not to treat, a group of blacks who were suffering from secondary syphilis. The press, on a tip from one of the researchers, finally blew the whistle, and subsequent investigations made clear just how sorry the behavior of the PHS was. Whatever rationalizations it could muster for not treating blacks in the 1930s (when treatment was of questionable efficacy and very complicated to administer), it could hardly defend instructing draft boards not to conscript the subjects for fear that they might receive treatment in the army; and worse, it could not justify its unwillingness to give the subjects a trial of penicillin after 1945. The PHS leaders' lame excuse was that with the advent of antibiotics, no one would ever again be able to trace the long-term effects of syphilis.[29]

Only a shade less notorious than Tuskegee were the experiments conducted at the University of Cincinnati General Hospital. The investigators, funded by the Department of Defense, applied whole and partial body radiation to patients with terminal cancer. The hospital claimed that the investigators had obtained the patients' consent and that the primary goal of the research was therapeutic. But critics insisted that the real purpose was to provide the Department of Defense with data that might protect the combat effectiveness of military troops who might be exposed to radiation. In fact, over the fifteen years that the experiments continued, therapeutic results were minimal, and the university never provided any documentation, such as signed forms, that consent had been obtained. Most damaging of all, the Cincinnati subjects closely resembled the Tuskegee ones: indigent, black, and with no more than a grade-school education. It was difficult to avoid the conclusion that once again investigators had chosen the underprivileged to be martyrs for scientific knowledge.[30]

Given the persistent interest of senators like Mondale, Jacob Javits, and Edward Kennedy in the regulation of biomedical research and practices, and the exposés in human experimentation, the opening months of 1973 witnessed an extraordinary burst of congressional bills and hearings. Senator Mondale reintroduced his resolution to establish a national advisory commission, Senators Javits and Hubert Humphrey reintroduced their bill to regulate human experimentation more closely, and they supported legislation that would place "an increased emphasis on the ethical, social, legal, and moral implications of advances in biomedical research and technology" in the education of health care professionals.[31] All of these bills became the occasion in the winter and spring of 1973 for Senator Kennedy to conduct hearings on the "Quality of Health Care—Human Experimentation."[32] Because of the recurrent scandals, human experimentation was most likely to rivet public attention and justify an increased surveillance and regulation of the laboratory. But the target was broader: really, all of medicine. The hearings' ultimate goal was to demonstrate that no wing of the medical profession could be trusted to keep its house in order—that medicine required a new kind of collective oversight. As Mondale put it: "Normally this committee finds itself at war with the medical profession over economics. But in this case we find ourselves at odds with the academic medical community, which says 'Leave us alone. Stay off our campuses. Send us the money but don't come in and see how we do our experimenting.' "[33]

Kennedy, more artfully than Mondale earlier, structured the hearings to demonstrate the need for outside intervention. The thrust of the opening testimony was to substantiate that physicians as well as researchers abused professional discretion; that the ethical and social dilemmas confronting medicine were not just futuristic but here and now; and finally, that all Americans, not just the poor and the institutionalized, were affected by these problems. "Human experimentation," announced Kennedy in his first statement, "is part of the routine practice of medicine." An absence of vigorous oversight, "coupled with the most unlimited freedom of action which physicians have in the treatment of their patients," allowed dangerous practices, including the premature use of unproven and untested drugs and procedures. "The question," insisted Kennedy, "is whether or not we can tolerate a system where the individual physician is the sole determinant of the safety of an experimental procedure. After all, it is the patients who must live the consequences of that decision."[34]

The case in point was the misuse of two drugs with contraceptive effects, Depo-Provera and DES (diethylstilbestrol). Both had been approved by the FDA for treatment purposes (Depo-Provera for the treatment of advanced cancers of the uterus and endometriosis, DES to prevent miscarriage), but neither was approved as a contraceptive. Once the FDA licensed a drug for one purpose, however, physicians were free to prescribe it for other purposes, and a parade of witnesses reported that many doctors were not only dispensing Depo-Provera and DES as contraceptives but failing to inform patients about potential side effects or obtain their consent.[35] The Senate committee learned that doctors at one Tennessee clinic injected a group of welfare mothers with Depo-Provera without explaining that it had caused breast cancer in a breed of dogs. Also, some fifteen university health clinics prescribed DES to women students as a "morning after" pill, without telling them of its cancer-causing potential for them and for their future children. As one witness declared, in precisely the terms that Kennedy wanted to hear, "Whether the subjects are prisoners, college students, military personnel or poor people, they share a common sense of captivity and the use of any drugs on them must be regulated with paramount regard for their well-being."[36]

Were these incidents not enough, there were still other examples wherein the poor in particular were the hapless victims of medical research and, indeed, medical practice. In 1972, Mexican American women who had gone to a clinic in San Antonio for contraceptives unknowingly became subjects in an experiment to identify whether the side effects of contraceptive pills were physiological or psychological; half the women were given contraceptive pills, the other half, placebos, in order to allow the investigators to match reported side effects with the active agent or the placebo. The problem, of course, was that the placebo group might well become pregnant, which ten of them promptly did. The experiment itself and the failure of the medical society to discipline the doctors involved not only confirmed the idea that "poor minority people" were particularly liable to be abused but also demonstrated, yet again, the inability of the profession to police its own members.

The hearings then moved from relatively ordinary concerns such as contraception to the extraordinary—to the use of psychosurgery to treat, in the words of its foremost advocate, Dr. Orlando Andy, a neurosurgeon at the University of Mississippi Medical Center, "aggressive, uncontrollable, violent, and hyperactive behavior which does not respond to various other medical forms of therapy." Kennedy first had the head of the National Institute of Mental Health (NIMH) establish that psychosurgery was an experimental procedure, and that the NIMH had no authority over a private doctor who wanted to practice it. The senator then made his point with Dr. Andy himself:

Q: Basically, then, you make an independent judgment whether to move ahead on this kind of operation?

A: Yes. The final decision is always mine in terms of whether or not an operation will or will not be done.

Q: Do you have any board or panel that continues to review the various bases for the psychosurgery in which you have been involved?

A: No. We don't have a board of supervisors or investigators or peer review type of activity over what we are doing.[37]

This was a surgeon ready to tamper with the human brain to control antisocial behavior, and no one—no peer group or federal regulatory body—was in a position to regulate him.

Next, after a brief discussion on genetic engineering, the hearings turned to experimentation in prison. Kennedy here aimed to demonstrate that prisoners in state penitentiaries and city jails were guinea pigs for medical researchers. In light of the impressive organization of rights groups and their important courtroom victories in the late 1960s and early 1970s, Kennedy was eager to define unbounded medical discretion as a problem in minority rights. "During the course of these hearings," he noted, "we have heard that those who have borne the principal brunt of research—whether it is drugs or even experimental surgery—have been the more disadvantaged people within our society; have been the institutionalized, the poor, and minority members."[38] The coalition, then, that would bring new rules to medicine would be composed of both ordinary citizens and rights activists, or in political terms, the center and the left.

That prisons were laboratories unto themselves was easily documented. Jessica Mitford, who had just published her exposé on the subject, recounted how pharmaceutical companies were altogether dependent on prisoners for testing new drugs, but the sums paid to them were "a pittance"—about a dollar a day, which was enough to attract many recruits because the dollar "represents riches when viewed in terms of prison pay scales."[39] Other witnesses made clear that the FDA was not kept informed on what transpired in prisons, or for that matter in jails, where pretrial detainees were also recruited for tests.

The unmistakable lesson that emerged from every aspect of the hearing was that outsiders had to regulate the medical and biomedical research community. Bernard Barber, a Columbia University sociologist, reporting on an extensive survey of existing practices, concluded that peer review was totally inadequate to the task of supervising research: "There has been no sign of the kind of intensive, imaginative, coordinated, persisting action with regard to the ethics of experimentation that the biomedical research profession has displayed in advancing the cause of medical research and therapy." Considerations of science still took precedence over considerations of ethics. Jay Katz, fresh from his service as chairman on the task force to examine the Tuskegee events, was also convinced that effective oversight would not come from inside medicine: "The research community has made no concerted effort either to impose any meaningful self-regulation on its practices or to discuss in any scholarly depth the permissible limits of human research. Therefore, I submit, regulation has to come from elsewhere."[40]

Others, too, like Willard Gaylin, the president of the Hastings Institute, were not at all hopeful that the professional associations, like the AMA, would be able to develop or enforce necessary safeguards. "These institutions," observed Gaylin, "were originally designed as protective guilds, and they still function primarily in that sense. . . . I suspect that they will always be more concerned with the protection of the rights of their constituents than with the public per se." He, for one, was eager to empower the patient: "Patient-consumers must no longer trust exclusively the benevolence of the professional. But basic decisions must be returned to the hands of the patient population whose health and future will be affected. . . . We should all share in the decision making."[41] Still others, like Alexander Capron at the University of Pennsylvania Law School, argued strongly on behalf of a greatly expanded federal role. "I do not share the view of the researchers who have expressed alarm and dismay over this growing scrutiny . . . by 'meddlesome intruders,' " declared Capron. "The objective of the 'outsiders,' like that of the biomedical scientists, is to reduce human suffering—a goal which requires not only the advance of knowledge through experimentation but also the protection of the experimental subjects."[42]

The legislative proposal that emerged from the Kennedy hearings called for the creation of a National Commission for the Protection of Human Subjects. Its eleven members were to be chosen from among "the general public and from individuals in the fields of medicine, law, ethics, theology, biological science, physical science, social science, philosophy, humanities, health administration, government, and public affairs." The very length of the roster as well as the stipulation that no more than five of the members could be researchers made clear just how critical the principle of external oversight had become. Kennedy repeatedly emphasized this point: Policy had to emanate "not just from the medical profession, but from ethicists, the theologians, philosophers and many other disciplines." Bernard Barber predicted, altogether accurately, that the commission "would transform a fundamental moral problem from a condition of relative professional neglect and occasional journalistic scandal to a condition of continuing public and professional visibility and legitimacy. . . . For the proper regulation of the powerful professions of modern society, we need a combination of insiders and outsiders, of professionals and citizens."[43]

The give-and-take of politics did not allow for the precise type of commission that Kennedy and his supporters envisioned. Although their version passed the Senate intact, the House enacted a variant proposal, and the resulting conference committee weakened the body. The commission became temporary, rather than permanent, and advisory (to the secretary of HEW), without any enforcement powers of its own.

Even in its reduced state, however, the commission represented a critical departure. First, it made apparent that the monopoly of the medical profession in medical ethics was over. The issues were now public and national—the province of an extraordinary variety of outsiders. Second, it gave an institutional expression to this change, because the commission provided a forum for outsiders that would command attention from both the media and public officials. The commission members had a national audience, and so did those who testified before them. Finally, although the commission was not permanent and was charged to investigate not all of medicine but only human experimentation, it had a vital and continuing presence. When its mandate was about to expire in 1978, Kennedy was able to transform it into the President's Commission for the Study of Ethical Problems in Medicine and give it the scope that Mondale had urged a decade before. By 1978, of course, the role of outsiders was much more firmly established. Bioethics was a field, would-be bioethicists had career lines to follow, and the notion that medical ethics belonged exclusively to medicine had been forgotten by most everyone, except for a cadre of older physicians and a handful of historians.

CHAPTER 10

No One to Trust

THE movement to bring new rules to medicine did not stop at the biomedical frontiers. Beginning in the early 1970s, the most elemental aspects of medicine—decisions on birth and death, on what lives were or were not worth living—became the center of public debate and controversy. Traditionally, these questions had been at the essence of bedside ethics, the exclusive preserve of doctors: they decided whether a newborn's deficits were so grave or an elderly patient's prognosis so poor that he or she would be better off untreated. But now, wearing a white coat was not a prerequisite—or, it seemed, even a qualification— for resolving these predicaments. Outsiders first superintended the work of physicians in the laboratory and then ultimately in the infant nursery and adult intensive care unit.

Although the progression from issue to issue seemed logical, even inevitable, the reality was more complex, and each shift was bitterly contested at every point. As in human experimentation, one again finds whistle-blowers and scandals, contentiousness and rancor, a deep mistrust among many physicians of inflexible rules that would interfere with their ability to make case-by-case decisions and a no less profound dissatisfaction among many laypeople with the exercise of medical discretion. In fact, resolving the conflicts in neonatal nurseries prompted still more outsiders to cross over into medicine. In human experimentation, two parties were at odds—the researcher and the subject. In the neonatal unit, three parties interacted—the doctor, the parent(s), and the infant—and the shadow of the state loomed larger here than elsewhere. In sorting out the best locus for decision making, some wanted to preserve a traditional physician hegemony, but most others were prepared to invoke parental and third-party input, albeit for very different reasons. Some believed that parents and third parties must participate if doctors were going to be able to terminate treatment; others saw in third parties the only protection against the conspiracy of doctors and parents to discriminate against the handicapped newborn. Still others saw in third parties the only way for parents to realize their choices against a doctor. Small wonder, then, that many commentators, unable to decide where to put their trust, opted to make medical decision making more collective and more responsive to outsiders. And small wonder that the judgment calls in the neonatal nursery became the focus of academic and popular discourse, and eventually legislative and judicial regulation.

Although there is something artificial about selecting a single starting point for this analysis, the case of the Johns Hopkins baby stands out. In 1969 a baby suffering from a digestive abnormality was born in a community hospital at Virginia's Eastern Shore. The infant was transferred immediately to the Johns Hopkins University Hospital, and his doctors discovered an intestinal blockage, a problem readily correctable through surgery. But the baby was also mentally retarded because of Down's syndrome. Upon being told of the situation, the parents refused to give permission for the surgery, and the hospital complied with their wishes. The infant was moved to a corner of the nursery, and over a period of fifteen days, starved to death.[1]

In the opinion of several physicians at Johns Hopkins, the case was not all that unusual. It was common knowledge, at least within the profession, that many infants born with spina bifida—a condition in which the spinal column is exposed and underdeveloped, causing paralysis, incontinence, and, frequently, mental retardation—never left the delivery room; the chart entry read "stillbirth." (When it later became the practice to intervene aggressively with spina bifida infants, the number of "stillbirths" went down almost to zero.) The Hopkins staff also believed that recourse to the courts was a waste of time because judges would always uphold the parents' desires.

Nevertheless, the baby's death deeply affected the resident who had pulled the feeding lines (William Bartholome), the chief resident (Norman Fost), and the chief of service (Robert Cooke, himself the father of two handicapped children). Indeed, they were so disturbed by the course of events that they took the issue outside the hospital. With assistance from members of the Kennedy family, whose concern for the treatment of the mentally retarded was exemplified in the work of the Joseph P. Kennedy Foundation, they oversaw the making of a short film about the incident, with a ten-minute segment devoted to the case and then a fifteen-minute panel discussion on the ethical principles involved.

The film opened with a close-up of a newborn baby crying lustily; included a sequence in which a couple, backs to the camera, discussed their preferences with the physician; and closed with a long shot of the bassinet at the far end of the nursery. It was extraordinarily moving—and misleading. A viewer would presume that the newborn shown on camera was *the* very baby, that the couple were the real parents, and what was being filmed was the short, unhappy life and death of the baby—not a re-creation made several years later. The credits only hinted that it was a re-creation, for the point of the film was to arouse indignation, which it certainly did.[2]

It was first shown in October 1971, at a three-day symposium on "Human Rights, Retardation, and Research," which the Kennedy Foundation sponsored. Although the conference covered a good deal of ground—from the "Ethics of New Technologies in Beginning Life" to "Why Should People Care, How Should People Care?"—and the conferees were exceptionally diverse—Mother Teresa was there, as were Elie Wiesel, James Watson, and B. F. Skinner—the Johns Hopkins incident became the lead story. The press had been invited to a special preview of the film, and journalists wrote about it extensively and provocatively.[3] Newspaper headlines were variations on the theme of "MDS WATCH AS SICK BABY STARVES." Shortly afterward, the ten-minute segment was shown on national television, and viewers as well as readers responded with indignation. Letters to the editor called the physicians' behavior "unspeakable" and "shocking."[4] Bags of mail came to Bartholome and Cooke. Almost all of the correspondents condemned the refusal to carry out the surgery, and many of them made analogies to the Nazis. Johns Hopkins was "something out of the bowels of Dachau" and its policies reminiscent of "Adolf Hitler's program." Said one correspondent: "We condemn Nazi Germany for what they did to exterminate the Jews. Is this country any better?"[5]

The level of indignation was so intense that the Johns Hopkins incident became the occasion to organize new forums to promote the analysis and discussion of ethical issues in medical decision making. Right before the opening of the Kennedy symposium, Georgetown University announced the creation of an institute that would join biology with ethics in what was now being called "bioethics."[6] "A determined effort has to be made," declared Georgetown's President Robert Henle, "to bring to bear on these human problems all the traditional wisdoms of our religions and our philosophy." With a $1.35 million grant from the Kennedy Foundation, the new institute aimed to "put theologians next to doctors." André Hellegers, an obstetrician-gynecologist, was appointed head of the institute; and not surprisingly, the illustrative cases had to do with disabilities, mental retardation, and medical care at birth. As Edward Kennedy declared, in a line he would be repeating in other contexts: "These problems should not be left to the politician and to the medical profession, or wholly to the theologian." Sargent Shriver made the same observation more aggressively: "I'd be happy to see one of the ethicists blast one of the doctors for doing something wrong."[7]

Bringing outsiders into medicine seemed ever so necessary to the three Johns Hopkins physicians as well. Bartholome responded to many of those who questioned him about the case that the "solution will come only if society is willing to support the formal investigation by physicians, lawyers, sociologists and moralists of these complicated issues."[8] The Johns Hopkins Hospital directors sought to counter the negative publicity by announcing, one week after the film's showing, that it was establishing a review board composed of a pediatrician, a surgeon, a psychiatrist, a clergyman, and a lawyer to advise on difficult ethical cases—and again the illustrative case was how to respond when parents of a retarded infant refused to allow life-saving surgery.[9]

The incident soon faded from the press, and for the moment, ethics institutes and hospital review boards remained the exception. But the

Johns Hopkins baby framed the first debates about life and death in the infant nursery, and the case's centrality gave both the discussions and the policies that emerged from them a very special emotional, as well as intellectual, cast.

It was physicians who first diligently pursued the implications of the case, attempting to achieve their own consensus. Within a year of the Kennedy forum, the prestigious Ross Conference on Pediatric Research, which previously had focused almost exclusively on scientific concerns (from endocrine dysfunction to the use of radioisotopes), devoted its deliberations to the "Ethical Dilemmas in Current Obstetric and Newborn Care." Just as the 1966 CIBA Foundation conference had helped raise considerations of ethics in transplantation, so the 1972 Ross Conference highlighted ethics in newborn nurseries. Because this meeting, like CIBA's, was an initial foray into the territory, most of the participants were physicians (twenty-two of the twenty-nine), but medicine was not as insular as it had been. Joining the physicians were a clergyman, a lawyer, and two of the new breed of bioethicists, Joseph Fletcher, now recognized for his pioneering work, and Robert Veatch, an associate at the Hastings Institute of Society, Ethics, and the Life Sciences.[10]

The two keynote speeches made abundantly clear that the departure point for this conference, like CIBA's, was the recognition that the inherited maxims of medical ethics were not sufficient to resolve the ethical questions at hand. Robert Willson, the chairman of obstetrics and gynecology at the University of Michigan School of Medicine, observed that "the obstetrician-gynecologist of the past was less often forced to make decisions which were contrary to his personal and professional code of ethics than is his contemporary counterpart." William Zuelzer, a pediatrician at Wayne State University, elaborated the point: "Until quite recently the very questions we are here to ask were taboo in a society whose medical ethic has not changed since Hippocrates. Our unconditional commitment to the preservation of life posed no moral or ecological problems." But this essential principle was no longer adequate to determine whether to "preserve life against nature's apparent intentions simply because we have the gadgetry that allows us to do so." Concluded Zuelzer, "Clearly, we are about to cast off from a hitherto safe anchorage without knowing where we may drift."[11]

Perhaps this fear of being morally adrift helped the conference participants forge an agreement. Their most acute concern was to ensure that the burdensome weight of a decision to discontinue treatment did not immobilize the physician. The nightmare case for them was not the unnecessary death of a defective newborn but the survival of such a newborn because physicians had been unable to make tough but necessary choices. Unless doctors took command, warned Zuelzer, the infant nurseries would stand as "the horror chambers we call intensive care units. . . . The operation is a success, the child will live, and now someone will brief the family with averted eyes that they have a mongoloid on their hands. A triumph of modern medicine—or medicine at its worst?"[12] Indeed, physicians' inertia was already beginning to make "the beep of the oscillograph . . . the voice of the new barbarianism."[13]

In this same spirit, Judson Randolph, a professor of surgery at George Washington University, attempted to spell out the conditions under which doctors could justifiably deny treatment in the "hopeless case." He came down on the side of the Johns Hopkins doctors: he would have recommended to the parents to forego surgery. The bioethicists present concurred with the general sentiment. Fletcher offered an admiring restatement of Robert Louis Stevenson's conclusion about the Polynesians: "Out of love for their children they practice infanticide, and at the same time their practice of infanticide makes them treasure their children all the more." Veatch, most concerned with maximizing parental input, testily criticized the physicians for what he took to be their arrogance: "The framing of the question in terms of 'how much the patient should be told or consulted' has been the standard formulation of this meeting. This grates me the wrong way. The question I would tend to ask is: Under what circumstances, if any, should the parents not have control of the decision?" But he, too, was ready to follow the parents' wishes with little concern for the interests of the newborn.[14]

Veatch's complaints notwithstanding, the Ross Conference demonstrated some readiness among the physicians to include in the decision making process not only parents but even third parties. The willingness to support such an unusual step reflected a widely shared sense that resolving the substantive issues was so far beyond the conventional boundaries of medical ethics that physicians had to adopt new strategies. "Here we are really playing God," declared Zuelzer, "and we need all the help we can get. Apart from giving parents a voice—or at least a hearing—we should enlist the support of clergymen, lawyers, sociologists, psychologists, and plain citizens who are not expert at anything, but can contribute their common sense and wisdom." Or, as Judson argued, there should be "an opinion body in every pediatric center to deal with ethical problems in the clinical setting. Such a board might be composed of physicians, administrators, lawyers, chaplains and other representative lay persons."[15]

No one was quite ready to define what such a body was to do, and many of those present feared it might set down rules that would interfere with the doctor–patient relationship. "We have to have some type of guidelines," Zuelzer noted. "I don't know what they are, but the danger lies not so much in our day-to-day decision-making process as in the prospect of some body some day pressing the bureaucratic button and saying: 'This is no longer an acceptable category of human beings and shall be eliminated.' "[16] But in the end, the shared sense of a desperate need for new policies led the conference attendees to two major conclusions:

The absolute obligation to prolong life under circumstances which impair its quality and dignity needs to be reexamined with a view to arrive at a humane philosophy and guidelines for medical practice.

One condition for reaching an acceptable ethic is the education of the public and the enlistment of the help of other professional and lay groups.

In short, the physicians were ready to strike a bargain: in order to be able to terminate treatment, they were ready to give nonphysicians a role in decision making. Presumably "a free flow of information from the profession to the laymen" would produce an ethic that would not require treating all patients at all times with all possible resources.[17]

• • •

The position adopted at the Ross Conference received a far more dramatic and attention-riveting formulation in Raymond Duff and Alexander Campbell's 1973 *New England Journal of Medicine* article on the "Moral and Ethical Dilemmas in the Special-Care Nursery." It was an almost exact analogue to Henry Beecher's 1966 article on human experimentation. Just as Beecher had demonstrated that ethical problems in human experimentation went well beyond the practices of an individual researcher, so Duff and Campbell revealed that the ethical dilemmas in neonatal nurseries extended far beyond the death of a single baby. Like Beecher, too, they were whistle-blowers exposing a secret shared by pediatricians—namely, that the cause of death for a considerable number of newborns was the physician's determination to withhold life-sustaining treatment. "That decisions are made not to treat severely defective infants may be no surprise to those familiar with special-care facilities," wrote Duff and Campbell.[18] The Johns Hopkins baby was merely one in a series.

Unlike Beecher, Duff and Campbell named names—indeed, named themselves. Rather than make a general argument about the ethical dilemmas in a neonatal unit, they were at once precise and specific: at the Yale–New Haven Hospital, 43 of 299 consecutive deaths in the special-care nursery between 1 January 1970 and 30 June 1972 (14 percent) occurred when physicians halted treatment. "The awesome finality of these decisions," they conceded, "combined with a potential for error in prognosis, made the choice agonizing. . . . Nevertheless, the issue has to be faced, for not to decide is an arbitrary and potentially devastating decision of default."[19]

In their exposé Duff and Campbell did not seek to denounce the withdrawal of treatment as unethical—the forty-three deaths were not the counterparts of Beecher's twenty-two cases on the roll of dishonor. Nor were they prepared to invite into the neonatal unit a hospitalwide committee staffed with ethicists and lawyers. Their goal was far more circumscribed: to have parents share in the determinations that once had been the doctors' exclusive preserve. They, like the Ross conferees, strongly supported the propriety of terminating treatment, provided that the decision was reached jointly by physicians and the parents: "We believe the burdens of decision making must be borne by families and their professional advisers because they are most familiar with the respective situations. Since families primarily must live with and are most affected by the decisions, it therefore appears that society and the health professions should provide only general guidelines for decision making." The parents, after all, would be the ones to bear the burden of care should the newborn survive in a compromised state (that is, physically or mentally handicapped, or both). Finally, like Beecher before them, they were convinced that parents, no less than human subjects, were intellectually and emotionally capable of giving informed consent to these decisions. Although some physicians believed that the mysteries of medicine were too esoteric for laypeople to grasp, or that the trauma of giving birth to a disabled infant was too disorienting, Duff and Campbell insisted that "parents are able to understand the implications of such things as chronic dyspnea, oxygen dependency, incontinence, paralysis, contracture, sexual handicaps and mental retardation."[20]

To buttress the case for parental involvement, Duff and Campbell contended that excluding parents would leave physicians to their own devices, which could well mean that the decisions would serve the doctors' purposes, but not necessarily the parents'. Physicians, they pointed out, often face conflicts of interest that "may result in decisions against the individual preferences"; they might, for example, decide to treat a newborn in order to learn more about experimental therapies that might save the life of the next low-weight baby or manage the information so as to aggrandize their own authority.[21] To read Duff and Campbell was to learn that the mind-set of the neonatologist was not significantly different from the mind-set of the researcher, for both might sacrifice the well-being of the particular patient in order to further the progress of medicine.

A companion piece to the Duff and Campbell article appeared in the same *NEJM* issue and adopted an almost identical approach. Anthony Shaw's "Dilemmas of 'Informed Consent' in Children" was more of an opinion piece, without hard data from a specific hospital unit, so it did not capture the same notoriety. But Shaw also centered his arguments on the Johns Hopkins case and rejected a "rigid right-to-life philosophy." Like the others, his fear was not discrimination against the handicapped but the survival of an infant with an unacceptably low quality of life. "My ethic," he wrote, "considers quality of life as a value that must be balanced against a belief in the sanctity of life." Because every year medicine gains the ability to "remove yet another type of malformation from the 'unsalvageable' category . . . we can wind up with 'viable' children . . . propped up on a pillow, marginally tolerating an oral diet of sugar and amino acids and looking forward to another operation." The only escape from the morass, Shaw also recognized, was to reach beyond the medical profession. "Who should make these decisions? The doctors? The parents? Clergymen? A committee? . . . I think that the parents must participate in any decision about treatment and they must be fully informed of the consequences of consenting and withholding consent." As to the standards to be followed: "It may be impossible for any general agreement or guidelines . . . but I believe we should bring these problems into the public forum because whatever the answers may be, they should not be the result of decisions made solely by the attending physicians. Or should they?"[22]

Despite Shaw's tacked-on last question, the message of the two articles—really, the consensus among the pediatric specialists who first tackled the issue—was unmistakable: the critical issue was to know when to terminate treatment, and in reaching this decision, it was valid to consider the quality of life and the consequences of treatment not only for the newborn but for the family. Substantive guidelines were probably too difficult to draw up and were potentially mischievous, but the process of decision making about termination of treatment should involve parents, and probably others as well. To adopt policies that were beyond the scope of traditional medical ethics, to terminate treatment despite injunctions to do no harm, required a new kind of legitimacy, namely, the sanction of the lay as well as the medical world.

This preliminary consensus was short-lived and, as it turned out, deeply controversial. The first critics came from within the profession: the idea that outsiders should participate in medical decision making sparked opposition, and so did the proposition that termination of treatment for handicapped newborns was sometimes ethically appropriate. The debates quickly spilled over from medicine to the laity, to become among the most divisive issues Americans faced in the post–Vietnam War era.

The first complaints about Duff and Campbell's and Shaw's articles came from conservative physicians who feared that these authors conceded too much authority to outsiders. Franz Ingelfinger, the outspoken, traditionalistic editor of the *NEJM*, wrote that what he liked best about the contributions was their case-by-case approach, their preference for "the principles of individualism" over "fairly rigid rules of ethical professional behavior."[23] (Ingelfinger's confusion of "individualism" with Duff and Campbell's commitment to an individual, case-by-case decision making may help explain his tenacity on the subject.) What he liked least about the articles was the suggestion that physicians invite in outsiders—a practice, he was convinced, that would produce "God squad" committees.

Although it was only 1973 and the bioethics movement's most impressive successes were yet to come, Ingelfinger was already bemoaning the fact that "this is the day of the ethicist in medicine. He delineates the rights of patients, of experimental subjects, of fetuses, of mothers, of animals, and even of doctors." And in a well-conceived comparison between the attitudes of the 1950s and those of the 1970s, he observed, "What a far cry from the days when medical 'ethics' consisted of condemning economic improprieties such as fee splitting and advertising." Ingelfinger had little patience with the ethicists whose work he considered to be "the products of armchair exercise," untested in the "laboratory of experience," and he advised his colleagues: "When Duff and Campbell ask, 'Who decides for the child?' the answer is 'you.' " He conceded that "society, ethics, institutional attitudes and committees can provide the broad guidelines, but the onus of decision-making ultimately falls on the doctor in whose care the child has been put."[24] To abdicate this responsibility was to subvert the ethics and standing of the profession itself. "Some will not agree with this thesis," Ingelfinger concluded, "but for those who do . . . a necessary corollary is that current attempts to de-mysticize and debase the status of the physician are compromising his ability to provide leadership (not exercise dictatorship!) when health and life are at stake." The issue came down to who would rule at the bedside—doctors or others.

Equally unhappy were a number of physicians who believed that the emerging consensus in favor of termination violated medicine's ethical norms. These critics condemned the Johns Hopkins Hospital for its handling of the case and denounced Duff and the others for their readiness to halt treatment. One of the first protests came from the Yale–New Haven nursery itself. Two of Duff and Campbell's associates, Doctors Joan Venes and Peter Huttenlocher, with a hostility not ordinarily found in letters to medical journals, disassociated themselves from the Duff–Campbell position. Accusing them of "hyperbole . . . throughout the article," Venes and Huttenlocher, like Ingelfinger, believed it "an abrogation of the physician's role . . . to argue conflicting opinions in the presence of already distraught parents or to leave with them the very difficult decision." But they went even further, rejecting the idea that physicians could use "active means to produce 'an early death' of the child," or should include in their calculus "the financial and psychologic stresses imposed upon a family with the birth of a handicapped child."[25]

This was only the start, though. Any notion of a consensus among physicians soon evaporated in the heat of antagonisms so bitter as to exceed anything heard in human experimentation or transplantation. Two of the physicians involved in the Johns Hopkins incident, Doctors Cooke and Fost, were soon condemning their own earlier behavior and colleagues who would follow that example. In a complete turnabout, Cooke now insisted that whatever the parental sentiments, "the physician must opt for [the] life of his patient. . . . The physician must recognize that the patient is neither his property nor that of the parents, to be disposed of at will." But if parents were too biased against the handicapped and too confused about the implications of a handicap to be trusted, and if Ingelfinger's advice seemed antediluvian, then how was one to proceed in the tough case where treatment might, or might not be, futile? Cooke opted for a "group decision," with input not only from ethicists and other professionals, but from "families who have been through such decisions themselves." In this way, "the handicapped or the potentially handicapped will be accorded treatment equivalent to that of his normal brother."[26]

Fost, also chastened by the Johns Hopkins experience, was even more insistent on treatment, whatever the parental wishes. At an academic conference that both he and Duff attended, he unleashed an impassioned attack on Duff's position: "Dr. Duff has been asked, 'What is to prevent families from deciding *arbitrarily* that a child shouldn't be kept alive?' He says, 'The doctors won't allow it.' I see institutions where children with Down's Syndrome . . . or myelomeningocele [spina bifida] with an excellent prognosis are allowed to starve, without specific criteria as to who is in this class and without a defined process for decision making. What is the definition of arbitrary if not the absence of criteria or a defined process?" He also rejected the simple definition of a "hopeless" case: "I do not understand what is hopeless about Down's Syndrome," [at which point another physician interrupted to say: "Have a child with it of your own—you will soon see."]. "Life, even impaired life, is very important. . . . We should not kill people or allow people to die just because they are going to wind up in wheelchairs or because they have only a 20 percent chance of a normal IQ."

Fost insisted on the need to open up and formalize the decision making process, not to facilitate decisions to terminate treatment, as some of his colleagues urged, but to protect the handicapped. "Dr. Duff rejects committees because members tend to be 'elite . . . quite powerful, and often seek more power. This tends to corrupt.' " But the power of a committee was minimal compared to the authority of physicians to disenfranchise the handicapped, "where an elite of the bright declares mental retardation to be equal to suffering, and an elite of the walking declares wheelchair existence to be 'massive disability.' " Not that Fost himself would treat every case maximally, but in the controversial cases and when long life was possible, he followed "a *process*—where facts, feelings, and interests not always perceived by parents and physicians, [are] brought to bear. . . . I assemble as diverse a group as we can—nurses, lawyers, students, secretaries, philosophers, to talk about it."[27] In sum, physicians were obliged to consult with outsiders to the case, even with outsiders to medicine.

Duff neither retreated from his readiness to terminate treatment at least in some cases, nor did he lack allies of his own. Perhaps the most controversial among them was John Lorber, the English surgeon who in the 1960s had been famous for his aggressiveness in treating spina bifida. In 1971, however, Lorber reversed his position, and as he explained to his American colleagues (at the same conference where Fost was taking on Duff): "The pendulum had swung too far, from one extreme of treating none to the other of treating all. The balance had to be restored. The case for selective treatment was overwhelming." To this end, Lorber formulated clinical criteria—the size of the lesion, degree of paralysis, and extent of hydrocephalus—and used them to guide (really, he conceded, to dictate) parental decisions. When a surgeon examined a newborn with extensive lesions, concluded Lorber, he "should think of the life that lies ahead for the baby. If he would not like such a child of his own to survive, then he should take the logical long-term strategic view and resist the temptation to operate."[28]

Anthony Shaw also continued to support the termination position, even going so far as to devise a mathematical formula that would ostensibly factor in all the relevant social and economic considerations: (N.E.) times (H. plus S.) equals M.L. That is, on a scale of 1 to 10, the child's natural endowments (N.E.) were multiplied by the home (H.) advantages (emotional, financial) plus the society (S.) resources (special education programs, foster homes) to determine a meaningful-life (M.L.) score. Shaw concluded that there could be no definition of a meaningful life, "except to point out that in this formula, a value of 200 would indicate the maximal meaningful life for an infant," and to imply that a score of 25 or 50 or 75 (a very handicapped child born to poor parents in a state unwilling to fund social services) would suggest a meaningless life, and thus permit (encourage?) a decision not to treat.[29]

With proponents like Lorber and formulas composed by Shaw, the termination position grew even more controversial; and for both obvious and less obvious reasons, those outside of medicine soon were drawn into the debate. For one thing, weighing of the issues here, as in human experimentation and transplantation, did not require a mastery of esoteric techniques or complex treatments. The clinical data about retardation, spina bifida, and low birth weights were accessible to laypeople; and the inevitable uncertainty about the neurological and social outcomes for the newborns in these categories heightened a sense that moral values, not medical facts, were fundamental to treatment decisions.

For another, it was ever so easy—and unsettling—to plot a slippery slope: Let the profession abandon a commitment to the preservation of life, and then the Lorbers and Shaws would devise value-laden formulas to decide who lived. Soon enough only the perfect child would be allowed to survive—and at the other end of life, only the perfect adult. This was not medicine but selective eugenics and the worst kind of social engineering, which raised the specter of Nazilike programs and brought greater acrimony to an already bitter dispute.

Still other considerations propelled outsiders to join in this debate. One cannot imagine an issue more likely to galvanize lay opinion and action than the treatment of the handicapped newborn, or imagine a time more auspicious for riveting attention on it than the early 1970s, or more precisely, 1973. Besides being the year of Duff and Campbell's *NEJM* article, 1973 was also the year of the Supreme Court's *Roe v. Wade* decision legalizing abortion. In 1973 Congress also enacted the Vocational Rehabilitation Act, and its Section 504 provided that no one "solely by reason of his handicap, be excluded from the participation in, be denied the benefits of, or be subjected to discrimination under any program or activity receiving Federal financial assistance."[30] The principles underlying both the court finding in *Roe v. Wade* and the congressional legislation in Section 504 were directly relevant to decision making in neonatal units. The difficulty was that the principles of the Court and the Congress were at conflict, pointing policy in opposite directions.

The thrust of *Roe v. Wade* was to maximize parental autonomy in that a mother who wanted a fetus aborted had the right to do so. To be sure, she had to act in cooperation with her physician, and her prerogatives, relative to the rule-making power of the state, declined as the viability of the fetus increased over time. But through most of the first two trimesters it was essentially the mother's choice—and not the doctor's or the legislature's—as to whether the fetus survived. In this way, *Roe v. Wade* expanded the domain of private decision making against both professional and state authority, and thus was most consistent, in the context of newborns and termination of treatment, with the recommendations that Duff and others were proposing. Under *Roe v. Wade* the parent determined whether the fetus would survive—and it was not much of an extension to add, whether a defective newborn would survive. Not that the Court spoke specifically to the fate of the handicapped newborn or that it sanctioned infanticide; rather, in the name of privacy, it championed parental decision making, which was precisely what Duff and others were advocating.

The very fact that *Roe v. Wade* did have this consistency with Duff, however, clarified for the public all the stakes in neonatal decision making and made it seem not only fitting but necessary for outsiders to enter the neonatal intensive care unit. The issue was not only how to respond to gravely ill newborns, which might be defined, in keeping with Franz Ingelfinger and John Lorber, as a medical question in which the doctor essentially calculated the odds and proceeded accordingly. It was also a question of defining life, and the Duff position seemed to exemplify the fears of not only the opponents of legalized abortion, who saw it as the first step on the road to destroying the sanctity of all life, but those essentially sympathetic with *Roe v. Wade* but apprehensive about an unbounded protection of family privacy. Did one begin by discounting the life of the fetus and then move, inexorably, to discounting the life of the newborn, and, eventually the elderly? Was the newborn nursery an inevitable extension of the abortion clinic? As a result of *Roe v. Wade*, the neonatal intensive care unit became a crystal ball in which one might see the future.[31]

Then, at the very moment the Supreme Court was expanding the scope of family privacy, Congress was expanding the rights of the disabled. Although the two developments might appear part of an enlargement of individual liberties, they were in fact on a collision course, destined to meet head-on in the newborn nursery.

According to the 1970 U.S. Census, almost 10 percent of Americans identified themselves as disabled. Despite their numbers, however, they had not yet been a visible or politically active group. Those handicapped by blindness had little to do with the deaf or with the wheelchair-bound, and almost no one among the physically disabled identified with the mentally disabled. Within a few years, however, not only was there a distinct disabilities community, but it was shaping public policy. Advances in medical technology, from prosthetic devices to surgical techniques, enabled the handicapped to live longer and do more. Consequently, the handicapped found their own disabilities less limiting than the social barriers they encountered, from too little access to public space to too much prejudice from potential employers and landlords. The diverse groups came together through a shared experience of exclusion and took as their model for political action the minority rights campaigns. The most notable success for the disabilities movement came in 1973. Just as Title VI in the Civil Rights Act of 1964 banned discrimination in federally financed programs on the basis of race, color, or national origin, and Title IX in the Education Amendments of 1972 banned discrimination on the basis of sex, so Section 504 of the Vocational Rehabilitation Act banned discrimination on the basis of handicap.[32]

The immediate impact of Section 504 on federal policy was negligible. The provision, one small paragraph in a lengthy vocational education bill, had not been debated in Congress; and none of its sponsors anticipated that by the end of the decade Section 504 would be the basis for the expenditure of well over a billion dollars to give the handicapped greater access to mass transportation, public housing, and employment and educational opportunities. But in 1973 Section 504 already reflected and reinforced a new attitude about disabilities diametrically opposed to the negative biases that many of the nonhandicapped, including physicians, shared. As one advocate (from the National Federation of the Blind) testified: "This civil rights for the handicapped provision . . . brings the disabled within the law. . . . It establishes that because a man is blind or deaf or without legs, he is not less a citizen, that his rights of citizenship are not revoked or diminished because he is disabled." Or as Senator Hubert Humphrey explained, "Every child—gifted, normal, and handicapped— has a fundamental right to educational opportunity and the right to health."[33]

It was still too early to foresee all the social consequences of this reorientation. No one, no matter how prescient, could have predicted that ten years later Section 504 would be tacked up on the walls of neonatal units or that medical care might come under its umbrella. But clearly, attitudes toward the handicapped were being transformed, and the impact was bound to be felt not only in modifications to make public buildings wheelchair accessible but in assessments of which conditions should or should not be treated in newborns, and who should be making the decision.

• • •

One more incentive for the public to focus on neonatal ethics arose in 1973: Mondale's long campaign to create a national commission finally succeeded, helped along by Kennedy's ability to use the newest scandals in human experimentation to press for both minority rights and patient rights. Kennedy himself tied all these strands together, convening a one-day hearing on "Medical Ethics: The Right to Survival." The very title made his own orientation toward neonatal decision making apparent; the key consideration for him was how to protect the rights of the newborn, not the prerogatives of doctors or parents. He opened the hearing by observing that just the previous week, Congress had formally established the National Commission for the Protection of Human Subjects, and the new body might well want to add to its agenda the treatment of the newborn, for the plight of handicapped neonates resembled the plight of many human subjects—both were vulnerable to discrimination, deprived of the right to consent, and in need of protection. "In our committee sessions," Kennedy reported, "we heard of prisoners being used in human experimentation . . . we learned of experimental drugs plus medical devices being used," and these experiments often were conducted without the consent of the subjects. "Now," he continued, "we are moving into a different area, but the question of consent still arises. Who has the right to give consent for infants? Is it only the parents? . . . Is it possible that some physicians and families may join in a conspiracy to deny the right of a defective child to live or to die?" The voice of the doctor and the parent were being heard, but not the infant's, and hence his fate might well depend on "which of you doctors the parents take him to."[34] Thus, physicians, even acting in concert with parents, should have an institutional review board–type committee looking over their shoulder.

Just how provocative these points were emerged in the testimony of the hearing's four witnesses. Two took their priorities from a sense of family privacy (staying with the *Roe v. Wade* model); two, closer to Kennedy, made their priority protecting the newborn (drawing on Section 504 and the lessons learned in human experimentation). Raymond Duff and Lewis Sheiner, a physician from the University of California–San Francisco (UCSF) medical school, advocated case-by-case decisions that ultimately reflected the choice of parents with their physicians. "It is disquieting," conceded Duff, "to discover that infants apparently have an identical condition and may be treated differently, and some may survive and some not . . . but that is the way it is." On the opposing side were Robert Cooke and Warren Reich, a bioethicist from the Kennedy Institute at Georgetown, who argued that parents might be so "very biased" that it was unconscionable to allow their preferences to condemn an infant to death. Nor were they persuaded that individual physicians had the insight or the moral authority to prevent such abuses. "Public awareness of the fallibility of its various priesthoods is increasing," noted Reich, "and medicine is no exception. The Tuskegee syphilis study debacle, or the Willowbrook hepatitis study make sensational news and arouse public distrust."[35]

The one point of agreement, although not very firm, was on the need for collective decision making. Far apart in substantive terms, all the witnesses still favored more open and formal decision-making mechanisms—notably, ethics committees with representatives drawn from medicine, the professions, and the lay public. Duff and Sheiner, for their part, emphasized the consultative character of the committee: "A dialogue must be begun." Reich stressed the need to equip such a group with explicit guidelines; otherwise, it, too, might discriminate against the handicapped. "Both Dr. Sheiner and Dr. Duff . . . lay great weight on procedures, as though procedures for decision-making are going to be our only salvation, since it is not possible to establish any kind of norms that can govern our conduct. I would like to say that procedures are indeed important, but they do not carry with them any assurance of truth. . . . Principles should be prior to procedures."[36] But everyone agreed that these committees were to educate both parents and doctors about handicaps, and rebut stereotypes about the effects of disabilities. Collective decision making in which physicians would share authority with a variety of outsiders seemed to be the only way out of the impasse.

The tensions between *Roe v. Wade* and Section 504, between the prerogatives of families, the authority of physicians, and the protections against discrimination due to handicap, also enlarged the cohort of philosophers interested in bioethics. In particular, Daniel Callahan, co-founder of the Hastings Institute, and Albert Jonsen of the UCSF Medical School followed a route into the field that began with abortion, continued through *Roe v. Wade*, and eventually entered the neonatal unit.

Although Callahan had earned a doctorate in philosophy from Harvard in 1961, he chose not to pursue a traditional academic career. He served on the editorial staff for the Catholic-oriented weekly, *Commonweal*, and held a variety of visiting teaching positions. Then, in the late 1960s, he became fascinated with the issue of abortion. With foundation support, he pursued his analysis, not attempting to resolve the controversies but "asking the question, as a philosopher, how one would go about thinking through an issue like that." In the process, Callahan discovered "the whole world of medical ethics, of which abortion was simply one part." In particular, he was drawn to the problems posed by heart transplantation, the definition of death, and the "possibilities and hazards in genetic engineering." He also discovered the critical need for an interdisciplinary approach: "One could see in any issue a philosophical problem, but then there was almost always a legal problem, a political problem, a socio-cultural problem as well."

From this starting point, Callahan joined with his Hastings, New York, neighbor, Willard Gaylin, a psychiatrist who was then writing a book on Vietnam war resisters, to found the Hastings Institute of Society, Ethics and the Life Sciences. The first items on its agenda, as might be expected, were population issues, behavior modification, death and dying, and genetic engineering. Its strategy was to bring together representatives of a variety of disciplines, both theoretical and policy oriented, to define the relevant issues, and, even more notably, to offer rules and guidelines for resolving them. Callahan both then and later insisted on the need for limiting physicians' "absolute autonomy," for devising "accepted ground rules." As he told an interviewer in 1977: "Doctors want . . . to make all the choices. Well, we're saying to them, no. There are some public interests at stake here and some general principles you have to abide by. . . . You're playing in a public ballpark now . . . and you've got to live by certain standards . . . like it or not."[37]

To be sure, not every philosopher who crossed over into medicine was quite so confrontational. Joseph Fletcher, for example, in his exceptionally popular 1966 book, *Situational Ethics* (which sold over

150,000 copies), emphasized the importance of doing right in a particular circumstance over rigidly following universal rules. "The situa-
tionist," he wrote, "enters into every decision-making situation fully
armed with the ethical maxims of his community and its heritage, and
he treats them with respect as illuminators of the problem. Just the
same he is prepared in any situation to compromise them or set them
aside *in the situation* if love seems better served by doing so." The idea
of ethics tied to the particulars of a situation fit well with medicine's
case-by-case orientation, and so amorphous a concept as "love" suited
the exercise of a very traditional kind of paternalism. But if such a
reading was popular among some physicians, Fletcher had other intentions. "Situation ethics" was hostile to what it labeled mindless legal-
ism, but it was also determined to elevate the lay voice, in the first
instance in religious controversies, and by implication, in medical controversies as well. Fletcher's aims were essentially democratic. In the
process of empowering the congregation against the bishop, he was
altogether comfortable in empowering the patient against the doctor.[38]

Albert Jonsen's approach was closer to Callahan than to Fletcher. In
May 1974, Jonsen, who had left the Jesuit order and was teaching in
the UCSF Health Policy Program, brought together colleagues from the
Department of Pediatrics with an interdisciplinary group of outsiders
to medicine to explore "Critical Issues in Newborn Intensive Care."[39]
At this meeting (and at many others thereafter), laypeople outnum-
bered physicians, and the recommendations reflected the altered balance of power.

The conference participants proposed "A Moral Policy for Neonatal
Intensive Care" (the prominence of "moral" in the title testifying to
the leading role of bioethicists). The lead proposition was that parents,
not doctors, had responsibility for the "ultimate decisions" affecting
the newborn. "Those who engender and willingly bring an infant to
birth are morally accountable for its well being. They are closest to the
infant and must bear the burdens of its nurture, especially if it is ill
or defective." Only as a last resort, when parents abdicated their rightful responsibility, should physicians assume "the heavy burden of rendering final decisions." Here again, as in human experimentation and
transplantation, the presumption was that physicians had a conflict of
interest. Echoing what had been said at the Ross Conference as well as

by Duff and Campbell, the participants explained in the report, "Physicians may feel that their duty extends not only to a particular infant under care but also to all children. For such a reason, some physicians may be devoted to scientific research aimed at improving the quality and effectiveness of neonatal care for all. While this dedication is necessary and praiseworthy, it may, on occasion . . . push a clinician, even unconsciously, to extend a course of care beyond reasonable limits of benefit to the patient."[40] The neonatal nursery was too close to the laboratory to trust to physicians.

The conference's second major recommendation was to urge the creation of guidelines for neonatal decision making. Establishing in advance a series of principles would rein in the discretionary authority of individual physicians and protect the interests of the newborn as well. The neonatologists should devise and circulate "clinical criteria which render more specific the general conditions of prolonged life without pain and the potential for human communication. Resuscitation criteria should be established. . . . Delivery room policy, based on certain criteria, should state conditions for which resuscitation is not indicated."[41]

To these same ends, the final recommendation was to open up neonatal decision making to outsiders: each unit should "establish an advisory board consisting of health professionals and other involved and interested persons." (Imagine how a once autonomous professional would respond to the idea of inviting in "interested persons.") The board would "discuss the problems of the unit and make a periodic retrospective review of the difficult decisions." Its purpose was not to supercede parental authority but to "provide, by bringing a variety of experience, belief, and attitude, a wider human environment for decision-making than would otherwise be available." Thus, the board would supplement—in effect, supplant—the narrow viewpoint of technicians.[42]

Although the recommendations were presented as the conference findings and published in a leading medical journal, *Pediatrics*, the consensus was less complete than it appeared. In quite self-conscious fashion, the bioethicists were laying down a challenge to the medical profession. They conceded that "this moral policy may seem unreal. This is the inevitable result of considering moral decisions apart from the agony of living through the decisions." But, they said, their intellectual distance from the bedside strengthened their position: "The air of unreality is, we believe, the necessary cool moment which philosophers say should precede any reasonable judgment. That judgment will have to be made amid the hard realities, but it may be better made in light of reflection on these propositions."[43] Armchair ethics was more cool, reasonable, and reflective than bedside ethics.

Although the physicians at the conference did not directly confront the philosophers, the split of opinion, particularly about the proper division of authority between doctor and parent, did peek through in the report. Dr. Clement Smith, of the Harvard Medical School, let it be known (albeit in a footnote) that "nonmedical members of the conference insisted . . . with unanimity . . . that life-and-death decisions must be made by the parents, while doctors of medicine with almost equal unanimity saw that as an avoidance of the physician's own responsibility." Dr. Smith preferred—and so did most physicians, he believed—"that the doctor, through intimate participation and full discussion with the parents, interpret their beliefs or wishes clearly enough to act according to those indications rather than confront parents directly with the act of decision."[44] His minority statement makes clear just how novel and controversial it still was to elevate the parent over the doctor.

Although many physicians shared Dr. Smith's frustration and discontent, they were unable to make their case persuasively. Inside the neonatal unit, they might convince parents to accept their advice; but in public forums devoted to exploring normative standards and the principles that should govern neonatal decision making, they were very much on the defensive, and their weakness affected the eventual design of public policy. To counter claims for expanding parental authority, Harvard's Dr. Smith and his peers invoked an almost discredited ideal of paternalism. Moreover, for them to claim that many parents did not want to carry the burden of the decision, and to live for the rest of their lives with the guilt of having "killed" their newborn—even though such instances were real enough—was an inadequate argument, for it conceded that if parents were strong enough and not guilt ridden, they should be making these decisions.

An alternative and potentially more powerful claim on behalf of the exercise of physician authority was to present the doctor as protector of the newborn against the potentially biased and self-interested parents, those who wanted a perfect child and were repelled at the prospect of raising a Down's syndrome baby. But this claim had problems of its own. The medical record was anything but spotless—as evidenced by the events at Johns Hopkins, the writings of Duff and Campbell, the formulas of Shaw, and the guidelines of Lorber. And to pit the doctor against the family even in the guise of the protector of the handicapped inevitably raised well-worn images of a heavy-handed medical paternalism. Indeed, it was against the prospect of continued medical paternalism that the parents of one low-birth-weight newborn wrote, first in an article and then in a book, one of the most widely read and emotionally moving attacks on physician hegemony. In *The Long Dying of Baby Andrew*, Robert and Peggy Stinson described their son's death with a bitterness matched only by ex–mental patients in denouncing psychiatric tyranny.[45] To read their account is to understand all the better why the public agenda gave so much prominence to neonatal decision making, why a variety of outsiders joined physicians in the nursery, and why physicians were not going to be recognized as defenders of handicapped newborns.

The Stinson story began in December 1976, when Peggy, five months pregnant with her second child, suddenly started to bleed heavily. Her physician diagnosed the problem as a low-lying placenta that was liable to hemorrhage, and he counseled her to remain in bed. Peggy and her husband, Robert, a historian teaching at Moravian College in Pennsylvania, considered, but decided against, an abortion. Although Peggy followed her doctor's advice, she entered spontaneous labor, rushed to her local hospital, and after many hours of difficult labor gave birth to an 800-gram baby boy, or what the Stinsons call a "fetal infant."[46] Almost immediately, they informed the physician that they did not want extraordinary measures used to keep the baby alive.

Even without heroics, the baby, Andrew, stabilized and survived his first several days of life. But then he experienced a fluid imbalance, a problem that the physician assured the Stinsons was readily correctable; with their agreement, Andrew was transferred to a tertiary care medical center in Philadelphia, with the expectation that he would remain there for a matter of days and return to the community hospital. However,

Andrew developed problems breathing and was placed on a respirator. When the Stinsons opposed this measure, the Philadelphia physicians summarily informed them that in their opinion Andrew should be treated, and should the Stinsons continue to object, the hospital would obtain a court order. "Mrs. Stinson," Peggy reports one doctor saying, "I wouldn't presume to tell my auto mechanic how to fix my car."[47]

The Stinsons each kept a journal of the events that followed Andrew's birth, and the entries make up *The Long Dying of Baby Andrew*. Their reason for publishing their record of the "tragic failures" and "perils" of the ICU, was, they explain, to help recapture medical decision making from the experts and return it to the family. "The general public—and that includes the parents and potential parents of the babies whose care the specialists are debating—has little exposure to the issues and no voice at all in the debate. While specialists argue abstractions and hospitals impose different 'policies,' suffering babies and their family can get, quite literally, trapped."[48]

One of the Stinsons's most bitter and telling complaints is the sense of exclusion and isolation they experienced throughout the ordeal. "Have they ever saved a baby like Andrew in this I[nfant] ICU?" they wondered. "Does Andrew have a real chance? . . . If only we had someone to trust."[49] Why this acute sense of an absence of trust? In part, because medicine deals with uncertainties. At every critical juncture, physicians (in retrospect, overly optimistic) assured the Stinsons that the interventions would be quick and effective. Place the infant into the tertiary care center to correct a fluid imbalance, or put the infant onto the respirator, and he will be back and stable in a matter of weeks. But Andrew never did leave the tertiary care center or get off the respirator. Indeed, from the start nothing happened as expected. The Stinsons had believed that her spontaneous labor was part of a miscarriage, only to learn to their astonishment that the fetus was breathing. Undoubtedly, other physicians might have been more effective at explaining to them the underlying uncertainties; but even so, the case of Andrew was like a roller coaster, and the parents felt helpless as they watched the ride.

Second, the Stinsons were strangers to the tertiary care hospital. The baby's transfer from the local hospital to the Philadelphia medical center took them, in every sense, away from home. Not only were they forced to travel several hours to visit Andrew, but the hospital itself, as Robert observed, was strange, "an entirely different world from the one I normally inhabit." The internal organization of the infant ICU only exaggerated the distance. Since this was a teaching hospital, a new group of residents rotated through the unit every month, with the result that over six months, the Stinsons met a bewildering number of doctors; no sooner did one face become familiar than the rotation was over and a new face was at the nursery door. "It's hard to find out how Andrew is," Peggy complained. "We never get the same person twice when we call the hospital." Her journal entry a month later noted: "Another stranger to explain ourselves to. . . . The bureaucracy controls Andrew. . . . It rolls inexorably onward. . . . Doctors come and doctors go—there's a schedule in the office somewhere." Ultimately, "The doctor-rotation thing is impossible from the point of view of the parent."[50]

Rotations meant not only adjusting to different styles of communication but to different information. It took weeks for the Stinsons to puzzle out whether or not Andrew had suffered a cerebral bleed, and some of the confusion had to do with a lack of continuity among the caretakers. So too, because the Stinsons continued to object to treatment, the medical teams labeled them difficult and uncooperative, and the label was passed on team to team, the way teachers tell each other about a troublesome student. Under these circumstances, it was virtually impossible for the Stinsons to form a relationship with any of the doctors.

Perhaps most important in understanding their feelings of distrust was the fact that the Stinsons were convinced (and, as we have seen, they were anything but alone in this) that the physicians did not share an identity of interest with them or, they thought, with Andrew. The physicians' primary commitment, they believed, was not to the particular newborn but to the accumulation of knowledge: the ICU was a laboratory, the physicians medical researchers, and Andrew the human subject. "It's not the technology per se that inspires fears—it's the mentality of the people employing it. Fallible people lost sight of their fallibility in the scramble to push back the frontiers of knowledge, to redesign nature and to outwit death." When they confronted one of the physicians directly with the question, "Isn't Andrew's life a kind of experiment, then?" he bridled at the idea, insisting that "our concern here is for the health of each patient." But the Stinsons were not persuaded. "Andrew is interesting to them in some detached way—their own private research project, conveniently underage so that they need no consent for whatever it is that they do. . . . Of course, they don't see it that way; they're saving the life of an unfortunate child. . . . And if it looks like Andrew can't be saved? Why stop there? They're still learning something." Health care in a tertiary center "could be a mask—a partial truth—which covers, however unintended, the research which is just as much a reason for [its] being."[51]

For the Stinsons the entire episode amounted to an unprecedented loss of control. "[Dr.] Farrell controls Andrew's life," Robert noted angrily. And Peggy repeatedly lamented that "everything is out of control. I am out of control. Even the disaster itself is out of control. . . . Andrew is not our baby any more—he's been taken over by a medical bureaucracy." This loss of control was all the more difficult for them to accept in light of *Roe v. Wade*. "A woman can terminate a perfectly healthy pregnancy by abortion at $24\frac{1}{2}$ weeks and that is legal," observed Peggy. "Nature can terminate a problem pregnancy by miscarriage at $24\frac{1}{2}$ weeks and the baby must be saved at all cost; anything less is illegal and immoral." It seemed hopeless to try to explain these points to the hospital staff. "We're irrelevant, just an annoyance, people for them all to patronize and categorize, and then shake their heads about."[52]

In their effort to cope, the Stinsons sought psychological counseling, and their therapist, as they report it, helped promote a sense of control: "You have been powerless. You have to get back in power." Apparently, the therapy helped, and toward the end of Andrew's six-month life, Peggy became pregnant again. The Stinsons interpreted the event as a symbolic victory: "The new baby is an act of will; we take control again."[53]

The Stinsons' account, as would be expected, struck a sympathetic cord in many of its readers (and eventually in many of the viewers of an adapted television program). The book jacket had a blurb from Raymond Duff that people should "apply the lessons from this classic story of irony and tragedy in modern medicine" and another from

Daniel Callahan that this was the story of "extraordinarily sensitive parents coping with a grievous moral problem." The doctors had apparently allowed "technological enthusiasm" to triumph over "human care." Two well-known ethicists, Peter Singer and Helga Kuhse, reviewed the book very favorably, applauding the Stinsons for sharing their ordeal with the readers.[34] Without doubt, many of the Stinsons' criticisms were on target and devastating: the alien character of the hospital setting, the frustrations of following house-staff rotations, and the arrogance of the senior physicians. Their story helps us understand the impulse to elevate the rights of parents against doctors, and by extension, the rights of patients against doctors. It also clarifies why, despite the very strong case that can be made in support of Andrew's doctors, physicians were destined to cede authority to a variety of third parties.

Like the film version of the John Hopkins case, *The Long Dying of Baby Andrew* is designed to impart a particular lesson and empower the Stinsons (and patients) against their doctors. But again, like the film, it is less than clear what this book actually represents. Ostensibly it is the diaries that the Stinsons kept; however, they themselves concede that it is not the complete and actual record, but an edited version, containing only what they have chosen to tell the reader. How many of the book's entries are tailored to make the case, to get revenge at the doctors, we cannot know (and the Stinsons are unwilling to allow an independent examination of the original entries). The opening sections of the journal, for example, do not have a ring of authenticity; it is doubtful that a woman who had never before kept a diary would start one when she began to hemorrhage in her fifth month of pregnancy and anticipated an immediate miscarriage. Nor is it likely that a parent given favorable news about her baby's prospects would on the spot react as skeptically as Peggy did. Rather, one suspects that much of the journal was written with the benefit of hindsight, reviewing the events when the outcome was known, when Andrew turned out to be a losing case.

It is important to keep these doubts in mind, for if we are to reverse the angle of vision and analyze these same events from the perspective of Andrew's physicians, a very different message emerges. After the fact, it is easy to fault physicians for making decisions to treat over parental objections. But go back to the start, bracket the ending, and simple judgments become complicated.

An 800-gram baby born in December 1976 was a newborn with a slim but real chance of survival. Hospitals with infant ICUs on a par with Philadelphia's, like University Hospital in Cleveland, had survival rates of 47 percent in infants between 501 and 1,000 grams.[55] Andrew, it is true, was born very early in the pregnancy, which reduced the odds, but not to the point of hopelessness. A range of neonatal units reported 10 percent success even here, and the Philadelphia hospital may well have been better equipped to treat such cases. What then were the physicians to do? The parents clearly did not want treatment; expecting an aborted fetus, they were having trouble coping with the fact of a breathing infant. But the first crisis of a fluid imbalance seemed to the doctors manageable, and the initial use of the respirator, reasonable; and the doctors were comfortable in not allowing the parents' displeasure to seal the fate of the infant. Over the next several months, when the prognosis for Andrew became more guarded and then dismal, the doctors had great difficulty in backing off—perhaps because the law on terminating treatment was still primitive; because neonatal units have a fierce protreatment ideology; or because the doctors did not want these parents, who had stopped visiting Andrew and were looking for ways to terminate their parental obligations, to be proven right. But being wrong in March or May was not the same as being wrong in December.

After all, what was at the root of the parents' case to terminate treatment? What arguments did they make to the doctors? Most of them had less to do with Andrew and more to do with their own concerns, such as their family, careers, and financial situation. From their perspective, the demands that Andrew would place on the family would deprive his older sister (and future siblings) of a fair share of parental attention. As Andrew's treatment persisted, the Stinsons faced the prospect that his hospitalization would outrun their medical coverage. Robert raised this possibility with one of the physicians, asking him whether, in the event of bankruptcy, he would lose his house. "I wanted to shock him into seeing how extensive and unrealized the consequences of his pursuit were, but he shocked me instead. 'I guess they will,' was all he said. . . . The social or financial consequences of his work, being literally beyond the glass walls of the IICU, are just not real to him. The unit is sterile and intensive in more ways than one thinks." Concluded Robert: "These doctors go on righteously about their business while our lives fall apart."[56]

Clearly, the physicians were not inclined to worry about the Stinson house or Andrew's impact on the Stinson family, however dismaying the predicament. Andrew was the patient, not the parents or the sister, and treatment decisions were not made with one eye on a bank account or the psychological state of siblings. Of course, the doctors should have been better at communicating uncertainties and much less arrogant. But these shortcomings notwithstanding, the crux of the problem was whether conditions external to the neonatal nursery should affect physicians' behavior in the neonatal nursery. The Stinsons insisted that the answer is yes—and Duff and others agreed. But then think of the objections of Cooke and Fost, and we are back to the deadlock of parental rights as against protection from harm.

However compelling the Stinsons' narrative, one has only to imagine a different set of circumstances to see its limits. What would have happened if Andrew had survived; if, despite his parents' reluctance to treat, the physicians had gone ahead and Andrew had made it through? The Stinsons would then have had no story. In other words, they got to publish their account precisely because this was one time (out of how many?) that the parents' reluctance to treat seemed justified by the end result. Had Andrew won, however, it would have been the physicians' turn to write about parents who quit too easily to be trusted with making treatment decisions, but even that would not have resolved the issues. In the end, the Stinsons found no one to trust, but neither does the reader. That Andrew lost does not support the case for parents' rights, any more than does the fact that other infants have won buttress the case for doctors.

Although the contest for control over neonatal decision making in the early 1970s did not yield definitive answers, it did exert a critical influence over how the larger issue of ruling medicine would be resolved. First, the era of the physician as unilateral decision·maker in the neonatal nursery (and elsewhere) was clearly over. It was still not apparent what combination of lawyers, legislators, administrators, bioethicists, patients, and parents would affect and control medical decision making. But whatever the mix, it was obvious that the ICU was no longer physicians' exclusive preserve. At the least, some kind of collective mechanism, along the line of the IRBs, was likely to come into place.

At the same time, the prospect was very real that politics would intrude. Whether spurred by reactions to *Roe v. Wade* or Section 504, the neonatal issues resonated with so many others that elected officials and candidates were likely to stake out a position that would win votes. Moreover, no organizations were at hand to reduce the controversies. In human experimentation, the NIH had been able to impose corrective action on the research community, and although the IRBs did not resolve all the social and ethical dilemmas and required a second round of redesign and reinvigoration (following on the exposés that Kennedy highlighted), still this mechanism defused, indeed depoliticized, the problem. Medicine, however, with no counterpart to the NIH, could not reach closure, and gave every opportunity for politicians to grandstand about medical cases.

Second, once the life-and-death decisions in the infant ICU were rendered visible, they could not again be buried. Some commentators tried to make the case for obfuscation, finding a virtue in maintaining unambiguous laws (such as ones condemning euthanasia) and ambiguous practices (such as letting some newborns die). But the curtain had lifted, the spotlight was trained, and there was very little room to maneuver.

Third, any policies adopted were likely to generate invective and hostility. There was no satisfying the views of all parties. Once the battleground for determining the limits of privacy against the state's protective power was the infant nursery, dissension was predictable. How unfortunate for physicians that the extraordinary tension between abortion, on the one hand, and protection for the handicapped, on the other, was fought out on their turf.

Finally, this encounter between physicians and outsiders helped frame what questions would be asked—or not asked—about medical decision making and neonatal care, and whose voice would be most prominent in answering them. Focusing on the Johns Hopkins case as prototypical meant that case-specific assessments of the morality of individual actions would dominate the intellectual and policy agenda, as though the only relevant considerations had to do with what happened in the neonatal nursery itself. The microissue—What should a doctor do about this baby?—not the macroissue—Are expenditures on the neonatal nursery the best use of social resources, or, why are most babies in the neonatal nursery from underprivileged families?—would be the focus of attention. Put another way, the Johns Hopkins case helped ensure that philosophy, not the social sciences, would become the preeminent discipline among academics coming into the field of medicine. This, in turn, meant that principles of individual ethics, not broader assessments of the exercise of power in society, would dominate the intellectual discourse around medicine. The meaning and implication of this fact will become more apparent as we examine the most celebrated of all the medical cases, the case of Karen Ann Quinlan.

CHAPTER 11

New Rules for the Bedside

THE culmination of the decade-long process of bringing strangers to the bedside came in the case of Karen Ann Quinlan. Its impact on opinion and policy outweighed even that of the scandals in human experimentation and the death of a newborn at Johns Hopkins. After Quinlan there was no disputing the fact that medical decision making was in the public domain and that a profession that had once ruled was now being ruled.

The bare facts of the case are well known and easily summarized. On the night of 15 April 1975, Karen Ann Quinlan, age twenty-two, was brought into a New Jersey hospital emergency room in a coma whose etiology was never fully explained and from which she never emerged. After several months of hoping against hope, her parents recognized that she would not recover, and they asked her doctors and the hospital, St. Clair's, to remove her from the respirator that had been assisting her breathing. Joseph and Julia Quinlan, practicing Catholics, had sought church guidance on the issue and had been told that respirator care was "extraordinary" and that returning Karen to her "natural state" (that is, taking her off the machine, even if she would then die) was a morally correct action. Although the Quinlans believed that their decision was in accord with the sentiments of Karen's doctors, the hospital denied their request. St. Clair's staff would not even consider removing Karen from the respirator unless a court formally appointed them Karen's legal guardians. Even then, the hospital reserved judgment, because by any criteria, including the Harvard brain-death standards, Karen was alive; and disconnecting her from the respirator—or "pulling the plug," as it came to be known in the popular jargon—might well violate the medical ethic to "do no harm" and open the doctors and the hospital to criminal prosecution for homicide.

The Quinlans went before the Superior Court of New Jersey to ask that Joseph be appointed Karen's guardian for the express purpose of requesting her removal from the respirator. In November 1975 the lower court rejected the petition, but the Quinlans appealed to the state's supreme court, which accepted the case. (Although the Quinlans did not initially know it, this court was especially active, having already ordered private hospitals to perform abortions and prohibited communities from using zoning statutes to exclude low- and moderate-income housing.)[1] The court heard arguments in January 1976, and on 31 March 1976 returned its verdict in support of the Quinlans. After another two months of wrangling with the hospital and the doctors, Karen was weaned from the respirator and transferred to a long-term-care facility. Despite predictions of imminent death, she survived, off the respirator, for another nine years.

Although the *Quinlan* case had many layers and contexts, legal, medical, theological, ethical, and popular, the heart of the decision involved not so much a patient's "right to die" but something more specific and elemental: Who ruled at the bedside? Strip away the rhetoric and the symbols, and the *Quinlan* case was a contest between physicians, on the one hand, and patients and their legal advocates, on the other. Once doctors had presumed to represent the patient's interest. With *Quinlan*, the role went, amazingly enough, to lawyers and judges.

Certainly, Joseph and Julia Quinlan experienced the shift to the legal arena. According to their account of the events, St. Clair's staff initially responded to their request to discontinue treatment matter-of-factly; the hospital had them sign a paper declaring: "We hereby authorize and direct Dr. Morse to discontinue all extraordinary measures, including the use of a respirator, for our daughter Karen Quinlan." The document noted that the physicians had explained all the consequences of the removal and were thereby released "from any and all liability." "When we left the hospital that night," Julia Quinlan recalled, "all I could think was Karen's ordeal is almost over. And so is ours." But the next day, Dr. Morse called Joseph Quinlan to tell him that he had a "moral problem" with the agreement, and he intended to consult a colleague; the day after, he called again to say he would not remove Karen from the respirator. When the Quinlans persevered and began to consider bringing the case to court, Paul Armstrong, about to become their lawyer, warned them not only of the extensive publicity that was likely to follow, but of the fact that "the medical profession is powerful, and they're not going to like an issue like this being taken to the courts."[2] The Quinlans, however, did not back off and so learned just how right he was.

In making the case for the Quinlans, Armstrong's briefs and oral presentation centered on Karen's (and her surrogate's) constitutional right to determine her own medical care. Relying on the expanded definition of privacy that the U.S. Supreme Court had established in 1965 in *Griswold v. Connecticut* (which guaranteed right of access to contraception) as well as *Roe v. Wade*, Armstrong argued that it is "the role and function of the physician to advise an individual of what his diagnosis is . . . that the physician should advise as to the nature of treatments that are available, what the options are. . . . Then that decision should be made either by the individual or his family."[3] The patient, not the doctor, was entitled to decide whether to pursue treatment.

The hospital and the physicians (as well as the state attorney general) took a different tack, not confronting the *Quinlan* argument directly but insisting that the court had no business interfering with physicians' medical judgments. "Removal of the respirator was not supported by accepted medical practice,"[4] and patients could not invoke the authority of the court to compel physicians to violate the Hippocratic oath. "No court . . . should require a physician to act in derogation of this sacred and time-honored oath."[5] In the past, judges had always "limited their review of the type of treatment prescribed by the physician to whether it was in accordance with ordinary medical practice and not to what the Court, in an exercise of its own judgment, determined to be the proper medical treatment." Thus, "plaintiff seeks relief which would inject the Court into the patient–physician relationship and override the medical treatment decided on by the treating physician."[6]

Leaving unclear whether the doctor or the patient had the last word in the examining room, the defendants insisted that the court did not belong there. "It's the decision of my client," argued the physicians' attorney, "that, from a philosophical point of view, they are opposed to the Court injecting itself into the relationship of the patient and the doctor; and the Court making a decision, so to speak, as to who shall live and who shall die." The attorney general agreed: "I think the difficulty that we have seen here today, and throughout the trial period of the case, demonstrates why, in my judgment, these problems should be left . . . to the medical profession."[7] In essence, the lower court had found that this was "a medical decision, not a judicial one," and the higher court ought to respect the ruling.

On 31 March 1976 the court handed down its opinion in a case it rightly labeled of "transcendent importance." First, it authorized the Quinlan family to have Karen taken off the respirator. Second, and no less remarkable and precedent setting, it installed judges at the bedside, allowing them to instruct doctors in what might or might not be done in the realm of treatment.

The court accepted Armstrong's argument, built on *Roe v. Wade*, that a constitutionally protected right to privacy overlay the doctor–patient relationship. "Presumably," declared the court, "this right is broad enough to encompass a patient's decision to decline medical treatment under certain circumstances, in much the same way that it is broad enough to encompass a woman's decision to terminate pregnancy un-der certain conditions." Nevertheless, the patient's right to privacy was not absolute; in the case of abortion, for example, the right carried little weight in the third trimester of a pregnancy. Thus, the court had to decide the degree to which the Quinlans' privacy rights were to be balanced or compromised by other considerations—namely, the inter-est of the state in preserving life and in allowing physicians to exercise their best professional judgment.[8]

Given the facts of the *Quinlan* case, the court disposed quickly of the state-interest question: "We think that the State's interest *contra* [withdrawal from the respirator] weakens and the individual's right to privacy grows as the degree of bodily invasion increases and the prognosis dims. Ultimately there comes a point at which the indivi-dual's rights overcome the State interest." And Karen Quinlan in a persistent vegetative state and on a respirator seemed to have reached the point.[9]

What of society's stake in the autonomy of the medical profession, and the charge that the court's "premise [in favor of withdrawal] unwarrantly offends prevailing medical standards?" The truly difficult issue was whether the court could dare to tell physicians how to treat, or not to treat, their patients. The court confronted the challenge of the *Quinlan* case head-on, insisting that the questions raised transcended medical authority. Whatever the physicians' prerogatives, judges should not be prevented from "deciding matters clearly justiciable nor preclude a re-examination by the Court as to underlying human values and rights." The court went even further, declaring that social values and medical values might well diverge, and then, medical practice "must, in the ultimate, be responsive not only to the concepts of medicine but also to the common moral judgment of the community at large." Who was to decide when such a conflict existed and how it should be resolved? The court, for it, and not physicians, was best situated to define and implement community standards.[10]

Such declarations notwithstanding, the court conceded that it still might seem daring or foolhardy for judges "having no inherent expertise . . . to overrule a professional decision made according to prevailing medical practice and standards." How could a court, then, have the temerity to contravene medical practice and medical ethics and order treatment to be discontinued? How could it substitute legal rulings for bedside ethics? The answer was by impeaching medicine; that is, by insisting that what doctors testified to in court and what they did at the bedside were two different things, and that physicians' efforts to smooth over the contradictions were lame. "The question," as the court framed it, "is whether there is such internal consistency and rationality in the application of such standards as should warrant their constituting an ineluctable bar to the effectuation of substantive relief for plaintiff at the hands of the court. We have concluded not."[11]

The court reasoned that while the principles of medical ethics required that physicians not remove life-preserving technologies from patients, the realities of medical practice revealed a "widening ambiguity," as evidenced by the fact that physicians refrained from putting hopelessly ill patients on advanced support systems or resuscitating them when they breathed what should have been their last breath. Doctors, in other words, did "distinguish between curing the ill and comforting and easing the dying," and to this latter end they were ready to use "judicious neglect" by writing in pencil on a patient's chart "the foreboding initials DNR [Do Not Resuscitate]."[12]

Admittedly, physicians saw no conflict between their standards and their practices. Dr. Morse, and the other physicians who testified on his behalf, scrupulously differentiated between withholding treatment in the hopeless case, which was allowable, and withdrawing treatment from the hopeless case, which ostensibly was not. They accepted sins of omission and condemned sins of commission. But the court was unimpressed with the reasoning: "The thread of logic in such distinctions may be elusive to the non-medical lay mind," for the end result was the same—whether by an act of commission or of omission, the patient died.

Why, then, were physicians in general so determined to maintain this distinction, and why, in the *Quinlan* case in particular, were they so unwilling to do for Karen Ann Quinlan what they did as a matter of course for other patients? The reason, concluded the court, had to do with physicians' fears of malpractice suits or, worse yet, of criminal prosecution. Put another way, self-interest and the fear of sanctions, not medical principle or an ethical commitment, explained their refusal to accede to the Quinlans' request. The court, therefore, took as its self-imposed duty to find "a way to free physicians, in the pursuit of their healing vocation, from possible contamination by self-interest or self-protection."[13]

The effort turned out to be more than a little confused and less than appreciated. Just as neonatologists had settled for agreement on process when agreement on substance was impossible, so did the *Quinlan* court. It called for the establishment of hospital ethics committees, expecting this mechanism to resolve the dilemma. The inspiration for its proposal was a 1975 *Baylor Law Review* article by Karen Teel, a pediatrician. Teel contended that physicians assumed unwarranted responsibility and risk in making difficult ethical decisions, for they were "ill-equipped" on intellectual grounds and, "knowingly or not, assumed civil and criminal liability." Along with a growing number of physicians, she recommended that they share responsibility with a formally constituted body, "an Ethics Committee composed of physicians, social workers, attorneys, and theologians." This committee would not only bring a new and valuable dialogue to medical decision making but appropriately, from a legal point of view, share and divide responsibility.[14]

The court took up Teel's suggestion, but with less interest in ensuring the interdisciplinary character of the committee than in promoting "the diffusion of professional responsibility for [termination] decisions, comparable in a way to the value of multi-judge courts in finally resolving on appeal difficult questions of law."[15] Without acknowledging it, however, the court transformed Teel's committee into a prognosis committee, charging it to decide not the ethical issues of a case but the narrower technical question of whether the patient was in a chronic vegetative state. If the committee found she was, the physicians could then remove her from the respirator "without any civil or criminal liability." Through this innovation, the court expected to rescue medicine from its internal contradictions. Once the committees were functioning, physicians would not have to worry about liability, and judges would not have to review decisions to terminate treatment.

The *Quinlan* case, in the tradition of Beecher and Duff and Campbell, exposed a well-hidden secret. Despite a rhetorical commitment to the maxims of "do no harm" and "preserve life," doctors had been in the business of managing death and, until now at least, doing so very much on their own. Writing on the op-ed page of the *New York Times* in 1975, Michael Halberstam, a practicing physician in Washington, D.C., expressed surprise that the case "is in court at all. Each day, hundreds, perhaps thousands, of similar dilemmas present themselves. . . . The decisions are difficult, often agonizing, but they are reached in hospital corridors and in waiting rooms, not courts." The *Quinlan* case, in other words, "represents a failure of the usual—often unspoken deliberately ambiguous—steps in caring for such a patient."[16] Halberstam expected that physicians would not change their pattern of "tacit cooperation with reality"; but, in fact, *Quinlan* changed the reality to make tacit cooperation suspect. Decisions to terminate or withdraw treatment that individual physicians had once made covertly now would take place before an audience. The stage was likely to be a courtroom, and lawyers and judges, the leading actors.

Not surprisingly, many physicians reacted hostilely to the decision, finding *Quinlan* an egregious example of the subversion of their professional discretion. A 1975 editorial in *JAMA*, actually written by a bioethicist, Richard McCormick, distorted the case to make this point. McCormick argued that "decision-making within health care, if it is to remain truly human . . . must be controlled primarily within the patient–doctor–family relationship, and these decisions must be tailor-made to individual cases and circumstances. If technology and law were largely to usurp these prerogatives—as they threaten to do as a result of the *Quinlan* case—we would all be the worse off."[17] (One could not know from his comments that the physicians had acted against the family, and that lawmakers were attempting to limit technology.) Physicians interviewed by the news weeklies generally voiced their opposition. A neurologist from the Massachusetts General Hospital (MGH) complained that to allow courts to make such decisions "is taking the judgment of a doctor and putting it in the hands of those not competent to make a decision."[18] A colleague from the University of Chicago insisted that "a court cannot decide in total detail what a physician is to do."[19] Even Dr. Teel, whose article the *Quinlan* court had cited, distanced herself from the opinion. Ethics committees were still a very novel and untested idea: "There are a lot of problems and I'd like to see them ironed out before everyone feels they must jump on ethics committees as the way to handle tough medical cases."[20]

With public scrutiny heightened, a few hospitals took steps to bring greater formality to the decision-making process. The *Quinlan* decision became the occasion for setting up committees to advise and review termination decisions and to formulate guidelines for individual physicians. But these measures represented more of an effort at damage control than an enthusiastic embracing of a new style of practice. Thus, the Massachusetts General Hospital administrators appointed an ad hoc committee to study "how best to manage the hopelessly ill patient," appointing to it a psychiatrist, two physicians, a nursing administrator, a layperson (who had recovered from cancer), and, in a wonderfully distancing phrase, "legal counsel." The committee recommended, and the MGH established, a four-point patient-classification system, ranging from A ("Maximal therapeutic effort without reservation") to D ("all therapy can be discontinued"), which would be "generally reserved for patients with brain death or when there is no reasonable possibility that the patient will return to a cognitive and sapient life." The MGH also organized an Optimum Care Committee to advise "in situations where difficulties arise in deciding the appropriateness of continuing intensive therapy for critically ill patients." The committee, however, met only at the request of the attending physician, and its recommendation went back to this physician, who was free to accept or reject its advice. In a six-month pilot trial of the system in 1976, the committee members reported that "requests for . . . consultation have been rare." They had reviewed the cases of fifteen patients, clarifying misunderstandings, reopening lines of communication, and, by their own estimate, "above all, maximizing support for the responsible physician who makes the medical decision to intensify, maintain or limit effort at reversing the illness."[21]

Boston's Beth Israel Hospital, also citing *Quinlan,* drew up guidelines for ordering a DNR code for a patient. When a physician believed a patient to be "irreversibly and irreparably ill," with death "imminent" (that is, likely to occur within two weeks), the physician could elect to discuss with an ad hoc committee, composed exclusively of doctors, whether death was so certain that resuscitation would serve no purpose. If the committee members unanimously agreed, and the competent patient made it his or her "informed choice," then a DNR order would be entered in the patient's chart; should the patient be incompetent, the physician was to obtain the approval of the family and then enter the order.[22]

Even these innovative measures were implemented with great caution and were not readily adopted in other settings. Both the MGH and Beth Israel committees were dominated by physicians and deferred to the "responsible physician." The MGH code did not emphasize the need to obtain the consent of the competent patient, and Beth Israel did not address the more general issue of termination or withdrawal of treatment. Nevertheless, even these modest innovations remained the exception and drew vigorous attacks. Most hospitals did not adopt guidelines or establish committees, and traditionalistic physicians disdained the new measures. "I am at a loss," observed one doctor, "to understand the need for the various [MGH] committees . . . if the final decision rests with the 'responsible physician.' " As for the Beth Israel

DNR guidelines, "I shudder to think of the innumerable unsalvageable poor souls who would undergo the assault of modern medical technology while awaiting the assemblance of an ad hoc committee . . . who could allow them the dignity of a peaceful departure from this world."[23] Another physician criticized the Beth Israel stipulation that physicians obtain the permission of the competent patient before writing a code: "The consultant-committee requirements are regrettable, but the requirement for the informed consent of the patient is intolerable. It is no longer enough that we let the terminal patient know that his prognosis is grave; he must know that it is utterly hopeless, and he must completely agree with us. If we allow him a slim thread of hope, if he persists in his natural denial of death, he must spend his last moments with someone pounding on his chest 60 times a minute."[24]

In effect, physicians and their institutions did not react any more forcefully to the *Quinlan* case and its aftermath than they had to the Johns Hopkins case and its aftermath. A handful of academic medical centers moved haltingly to meet the challenge, but they did not become the models for emulation. More typically, the professional response amounted to a repetition of now familiar refrains: Trust to the doctor and do not intrude on the doctor–patient relationship. Keep courts and formally constituted committees out of the ICU. But these wishes were destined not to be respected by attorneys, judges, or the patients themselves.

Soon after the *Quinlan* decision came down, the *NEJM* ran an editorial entitled "Terminating Life Support: Out of the Closet," written by a professor at Harvard Law School, Charles Fried. The fact that a lawyer authored a column normally reserved for doctors reinforced its very argument. "That [life-prolonging] measures are in fact regularly withheld or withdrawn is an open secret," observed Fried, "but the course of decision and the testimony in the *Quinlan* case show how wary the medical profession can be when the spotlight of publicity illuminates its practices." However uneasy the physicians were, Fried was certain that lawyers would have "the last word." Conceding that lawyers had typically been involved in medicine through malpractice litigation, and that they had not "been a constructive force in the shaping of the relation of the public to the health professions," Fried

STRANGERS AT THE BEDSIDE

contended that "for better or for worse we still shall have to fall back
on the lawyers' skills, for they are not only an unavoidable nuisance
but the professional adjuvants of the ordinary citizen's autonomy, particularly when this autonomy is threatened by complexity or adver-
sity."[25] Fried spotted what the physicians had missed: that lawyers and
judges had not pursued some imperialistic imperative and invaded
medicine's domain but, rather, were in alliance with patients in an
effort to right an imbalance of power and establish the principles of
patient autonomy. This process, shrewdly concluded Fried, would continue. *Quinlan* was a portent of things to come.

His prediction was quickly borne out, for *Quinlan* sparked a new
and more sustained involvement of lawyers and judges in medical decision making. It had little in common with compensation-minded malpractice litigation, which only looked back on events to see whether
harms had occurred. It was closer to the type of law inspired by human
experimentation, especially the substantial case law and legal analyses
devoted to informed consent. To be sure, decisions around transplantation had found their way into the courts, with judges ruling that
parents could have one child donate a kidney to another. On occasion,
so too had withdrawal of treatment issues; for example, in the aftermath of the Johns Hopkins case, a judge in Maine had ordered treatment for a handicapped newborn. But all of these interventions were
completely overshadowed by the fallout from the *Quinlan* decision.
What had been exceptional now became the rule.

After *Quinlan* a self-perpetuating dynamic took hold. Hospitals that
attempted to alter practice in accordance with the ruling required the
services of a lawyer to insure that it was on the right track. Thus, both
the MGH and Beth Israel, as Fried noted, had used lawyers to help
them design their new procedures. Moreover, the *Quinlan* decision provoked questions, analyses, and then in short order, more decisions.
Here was a far-reaching case replete with ambiguities and covered with
maximum intensity in the press—the only cases more prominent were
the Supreme Court decisions in *Brown v. Board of Education* and *Roe
v. Wade*. If physicians took comfort in the gaps that the *Quinlan* case
left open, the lawyers rushed in to fill them. Just as nature abhors
a vacuum, legal minds abhor contradictory standards or confusing
stipulations, and *Quinlan* had more than its fair share of them.

232

Hence, it served as the bridge for lawyers and judges to cross over into medicine.

Take the matter of ethics committees. The *Quinlan* court had responded by the seat of its pants—apparently unaware, to judge by an absence of references, that ethics committees had first been discussed in the context of treatment decisions for newborns. The decision cited Dr. Teel, but her *Baylor Law Journal* article was not so much an article as a short and highly general comment inspired by the Johns Hopkins baby case. Teel did not set out a model for the committees, and she was astonished that the court had picked her suggestion. She got the idea, she later remarked, from a program on educational television (probably the film about the Johns Hopkins baby) and had even expressed some reservations about it in the piece itself. Thus, the court left open even more questions than it answered. "The ethics committee aspect of the *Quinlan* decision is the subject of much confusion, disagreement, and concern," noted a *Rutgers Law Review* article. "For example, would the role of such a body be solely advisory or would its determinations be mandatory? What should be its composition— totally professional or representative of various disciplines? Who should select the members? . . . And of particular importance, is the requirement of committee concurrence in a termination decision reached by a physician and family or guardian constitutional?"[26] The court not only failed to define the role and duties of such a committee, but actually compounded the confusion by mixing ethics with prognosis. Were the committees to address moral values or neurological outcomes? Was this a committee to evaluate the wishes of the patient or the accuracy of medical predictions? The *Quinlan* decision obfuscated the issues, inviting others to clarify them.

Not only the substance but the fact of *Quinlan* set off a reaction that brought more such cases to court, expanding the direct involvement of law in medical decision making. Although the ruling of a New Jersey court was not binding in any other jurisdiction, cautious and prudent physicians and hospital directors elsewhere were soon preparing to go to court rather than unilaterally terminate treatment. Less than a month after *Quinlan*, a Massachusetts court (in the case of *Superintendent of Belchertown State School v. Saikewicz*) was asked by the superintendent of a state school for the retarded to decide whether chemotherapy could

STRANGERS AT THE BEDSIDE

be withheld from a mentally retarded adult suffering from leukemia, particularly when similarly situated nonretarded adults would almost certainly take the treatment. The Massachusetts court not only found the issue justiciable and ruled that such withholding of treatment was permissible, but went on to say, even more vigorously than *Quinlan*, that these questions had to come before a court. As against the *Quinlan* court's expectation that ethics committees would obviate judicial involvement, the Massachusetts court insisted:

> We take a dim view of any attempt to shift the ultimate decision-making responsibility away from the duly established courts of proper jurisdiction to any committee, panel or group, ad hoc or permanent. . . . We do not view the judicial resolution of this most difficult and awesome question—whether potentially life-prolonging treatment should be withheld from a person incapable of making his own decision—as constituting a "gratuitous encroachment" on the domain of medical expertise. Rather, such questions of life and death seem to us to require the process of detached but passionate investigation and decision that forms the ideal on which the judicial branch of government was created. Achieving this ideal is our responsibility and that of the lower court, and is not to be entrusted to any other group purporting to represent the "morality and conscience of our society" no matter how highly motivated or impressively constituted.[27]

Once the secret was out, a number of judges defined themselves as the properly constituted authority to render such decisions, unwilling to rely on ad hoc groups with ad hoc procedures.

Not surprisingly, the *Saikewicz* decision infuriated and frightened physicians. Arnold Relman, who succeeded Ingelfinger as the editor of the *NEJM*, could reconcile *Quinlan* with traditional medical ethics, for the court assumed that doctors and patients (if not the doctor alone) should reach life-and-death decisions. But *Saikewicz* represented an all-out war on physicians' authority. The decision, declared Relman, left "no possible doubt of its total distrust of physicians' judgment in such matters. . . . Physicians must not be allowed to use their own professional judgment, but should be guided instead by government regulation." Unhappily, but very accurately, he concluded: "This astonishing opinion can only be viewed as a resounding vote of 'no confidence' in the abilities of physicians and families to act in the best interest of the incapable patient suffering from terminal illness. . . . The court thus asserts in effect that its duty is not simply to remedy abuses and settle disagreements that arise in the practice of medicine but also to take routine responsibility for certain types of medical decisions frequently needed for terminally or hopelessly ill patients."[28]

To be sure, a number of legal scholars and judges shared Relman's conviction that the court was the wrong forum for resolving these issues. They objected to the interventionist position of *Quinlan* and, even more so, of *Saikewicz*, and they were not at all content with so ill-defined a creature as an ethics committee. But the outlook of even these critics was much closer to that of their legal colleagues than that of physicians, for they, too, were unwilling to trust to the discretion of the physician without formulating coherent procedures and a body of agreed-upon principles. They preferred that the legislature, not the court, set policy, but from medicine's perspective that was a minor distinction. For whatever the disagreements among lawyers and judges about the specifics of *Quinlan* and *Saikewicz*, they all wished to narrow the discretion of physicians and enhance predictability through formal rules and regulations.

An example that aptly illustrates both the dynamic set off by the *Quinlan* case and what it means to bring a legal mind-set into medicine, is the grand jury investigation and report of the DNR procedures in effect at New York's La Guardia Hospital as of 1983.[29] The facts of the case were not as unique as one might expect. (An almost exact replay took place several years later at New York Hospital.) Mrs. M., a seventy-eight-year-old woman, was on a respirator in the hospital's ICU, suffering from breathing difficulties of uncertain cause, with no diagnosis of a terminal illness. Although she may have on a few occasions tried to disconnect her respirator, neither she nor her family had asked that treatment be discontinued or given any indication that she wished to die. One night Mrs. M. was found off the respirator (the tube neatly wrapped under her pillow and the monitor alarm turned off) and in the midst of a cardiac arrest. The medical student on duty in the ICU, according to the grand jury finding, "began administering closed chest massage while the nurse reconnected the tubing. Another nurse arrived and asked the student whether she should call a 'Code 33' emergency, the hospital's signal for all available personnel to respond and administer cardiopulmonary resuscitation. . . . As the nurse started to do so, the student indicated that Mrs. M. was not to be coded. According to the testimony of both nurses, the medical student said: 'What am I doing? She's a no-code,' and then ceased the cardiac massage." Mrs. M. died a few minutes later. The next morning the hospital told the patient's relatives that everything possible had been done for her, but an anonymous phone call to the family from someone who identified herself as a nurse at the hospital reported that the patient "had died 'unnecessarily' because 'a no-code' was sent out."

The grand jury investigation did not resolve precisely what happened that night—the medical student denied the nurses' version, and there was no finding on who disconnected the respirator. But the grand jury did evaluate the procedures around the DNR code and found "shocking procedural abuses." The system was arbitrary, capricious, and without accountability. The hospital officials, reported the grand jury, prohibited "any written mention of [DNR] orders on the patients' charts. Instead they instituted a process of designating 'no code' patients by affixing so-called 'purple dots' to file cards which were kept solely by the nurses and only until the particular patient died or was discharged. . . . As a result, the 'no-code' order could never be attributed to any physician and the only record of it would disappear after it was carried out." There was also "no officially formulated policy which required physicians to obtain consent from, or even inform, the patient or his family before the 'no-code' order was given."

The grand jury response, with a good deal of guidance from the state's attorneys, exemplified both the strength of the patient–lawyer alliance around autonomy and the differences between a legal and medical orientation. The grand jury recommended, first, that DNR decisions "be reached jointly" by the physician and the patient; so significant a measure could not be entrusted to the physician alone. Recognizing that many doctors believed that this consultative requirement was a cruel burden to put on a dying patient, the grand jury still insisted that it was an essential aspect of patients' rights and that doctors must not have the authority to decide unilaterally who should be resuscitated and who should be left to die. Second, although the grand jury did not want to impose rigid rules on hospitals—recognizing that all patients were not alike—and did not want to define precisely all the circumstances under which it was proper not to resuscitate a patient, it did insist on "explicit procedural safeguards to prevent the decision from being made carelessly, unilaterally or anonymously." DNR decisions were to be "accurately and permanently documented," entered on the patient's chart, and signed by the responsible physician.

The La Guardia report did not immediately accomplish its aims. Not long afterward, a New York daily newspaper published a photograph surreptitiously taken of Memorial Hospital's "confidential" chalkboard entries of which patients should be treated with maximum therapy and which should not; and New York Hospital faced a well-publicized suit when its staff not only refused to resuscitate a woman patient but prevented her nephew, a doctor who by coincidence was at her bedside when she arrested, from doing so. But the grand jury report, by publicizing how haphazard DNR standards were and recommending more rigorous procedures, helped reduce the tolerance for the individual exercise of discretion without accountability—what physicians considered the exercise of professional discretion. Within a few years New York became one of many states that required extensive consultation with patients, properly executed forms, and properly annotated charts before a patient could be coded DNR.

The *Quinlan* case also helped make medical decision making the stuff of everyday, popular discourse, which had the effect of strengthening the alliance of lawyer and patient against the doctor and the hospital and bringing still more forms, and more formality, to medicine. The case of Brother Fox demonstrates the process at work. A member of a Catholic religious order, Brother Fox, in 1979, at the age of eighty-three, underwent a hernia operation. In the course of the procedure, he suffered a cardiac arrest, and the loss of oxygen to the brain left him in a persistent vegetative state. The brothers in his order asked the hospital officials to disconnect his respirator, which they refused to do without court permission. At the subsequent hearing, the brothers explained that right after the *Quinlan* case, their community, including

Brother Fox, held lengthy discussions about the ethics of withdrawal of treatment, and Brother Fox had firmly stated that were he ever to fall into such a state, he would want the respirator disconnected.[30]

The discussions that Brother Fox and his religious community conducted formally, many other Americans conducted informally, for *Quinlan* took the issue of termination of treatment not only into law review journals but magazines on supermarket racks. The case had almost every necessary ingredient for capturing public and media attention. It had elements of a good-girl-gone-bad story—a twenty-two-year-old from a devout Catholic family who may have used drugs. It also had a grade-B horror-movie quality: Why had Karen Ann Quinlan fallen into a coma, and was there any chance she would awake from it? But perhaps most important, Quinlan's case personalized an issue that had previously seemed abstract. It was one thing for Senator Mondale to inveigh against the future implications of medical technology, but quite another to think about Karen—and to a remarkable degree this became the story of Karen, to the point that even the court decision referred to her by her first name. There she lay, tethered to a machine that kept her alive for no purpose.

Although the media tended to frame the story as a case of the "right to die," as though the villain in the story was the respirator technology itself, many people understood that the real issue at stake was who ruled at the bedside. The cautionary lesson that emerged from *Quinlan* was the need for individuals to find a way to have their wishes respected. Almost no one argued against the Quinlan family's request; the overwhelming majority of the public agreed that families "ought to be able to tell doctors to remove all life-support services and let the patient die." (In 1977, 66 percent of respondents to a poll by Lou Harris approved the proposition and 15 percent were undecided; four years later, 73 percent approved and only 4 percent were undecided.)[31] Rather, the pressing issue was how to avoid the Quinlans' predicament.

The answers were not long in coming. In casual ways, people expressed their preferences to family and friends, more or less as Brother Fox had done. (Numbers here are imprecise, but when termination-of-treatment cases entered the courtroom, judges certainly assumed that once-competent patients would have expressed a preference, and relatives and friends often reported that they had.) There was also mounting interest in more formal documents, such as "living wills." The idea of an advance directive by which individuals could instruct physicians not to use heroic treatment in the event of terminal illness grew apace with respirators and intensive care units. In the early 1970s, the Euthanasia Educational Council drew up a model living will, and when the "Dear Abby" column described it, 50,000 people wrote in for a copy. In April 1974, Dr. Walter Modell published in the *NEJM* a one-page directive "On Medical Intervention." "Because medical advances have outdistanced our expected forms of ethical behavior," the form read, "I believe it is therefore wise to establish an order of preference which can be used to guide those physicians who care for me." Two months later, the *New York Times* Sunday magazine devoted an article to the living will, under the banner: "Thousands have signed a document that says, in effect: If I'm terminally ill, pull the plug." But in these first appearances, the living will was highly controversial. A number of leaders in gerontology and thanatology, concerned that people in good health would be making wrong-headed decisions about what they might want done when they were in poor health, condemned it as a "cop-out."[32]

The *Quinlan* case brought a more favorable consensus and new popularity to the living will. Sissela Bok, a philosopher interested in health policy, explored the "Personal Directions for Care at the End of Life" in the *New England Journal of Medicine*, openly seeking to empower the patient (through a legal document) against the physician and the hospital. "The plight of Karen Quinlan and her family," declared Bok, "touched many readers. More than the fear of death itself, it is the fear of lingering before death and of creating heavy burdens for families that troubles many. . . . Accordingly, a growing number of persons are now signing statements, often known as Living Wills, requesting that their lives not be unduly prolonged under certain conditions." Although the legal status of such documents was uncertain, Bok believed that they should guide physicians' decisions, and she offered a model form:

I,_____, want to participate in my own medical care as long as I am able. But I recognize that an accident or illness may someday make me unable to do so. . . . If my death is near and cannot be avoided . . . I do not want to have my life prolonged. I would then ask not to be subjected to surgery or resuscitation. Nor would I then wish to have life support from mechanical ventilators, intensive care services, or other life prolonging procedures.[33]

Bok insisted that the general tenor of the document was as important as the specific stipulations. As befit the contentious quality of so many of the cases, her first point was that a living will "should use a tone of requesting what is one's due rather than a tone of pleading or begging for consideration." The living will was an expression of a patient's rights—the right to die was part of a right to "participate" in medical care, not only while competent, but even when incompetent.

Neither the real nor the symbolic quality of the living will was lost on doctors. One oncologist suggested an alternative model:

> I . . . having been under the care of my physician for a reasonable enough time to realize that he is compassionate, skilled and has my best interests at heart, in the event my conditions become critical and death appears imminent, trust him to continue to act in this manner. . . . I believe he is my best advocate in matters relating to my care. . . . He is a friend and understands my feelings. I do not wish to place potential and real barriers between myself and him by authorizing a third party to act on my behalf.[34]

That the document has the aura of a parody, if not fantasy, demonstrates both the degree to which doctors had actually become strangers (the phrases about friendship and feelings ring hollow) and the extent to which medical paternalism had lost legitimacy.[35] Thus, the reactions to the *Quinlan* case drew on and reinforced the ideology of patients' rights. The living will took its place alongside the AHA Patient Bill of Rights in asserting the new stand against doctors.

These attitudes also increased the pressure on legislatures to regulate medical decision making at the end of life. By the mid-1970s, some dozen states had enacted brain-death statutes, but the fallout from *Quinlan* and similar cases brought to the fore issues that bore even more intimately on the doctor–patient relationship. For one thing, the courts kept asking for legislative guidance in this area. Although a number of judges were ready to pronounce on termination of treatment, they consistently urged the state to enact legislation clarifying the duties and responsibilities of physicians and eliminating the fears of civil or criminal liability. Even the *Saikewicz* court, for example, refrained from formulating comprehensive guidelines to govern the treatment of incompetent patients, insisting that this effort should be left to the legislative branch. For another, the popular interest in living wills prompted calls for legislation that would make the documents binding on doctors and hospitals.

A few months after the *Quinlan* decision, California enacted a living will statute, and although its many qualifications made the document very difficult to use—the patient had to be suffering from a terminal disease, the living will could not be over five years old, and it must have been reexecuted no sooner than fourteen days after the patient learned about a terminal disease—it was still perceived as moving in the right direction. The living will now had legal standing as "the final expression of [the patient's] legal right to refuse medical or surgical treatment and accept the consequences from such refusal," and it absolved physicians who followed the will's instructions from charges of homicide. (It also protected next of kin from losing insurance benefits cancelable in the event of suicide.)[36] To be sure, there were good reasons for legislators to avoid acting on termination of treatment, for the potential to antagonize one or another religious group or state medical association was considerable. Nevertheless, after *Quinlan* it was not only the courts but the legislatures that entered medicine, typically to the end of expanding patient choices and narrowing physician authority.

Finally, the *Quinlan* case not only brought new players into the realm of medical decision making but solidified the position of one group of outsiders already there, namely, the bioethicists. After *Quinlan*, the bioethics movement in the United States had a vitality and a standing that were in every way remarkable. Every national commission addressing medical issues would have among its members a bioethicist, and no media account of a medical breakthrough would be complete without a bioethicist commenting on its implications. Within the decade, most medical schools would have a philosopher teaching a course on bioethics, and many tertiary care centers would have bioethicists serving on one or another of its critical care, IRB, transplant, or human reproduction committees. Once it was assumed that anyone on ward rounds who was not wearing a white coat was a chaplain; after *Quinlan*, he or she was assumed to be a bioethicist.

Renee Fox, one of the leading contemporary medical sociologists, was among the first to analyze this change and to decry both the methods and intellectual assumptions of bioethics. The very year of the *Quinlan* decision, 1976, she wrote an article exploring "the emergence of a new area of inquiry and action that has come to be known as bioethics." Quoting Daniel Callahan, of the Hastings Institute, to the effect that bioethics was "not yet a full discipline," that most of its practitioners "had wandered into the field from somewhere else, more or less inventing it as they go," Fox documented its growing influence. Not only were several academic centers studying and teaching bioethics, but an "impressive array of private foundations, scholarly bodies and government agencies" were supporting such efforts; and an equally impressive interdisciplinary group, composed predominantly of philosophers and concerned physicians, were pursuing them.[37]

Fox was disturbed, however, that bioethics had made such quick and thorough inroads, for she was convinced that it was bringing the wrong set of values to medicine. Some of her dissatisfaction reflected a struggle over turf, for as the bioethicists had moved into medicine, sociologists had moved out; she noted "a remarkable paucity of work by sociologists or other social scientists in this area."[38] But the point of Fox's attack was to criticize bioethicists not so much for excluding sociologists but for excluding the sociological approach. In a formulation that she later repeated and elaborated, Fox charged that bioethicists had no sense of time or place—that is, no awareness of why the movement had succeeded when it did or where it did, nor of why over the past ten years bioethics had become more important in the United States than in any other industrialized nation. Lacking this broader perspective, bioethicists could not recognize their own particular biases and predilections. In particular, they did not understand that they were elevating to a universal status beliefs that reflected nothing more than their own views. Indeed, in their eagerness to extend their reach, they transformed religious questions into ethical questions, giving a narrowly secular quality to discussions that had once been more wide-ranging.

The net result of this failure, Fox contended, was to entrench within bioethics an unyielding and unqualified commitment to individual rights, thereby minimizing all other communal or societal considerations. Insisted Fox:

> In the prevailing ethos of bioethics, the value of individualism is defined in such a way, and emphasized to such a degree, that it is virtually severed from social and religious values concerning relationships between individuals; their responsibilities, commitments, and emotional bonds to one another.... To this narrowly gauged conception of individualism bioethics attaches an inflated and inflationary value. Claims to individual rights phrased in terms of moral entitlements tend to expand and to beget additional claims to still other individual rights. In these respects, the individualism of bioethics constitutes an evolution away from older, less secularized and communal forms of American individualism.

Her conclusion was partly judgmental, partly wishful thinking: "It is unclear whether bioethics truly reflects the state of American medical ethics today and whether it can—or ought to—serve as the common framework for American medical morality."[39]

In her determination to fault bioethics for adopting so individualistic an approach, Fox was herself guilty of some of the very charges she leveled at bioethics. She, too, failed to set the movement in a societal framework, leaving the impression that bioethicists were a self-seeking and self-promoting group of academic entrepreneurs, which would hardly suffice to explain their broad appeal. What Fox missed, or was unwilling to consider, was that the movement's strong commitment to individual rights was at the core of its success. This orientation may well have alienated doctors, but it allied bioethicists with other outsiders to medicine—namely, lawyers, public officials, the media, and, even more, patients and their families who, like the Quinlans, had confronted unyielding medical authority.

Just how close the fit was emerges from one telling incident. When the Quinlans' lawyer, Paul Armstrong, was preparing for oral argument before the New Jersey Supreme Court, he first flew to Washington to consult with the bioethicists at Georgetown's Kennedy Institute and then went to the Hastings Institute to review his arguments with Robert Veatch. They peppered him with questions—"Mr. Armstrong, can you draw a distinction between allowing someone to die and actively advancing death? How do we know what Karen's wishes are since she is incompetent?"—and helped him frame answers.[40] In this way, the *Quinlan* case represented both the emergence of a new authority over medicine and a new alliance among outsiders to medicine. The Quinlans first took counsel with the clergy, but to effect their wishes, they had to turn to a lawyer, who, in turn, consulted with bioethicists so as to sharpen his argument before a court.

The great majority of bioethicists, as this incident suggests, came down on the side of the Quinlans, elevating individual rights over medical authority. If Fox was likely to give greater weight to medical traditions, the bioethicists were adamant in championing the patient's claims. *Quinlan* became the occasion for one after another of them to speak out for patient autonomy. Edmund Pellegrino, then a professor of medicine at Yale University and later the head of the Georgetown program in medical ethics, warned against "putting excessive powers into the hands of professionals of any kind. . . . Give the physician too much power, and it can be abused."[41] The proper task for the doctor was to provide patients and their families with the information necessary for them to reach a decision. Tristram Engelhardt, then on the faculty at Georgetown, put the *Quinlan* decision into the framework of the Patient Bill of Rights for strengthening the voice of the patient.[42] And Robert Veatch, having counseled Armstrong, celebrated the court decision, hopeful that it would become the guiding precedent.[43]

Was anything lost by the almost exclusive dedication of bioethics to the principle of patient autonomy? Perhaps the thoroughgoing commitment to autonomy did encourage a polarization of issues, pitting tweed coat against white coat, but it is doubtful whether any modifications in this stance would have made the medical profession more comfortable about losing discretionary authority. More important, as witnessed in the cases of both Karen Ann Quinlan and the Johns Hopkins baby, the individualistic approach of the bioethicists focused their attention more on the one-to-one encounter of patient and doctor than on the societal context of American medicine. A commitment to patient autonomy presumed that the most critical problem in American medicine was the nature of this doctor–patient relationship and that, by implication, such issues as access to health care or the balance between disease prevention and treatment were of lesser import. In this sense Fox was right to observe that bioethics lacked a sociological imagination. Nevertheless, protecting the rights of the individual patient often had a relevance that transcended class lines—emphasizing concepts like consent meant protecting both the poor and the well-to-do from the unscrupulous researcher, and insisting on patient dignity had implications at least as vital for the ward service as for the private pavilion.

In the end, the initial commitment of bioethics to patient rights helps account for its extraordinary accomplishments in the decade from 1966 to 1976. The fit between the movement and the times was perfect. Just when courts were defining an expanded right to privacy, the bioethicists were emphasizing the principle of autonomy, and the two meshed neatly; judges supplied a legal basis and bioethicists, a philosophical basis for empowering the patient. Indeed, just when movements on behalf of a variety of minorities were advancing their claims, the bioethicists were defending another group that appeared powerless— patients. All these advocates were siding with the individual against the constituted authority; in their powerlessness, patients seemed at one with women, inmates, homosexuals, tenants in public housing, welfare recipients, and students, who were all attempting to limit the discretionary authority of professionals. In fact, the bioethicists had far more in common with the new roster of rights agitators than many of its leaders recognized or would have admitted. Ph.D.s, often trained in philosophy, many with a Catholic background, who typically followed conventional life-styles, may not have been personally comfortable with still more left-leaning, agnostic, and aggressive advocates committed to alternative life-styles. But however glaring these differences, the conceptual similarities were critical. All these movements looked at the world from the vantage point of the objects of authority, not the wielders of authority.

Of course, bioethics had one critical advantage that gave it more staying power than these other groups, assuring its successes not only in the late 1960s and early 1970s, but through the 1980s. Bioethics crossed class lines. It was at least as responsive, and perhaps even more so, to the concerns of the haves than the have-nots. Not everyone is poor or a member of a minority group or disadvantaged socially and economically; but everyone potentially, if not already, is a patient. This fact gives a special character and appeal to a movement that approaches the exercise of medical authority from the patient's point of view.

EPILOGUE

IN the fifteen years since the Quinlan decision, the trends that first emerged in the 1966–76 decade have become all the more prominent and powerful. Outsiders to medicine, more conspicuously and successfully than physicians, now define the social and ethical questions facing the profession and set forth the norms that should govern it. The most impressive and thorough undertaking in this area, the President's Commission for the Study of Ethical Problems in Medicine and Biomedical and Behavioral Research, was dominated by lawyers and philosophers (from academic departments rather than schools of theology). Created by Congress in 1978 as the successor organization to the 1973 National Commission on the Protection of Human Subjects, it, too, owed its existence to the energetic intervention of Edward Kennedy. Invoking, once again, the great scandals in human experimentation—Willowbrook, Tuskegee, Brooklyn Jewish Chronic Disease Hospital—Kennedy successfully moved for the establishment of "an interdisciplinary committee of professionals . . . to work together to try to give the society guidance on some of the most difficult, complex, ethical and moral problems of our time."[1] In 1978 substantial political mileage could still be gained from these scandals, bringing more rules and players to the bedside.

The appointment of Morris Abram to the commission chairmanship is inexplicable without an appreciation of the events of 1966–76. In no other way can one fathom the selection of a former civil rights lawyer to head a study of medical ethics. In fact, Abram exemplified not only the influence of lawyers on medicine, but the formidable new authority of the patient as well. Stricken a few years earlier with leukemia, Abram had been as active in directing his own treatment as any patient could be. He arranged for the importation from abroad of an experimental drug (no mean feat in the 1970s), and ordered every doctor who touched him (in his immuno-compromised state) to scrub in his presence; when, after multiple blood drawings, his veins started to close down, Abram compelled the physicians to devise a routine that would satisfy all their daily requirements with one needle stick.[2] Not surprisingly, Abram selected another lawyer, Alexander Capron, to serve as executive director for the commission. Capron, one of the first professors of law to cross over into medicine and an active member of the Hastings Institute, had written extensively and perceptively on many of the issues that composed the bioethics agenda.

Outsiders to medicine dominated the commission's membership. Five of the first eleven commissioners came from bioethics, law, and the social sciences, and three from behavioral research. The group designated to pronounce on ethical problems in medicine had only five M.D.s, of whom three were practicing physicians. The professional staff was even further removed from medicine. Only one was an M.D., while four had law degrees, and five, Ph.D.s. In short, this group was not likely to give great deference to the traditions of bedside ethics.

Structure and personnel did shape substance. Between 1980 and 1983, the commission published over a dozen reports devoted to such concerns as establishing a uniform definition of death, obtaining informed consent, compensating for injuries to research subjects, securing access to health care, and, of course, terminating life-sustaining treatment.[3] In addressing this exceptionally broad range of subjects, the commission was guided by a series of now well-established principles. First, the relationship between patient and doctor should be marked by "mutual participation and respect and by shared decisionmaking."[4] The patient was to be active and involved, the physician, responsive and sharing. Second, the commission insisted that medical decision making conform to explicit principles that would be consistently applied, eschewing case-by-case resolutions. Finally, when confronting almost insoluble ethical problems, the commission opted for collective as opposed to individual judgments; when the issues became intricate, it frequently invoked procedures modeled on IRB deliberations. The commission strove to make medical decision making visible, formal, and predictable, and altogether responsive to the patient's preferences.

Consistent with these ends, the commission made informed consent the cornerstone of its design. "Ethically valid consent is a process of shared decisionmaking based upon mutual respect and participation, not a ritual to be equated with reciting the contents of a form. . . . Patients should have access to the information they need to help them understand their conditions and make treatment decisions. . . . Health care providers should not ordinarily withhold unpleasant information simply because it is unpleasant."[5] Thus, in framing policy for terminating treatment, arguably its most important contribution, the commission gave precedence to "the voluntary choice of a competent and informed patient." It recognized that in some instances the conscience of physicians or the mission of a hospital might conflict with the patient's wishes, and it did not wish to ride roughshod over these differences. It hoped that some of the disputes would be worked out between doctor and patient and that hospitals would develop review mechanisms and policies "to ensure the means necessary to preserve both health and the value of self determination." But when conflict was unavoidable, "the primacy of a patient's interests in self-determination and in honoring the patient's own view of well-being warrant leaving with the patient the final authority to decide."[6]

The commission was equally adamant about protecting the rights of the incompetent patient. It strongly advocated the development of legal mechanisms that would allow patients to make their wishes known in advance, either by living wills or through the appointment of a surrogate decision maker. In the event that the patient had been silent, or had never achieved competence (as in the case of newborns or persons with severe mental disability), the commission again looked to hospital review committees, not individual physicians, to advise on the decisions. Hospitals should formulate "explicit, and publicly available policies regarding how and by whom decisions are to be made."[7]

The initial reception accorded the commission's publications demonstrates the persistence of the distinction between medical insiders and outsiders. Most medical journals ignored the enterprise, not reporting on the commission's birth or passage, or on its substantive findings; well into the 1980s, it was the unusual physician who had read any of its reports. (The one exception was the commission's draft of a Uniform Determination of Death Act, which was endorsed by both the American Medical Association and the American Bar Association, and enacted by many states; but this was primarily a technical matter that did not divide the profession.) Outsiders, on the other hand, were, and still are, far more attentive to the commission's findings. Let a termination-of-treatment case make headlines, and the courts, the media, and the legislature, as well as an enlarged community of concerned academics, will consult and cite the commission's recommendations.

The commission's work, however, has not escaped substantive criticism, and one particular charge casts a harsh light not only on the commission itself but on the degree to which medical decision making has actually changed over the past twenty-five years. Jay Katz, who was among the first to explore in depth the ethics of human experimentation (Capron was his student at Yale Law School), has argued that the commission was far too complacent about the prospect of doctors entering a partnership with patients. Convinced that the hallowed tradition in medicine is for physicians to be silent with patients so as to exercise their own discretion, Katz remains unpersuaded that a fundamental redressing of the balance of authority has come to mark the doctor-patient relationship. Committed to empowering the patient, he is dismayed by the difficulty, if not impossibility, of the task. "I have nothing but admiration," he declared, "for the Commission's remarkable vision, which is so contrary to the medical profession's view of how physicians and patients should converse with one another." But no one should be misled into thinking that such rhetoric has engendered a new reality. The commission, for example, cited an opinion poll which found most physicians ready to share information about a fatal diagnosis with patients; Katz countered that sociologists who observe interactions in psychiatric wards report that physicians manipulate the consent process to render it meaningless. The old attitudes and practices persist, for medicine lacks a tradition of communicating uncertainties to patients and sharing decision making.[8]

Katz is not alone in minimizing the import of the changes that have come to medicine. A number of sociologists contend that medicine's privileged status has not eroded over the past twenty-five years. In the words of one student of the debate, medicine has not lost "its *relative* position of prestige and respect, or expertise, or monopoly over that expertise." Eliot Freidson, one of the most prominent sociologists of medicine, insists also that "the professions . . . continue to possess a monopoly over at least some important segment of formal knowledge that does not shrink over time." Conceding that doctors have lost some individual autonomy over decision making, he believes that this authority has simply been transferred to other doctors, not to outsiders. The internal organization of the profession has been altered, but not the external position of the profession in society.[9]

How accurate are these judgments on the events of 1966–76 and their aftermath? Have physicians merely adopted a different stance toward the pollster but not toward the patient? Have the new rules and players truly made a difference?

The record since 1966, I believe, makes a convincing case for a fundamental transformation in the substance as well as the style of medical decision making. Certainly this is true for the conduct of human experimentation. Although the regulatory performance of the Institutional Review Boards is not without flaws, the experiments that Henry Beecher described could not now occur; even the most ambitious or confident investigator would not today put forward such protocols. Indeed, the transformation in research practices is most dramatic in the area that was once most problematic: research on incompetent and institutionalized subjects. The young, the elderly, the mentally disabled, and the incarcerated are not fair game for the investigator. Researchers no longer get to choose the martyrs for mankind.

To be sure, gaps and deficiencies remain. IRBs in different institutions work with different standards, and just the way that liberal incorporation laws in one state (like New Jersey in the 1900s) undercut regulation elsewhere, so a researcher unhappy with IRB supervision at his home institution can pick up and move his shop—which apparently is what heart surgeon William DeVries did. More, the structure of the IRBs remains flawed. Although mandated to include "community representatives" among their members, the IRBs are at liberty to define the category, to select almost anyone they wish to fill it, and to dismiss out of hand anyone whose performance displeases them. More telling, the IRBs almost never investigate or scrutinize the actual encounter of researcher and subject. They examine the language of the consent form, but do not monitor the consent process or the interaction between investigator and subject.[10]

On the balance, however, the procedures to protect human experimentation are so firmly entrenched that the central issue now, in view of the AIDS crisis, is not how to protect the human subject from the investigator but how to ensure that all those who wish to be human subjects have a fair opportunity to enter a protocol. The nightmare image has shifted from an unscrupulous researcher taking advantage of a helpless inmate to a dying patient desperate to join a drug trial and have a chance at life. The backlash against the IRB is spurred not by researchers impatient with bureaucratic delays but by patients who want to make their own calculations of risks and benefits and to decide for themselves, without the veto power of an IRB, whether a protocol is worth entering. Although this reorientation in large measure reflects the grim fate confronting persons with AIDS, it also testifies to how effectively the IRBs have trained, really tamed, the researcher.[11]

To turn to the examining room, it is evident that the changes that have occurred there since the mid-1960s resemble the changes that followed in the aftermath of *Brown v. Board of Education.* Just as in civil rights one witnessed a powerful legal and societal endorsement of the idea of integration which practice never quite managed to realize, so in medicine one also witnessed a powerful endorsement of patient sovereignty with practice, again, falling short of the model. This has been a period of transition, marked by an exceptional variety of styles characterizing medical decision making. One finds, particularly among older physicians and older patients, a reluctance to adapt to a new set of expectations. Some physicians are unwilling to relinquish the discretionary authority that they exercised for so long, and some patients are unable to exercise the authority that they have won.

Nevertheless, the examining room, like the laboratory, gives ample evidence of the impact of new rules and new players. An unprecedented degree of formality now accompanies a resolution to forego life-sustaining treatment. Some states, and an even larger number of hospitals, require physicians to complete detailed forms and obtain the competent patient's signed consent before entering a Do Not Resuscitate code. Predictably, physicians have complained that, in compelling patients to confront their impending death, these discussions are cruel. For to justify a DNR code, the physician will have to explain that the disease is terminal and death imminent, that resuscitation is medically futile, and that the pounding on the chest, the likely breaking of ribs, and going on a ventilator are more painful than useful. But these protests notwithstanding, public policy and opinion demand that this explicit dialogue occur, preferring such conversations to pencilled notations on nursing charts or chalk entries on blackboards.

To be sure, subterfuge is possible and undoubtedly happens. Hospital resuscitation teams may follow a "slow code," walking, not rushing, to the bedside, and when a patient is incompetent, the physician may manipulate the family into following orders, if not on the first day then on the third. There is also evidence that some physicians find the obligation so distasteful or difficult that they postpone the discussions to the last minute, and then, with the patient in a coma, talk to the family. (This tactic helps explain why one retrospective study of DNR orders found that the family was far more likely than the patient—86 percent compared to 22 percent—to have authorized a DNR code, and another study reported that most DNR orders were written within three days of death.)[12] Still, it is apparent that new procedures have taken hold. Medical decisions now leave a well marked paper trail, and the stacked DNR forms are becoming as prominent on the nursing station desk as any other order sheets.

What is true for DNR orders holds as well for decisions to refuse or withdraw life-sustaining treatment. Ask a medical school class whether physicians should respect the wishes of a competent adult who is a Jehovah's Witness to be allowed to die rather than accept a blood transfusion, and the immediate and unanimous response is yes. That the competent, terminally ill patient can refuse not only high-technology interventions but food and water is now a well established principle, not only in bioethics tracts but in case law, and many physicians have come to respect, and even be comfortable with, this exercise of patient autonomy. (One surgeon recounted to me how much easier it is to function in an atmosphere where openness about prognosis is the norm. In the old days, he would have to pause outside the room to try and recall precisely which deceit he had perpetrated on the patient; now he only had to consult the chart, read the entries, and begin the conversation.) Again, physicians have retained some degree of discretion. They may well consult with patient and family about the use of a respirator or the administration of antibiotics, but reserve for themselves more technical (and covert) decisions about raising or lowering drug dosages that alter cardiac output or blood pressure. Taken as a whole, however, the cloak that covered medical decision making when the end of life approached has been lifted, and determinations on whether to continue or halt treatment are the focus of open deliberation.

These decisions are the substance of hospital committee deliberations as well. The idea of an ethics committee, as we have seen, first captured national attention in the Quinlan decision and commentators were soon suggesting that these committees should address not only the purely medical question (is the illness terminal?), but the truly ethical ones (for example, by what standard should decisions be made on behalf of the incompetent patient?). The catalyst for the spread of ethics committees, however, was not only academic analysis but several well-publicized incidents between 1982 and 1984 in which treatment was withdrawn from handicapped newborns. In these so-called "Baby Doe" cases, replays of the earlier Johns Hopkins case, parents refused to give permission for life-saving surgery because the newborn seemed too severely disabled. Media coverage of these incidents was extensive (confirming the extent to which consciousness had been raised about bioethical questions), and the Reagan administration tried to gain political capital with right-to-life groups by insisting upon life-sustaining treatment under almost all circumstances. The Department of Health and Human Services (HHS) opened an 800 telephone number to receive tips about possible discriminatory treatment of a disabled newborn and organized a Baby Doe squad that would rush to investigate cases and compel treatment. Individual right-to-life proponents joined the campaign. One of them, upon learning that a New York hospital was about to accede to the joint decision of family and physicians to withhold surgery from a severely impaired newborn, asked the state court to order treatment.

Both federal and state courts have rejected these efforts. They found no statutory basis for the federal government to reach into the neonatal nursery, and preferred to empower families and physicians rather than third-party advocates to make the decisions. The Reagan administration persisted, and HHS issued regulations to expand the oversight role of state child protection agencies. At the same time, it urged, but did not require, that hospitals establish neonatal ethics committees.

These same incidents also encouraged other, very different groups to endorse ethics committees. The President's commission urged hospitals with high-tech neonatal units to formulate "explicit policies on decision-making . . . for these infants," and it hoped that an ethics committee would conduct reviews whenever the family and the physician differed about life-sustaining interventions or whenever a dispute occurred on the futility or benefit of such an intervention.[13] In addition, a variety of medical associations, including the American Academy of Pediatrics, the American Medical Association, and the American Hospital Association, went on record favoring ethics committees. Surveys of hospitals between 1983 and 1985 reported that the percentage of hospitals with these committees doubled, with teaching hospitals and large tertiary care centers taking the lead.[14] At the least, ethics committees may obviate the need to go to court (or forestall another effort to bring 800 numbers into the nursery). At best, they may provide a forum for resolving conflicts in which both sides could invoke strong ethical principles.

Although hospital ethics committees come in an almost bewildering variety of shapes and forms, even more so than the IRBs, they do share a number of essential characteristics. Membership is heavily weighted to clinical personnel, with a bioethicist and community representative (again undefined) included. The committees often design and implement teaching programs for staff or assist in drawing up guidelines and procedures for their hospitals, and these activities are generally well accepted. Controversy begins when ethics committees address individual cases, when their members take a place around the bedside. Critics of ethics committees, like critics of IRBs, come both from those who believe they go too far and from those who believe they do not go far enough. One side feels that they violate the privacy of the doctor-patient relationship and promote consensus at the cost of principle; the other complains that the committees mainly serve the needs of the clinician (patients do not always have the right to convene them) and lack real authority (most are only advisory in character). Thus one prefers to trust to the doctor and the family, the other, to a full-fledged court hearing.

Ethics committees are still too new and the data too thin to resolve these differences. Lacking a clear federal mandate, they do not have the authority of the IRB, and their advisory role can be impeded by state legislation. A number of states, for example, have mandated the treatment of all surviving newborns. (Louisiana law, for example, declares that "no infant born alive shall be denied or deprived of food or nutrients, water, or oxygen by any person whatsoever with the intent to cause or allow the death of the child.")[15] A neonatal ethics committee responsive to such laws might find nothing to do. Moreover, the committees may not consistently or meaningfully enhance the voice of the patient. To the degree that they are doctor-convened, they may be doctor-dominated. Nevertheless, their potential benefits are likely to promote their spread and use. Ethics committees, more than courts, may provide a relaxed atmosphere in which to clarify implicit but unexamined assumptions, by the family or the physician, about what it means to have disability and how to cope with it. The committees may also operate without paying scrupulous attention to the letter of the law or by finding a loophole that will sanction their recommendation. For example, even under restrictive state legislation that mandates treatment, an exception may be made when the intervention would be "futile," a term that does not lend itself to strict definition. Thus ethics committees may be able to recommend withholding or foregoing "futile" treatment in a particular situation, whatever the statute's general thrust.[16]

No estimate of the recent impact and future direction of the changes we have been analyzing can be complete without reckoning with the extraordinary growth of economic regulation of medicine over the past twenty-five years. As we noted at the outset, the movement to bring law and bioethics to the bedside was not driven by cost considerations. There was hardly a mention of fiscal matters in the Mondale or Kennedy hearings, in the reports of the national commissions addressing human experimentation or bioethics, in the debates over defining death and facilitating transplantation, or in the controversies that enveloped the Johns Hopkins baby or Karen Ann Quinlan.

This dynamic is not, however, altogether separable from the one that brought federal, state, and corporation administrators to the bedside. In fact, it is difficult to sort out the relationship between these two trends, or to plot which way the arrow of influence points. Both worked to reduce discretion in medical decision making, empowering not only courts, legislatures, and committees but government and business regulatory bodies—who now require (before allowing reimbursement) unambiguous evidence that the patient was sick enough to warrant hospital admission, a stay of however many days, and the particular procedures used. After all, 1966 was not only the year that Beecher published his exposé, but the year that the federal government, through the enactment of Medicare and Medicaid, became the single largest purchaser of services.

Without being dogmatic, it may be that the concerns about trust, deference, and discretion helped to promote the change in regulatory policy. The new and enormous stake of the federal government in medical costs may have been in itself sufficient to explain the origins of cost containment. But it is also worth noting that this effort gathered momentum from the dynamics we have been exploring here. Because the doctor had become a stranger, because the levels of trust had diminished, because technology placed the doctor's hands more often on dials than on patients, it became more legitimate to treat the physician as one more seller of services and medical care as a commodity that should be regulated like any other.

Whatever the causal relationship, it is indisputable that the two trends have been mutually reinforcing. Each of them separately and then both together have brought more outsiders to medicine, and more formality and collective judgment as well. Whatever gaps one has left open, the other filled in. One cannot always be certain which of the two is ultimately responsible for a development, but since they both drive policy in the same direction, the route of change is marked in bold.

There is every reason to expect that for the foreseeable future medical decision making will be a shared enterprise and physicians will not regain the discretionary authority they once enjoyed. The outsiders who have entered medicine will probably remain there, bringing in like-minded successors. Medicine is and will continue to be in the public domain. Programs in bioethics are now entrenched in the medical schools, delineating a relatively fixed career line. The body of law around medical decision making and, concomitantly, the number of jobs in law and health care are great enough to ensure that a new cadre of lawyers will be engaged with these issues. Moreover, the media have their health reporters with refined sensibilities about the legal and ethical dimensions of a story. It is not simply that ethical and legal issues in medicine now abound, but that a cadre of journalists are trained to perceive and pursue them. Let an announcement of a medical advance be made, whether in mapping a gene, prescribing a growth hormone, or transplanting fetal tissue, and the reflex response is to analyze the ethical dimension of the innovation. All the while, of course, the vigorous attempt to contain medical costs will keep a small army of budget-minded officials involved as well.

Patients are also likely to be sparing with the deference and trust they accord to physicians or hospitals, reserving for themselves critical decisions about treatment. Attitude and practice will vary by class, gender, and generation—younger middle-class women are likely to be more assertive than elderly lower-class men. But in crisis situations, particularly around life-sustaining treatments, patients and their families will forcefully advance their own preferences. The structural considerations that originally helped to secure this change have only assumed greater prominence. Doctors are all the more strangers and hospitals the more strange places as the number of physicians in group practice (whether a health maintenance organization or health center) mounts, along with the degree of subspecialization. Simultaneously, the number of community and sectarian hospitals is shrinking and the rural hospital is becoming a relic of the past.

Judicial decisions, directly and indirectly, will encourage patient prerogatives and reinforce proceduralism. State and federal courts have become deeply immersed in medical decision making—by one recent count, between 1976 and 1988 there have been fifty-four reported decisions involving the right to refuse life-sustaining treatment, and the Supreme Court, in the 1990 *Cruzan* decision, has now addressed the issue. The clear consensus, joined by the Supreme Court, is that competent patients have the right to make their own decisions about life-sustaining treatment, and such treatment is to be broadly defined, including the provision of food and water. The principal area of disagreement is on the standards that should be applied in decision making for the incompetent patient. Must the once-competent patient have left clear and convincing evidence of his or her wishes? Can a lower standard suffice, especially when parents are requesting that treatment be terminated?

The case of Nancy Cruzan exemplifies the controversies. As a result of an automobile accident, Cruzan suffered brain damage and loss of oxygen. She remained in a coma for several weeks, then entered a persistent vegetative state. To keep her nourished, the hospital inserted a feeding and hydration tube. When it became apparent to her parents that their daughter would never regain mental functioning, they asked the hospital to remove the tube. The hospital refused, and, as in the case of Karen Ann Quinlan, the dispute entered the courts.

A lower Missouri court sided with the parents, crediting their report of a "somewhat serious conversation" in which Nancy stated that she did not wish to be kept alive unless she could live a halfway normal life. The Missouri Supreme Court adjudged this testimony "unreliable," and ruled that a state may insist, as Missouri does, on "clear and convincing" evidence before terminating treatment for an incompetent patient. The majority opinion from the U.S. Supreme Court agreed, finding this higher standard reasonable and not in contravention of a right to privacy. Although proponents of patients' rights interpreted the *Cruzan* case as a defeat, the initial effect of the Supreme Court ruling has been to publicize the need for competent adults to record their wishes through a living will or the formal appointment of a surrogate decision maker. So too, *Cruzan* is prompting state legislatures to make these stipulations binding on health care personnel and facilities. The fallout from *Cruzan* may thus help to persuade even more Americans to declare their preferences in advance and to secure the legality of such directives. It may soon become standard practice for hospital admission offices to ask patients not only for their insurance card but for their living wills.

Indeed, let a family for one reason or another be frustrated in fulfilling its wishes, and it may even take vigilante action. In one recent case a father, brandishing a revolver to keep the hospital staff from intervening, disconnected the respirator that was keeping his infant daughter alive in a persistent vegetative state. In another incident, a family disconnected the respirator that was keeping their brain-injured father alive, and physically barred hospital personnel from reconnecting the machine. Although one would have thought that vigilante actions had no place in an ICU, neither case led to an indictment. Still more startling, both stories became the occasion for commentators to disparage the tyranny of medicine and the machine over the patient.[17]

By almost every account, these changes have disturbed many physicians and may adversely affect recruitment to the profession. Physicians lament the loss of status and authority, which they link directly to a loss of professional autonomy and discretion. Writing in the *NEJM* in January 1990, Dr. Saul Radovsky asked "why the morale of today's doctor is low," and found much of his answer in the extent to which their professional lives "are more hemmed in and complicated" by rules. "Doctors ethics, morality, and commitment to public service have largely been legislated or are regulated." Physicians now see themselves "cast as wrongdoers and incompetents who yearly require new laws, regulations, admonitions, court decisions, and exposés to make them more honest, ethical, competent, corrigible, and contrite. Perhaps it is no wonder if many of them now look for a change or exit."[18] Reporting in the *New York Times* a month later, Lawrence Altman and Elisabeth Rosenthal found that "the degree of dissatisfaction among doctors is astonishingly high," and they cited a 1989 Gallup Poll that almost 40 percent of physicians questioned said that if they knew then what they know now, they would not have entered medical school.[19] These complaints are in large measure responsible for a notable decline in applications to medical school—among white males, the pool has decreased by half—and one is left to ponder whether this decrease presages a more general demoralization of the profession.

Which brings us to our final consideration. Reviewing these events, and speculating about the future, suggests that the transformations in medical decision making, as vital as they are, have come with a price. To alter the balances between doctor and patient and medicine and society encouraged, unavoidably, the intervention of a greater number of third parties. Ironically, to cope with the doctor as stranger and the hospital as strange, to respond to perceived conflicts of interest and to the power of new technologies, it appeared necessary to bring still more strangers to the bedside. Constraining one authority figure required creating other authority figures. To make certain that the patient's voice would be heard and respected demanded the support of a chorus, and as sometimes happens, the chorus can overwhelm the soloist.

The crowding of so many people around the bedside may be a transitional phenomenon in the history of medical decision making. Successor generations may find it less necessary to draw on outsiders to enhance the prerogatives of the patient; they may be more ready to trust to the patient alone, or the patient together with the doctor. Indeed, one glimpses signs of new alignments, such as doctors and patients uniting against government and corporate officials who attempt to curtail medical expenditures. By the same token, court cases on termination of treatment at times pit patient against hospital, with the doctor siding with the patient. And in the case of handicapped newborns, doctors, families, and courts have closed ranks to keep out third-party, right-to-life advocates and government bureaucrats. Thus, with new configurations emerging, the crowd now gathered around the bedside may disperse.

The process of change may be accelerated because if patients today are more sovereign than ever before, medicine itself is more bureaucratic, enmeshed in forms, committees, and procedures. This bureaucratization can adversely affect patients as well as practitioners. Signing a DNR code sheet is a proper exercise of patient autonomy, but one may still wish for a less formal and cumbersome mechanism. That dying has become a legal process is not an unqualified sign of progress.

In effect, one more aspect of modern life has become contractual, prescribed, and uniform. One more encounter of a primary sort now tends to be disinterested, neutral, and remote. To be sure, medical schools, medical societies, institutes, foundations, and government agencies are attempting to ameliorate the situation. Perhaps bringing the humanities into medical education will humanize the doctor; perhaps there are new ways to teach students not only how to take a case history from a patient but how to give information to a patient. Perhaps the incentives to train family doctors will alter recruitment patterns and strengthen the doctor-patient relationship. And perhaps all the energies devoted to these programs and the discussions that accompany them will help us as a society to resolve the daunting questions of what values we wish to preserve, or abandon, in the effort to prolong human life.

The prospect of accomplishing such an agenda does not breed an easy confidence or optimism. In the end, patients may well continue to experience medicine as modern: powerful and impersonal, a more or less efficient interaction between strangers.

APPENDIX A

Citations to Henry Beecher's 1966 Article

1. Captain Robert Chamovitz, MC, USAF, Captain Francis J. Catanzaro, MC, AUS, Captain Chandler A. Stetson, MC, AUS, and Charles H. Rammelkamp, Jr., M.D., "Prevention of Rheumatic Fever by Treatment of Previous Streptococcal Infections: I. Evaluation of Benzathine Penicillin G," *New England Journal of Medicine* 251 (1954): 466–71.

2. Captain Alton J. Morris, Captain Robert Chamovitz, MC, USAF, Captain Frank J. Catanzaro, MC, Army of the United States, and Charles H. Rammelkamp, Jr., M.D., Cleveland, "Prevention of Rheumatic Fever by Treatment of Previous Streptococcic Infections: Effect of Sulfadiazine," *Journal of the American Medical Association* 160 (1956): 114–16.

3. Pedro T. Lantin, Sr., M.D., Alberto Geronimo, M.D., and Victorino Calilong, M.D., Manila, Philippines, "The Problem of Typhoid Relapse," *American Journal of the Medical Sciences* 245 (1963): 293–98.

4. Howard E. Ticktin, M.D., and Hyman J. Zimmerman, M.D., "Hepatic Dysfunction and Jaundice in Patients Receiving Triacetyloleandomycin," *New England Journal of Medicine* 267 (1962): 964–68.

5. James L. Scott, M.D., Sydney M. Finegold, M.D., Gerald A. Belkin, M.D., and John S. Lawrence, M.D., "A Controlled Double-Blind Study of the Hematologic Toxicity of Chloramphenicol," *New England Journal of Medicine* 272 (1965): 1137–42.

6. Robert M. Zollinger, Jr., M.D., Martin C. Lindem, Jr., M.D., Robert M. Filler,

M.D., Joseph M. Corson, M.D., and Richard E. Wilson, M.D., "Effect of Thymectomy on Skin-Homograft Survival in Children," *New England Journal of Medicine* 270 (1964): 707–9.

7. A. A. Lurie, M.D., R. E. Jones, M.D., H. W. Linde, Ph.D., M. L. Price, A.B., R. D. Dripps, M.D., and H. L. Price, M.D., "Cyclopropane Anesthesia. 1. Cardiac Rate and Rhythm during Steady Levels of Cyclopropane Anesthesia at Normal and Elevated End-Expiratory Carbon Dioxide Tensions," *Anesthesiology* 19 (1958): 457–72.

8. Frank A. Finnerty, Jr., Lloyd Witkin, and Joseph F. Fazekas, with the technical assistance of Marie Langbart and William K. Young, "Cerebral Hemodynamics during Cerebral Ischemia Induced by Acute Hypotension," *Journal of Clinical Investigation* 33 (1954): 1227–32.

9. Angelo G. Rocco, M.D., and Leroy D. Vandam, M.D., Boston, "Changes in Circulation Consequent to Manipulation during Abdominal Surgery," *Journal of the American Medical Association* 164 (1957): 14–18.

10. Eugene Braunwald, Robert L. Frye, Maurice M. Aygen, and Joseph W. Gilbert, Jr., "Studies on Starling's Law of the Heart. III. Observations in Patients with Mitral Stenosis and Atrial Fibrillation on the Relationships between Left Ventricular End-Diastolic Segment Length Filling Pressure, and the Characteristics of Ventricular Contraction," *Journal of Clinical Investigation* 39 (1960): 1874–84.

11. Eugene Braunwald, M.D., and Andrew G. Morrow, M.D., "Sequence of Ventricular Contraction in Human Bundle Branch Block: A Study Based on Simultaneous Catheterization of Both Ventricles," *American Journal of Medicine* 23 (1957): 205–11.
12. Douglas R. Morton, M.D., Karl P. Klassen, M.D., F.A.C.S., Jacob J. Jacoby, M.D., Ph.D., and George M. Curtis, M.D., Ph.D., F.A.C.S., "The Effect of Intrathoracic Vagal Stimulation on the Electrocardiographic Tracing in Man," *Surgery, Gynecology and Obstetrics* 96 (1953): 724–32.

13. Stanley Reichman, William D. Davis, John Storaasli, and Richard Gorlin, "Measurement of Hepatic Blood Flow by Indicator Dilution Techniques," *Journal of Clinical Investigation* 37 (1958): 1848–56.

14. Gerald B. Phillips, M.D., Robert Schwartz, M.D., George J. Gabuzda, Jr., M.D., and Charles S. Davidson, M.D., "The Syndrome of Impending Hepatic Coma in Patients with Cirrhosis of the Liver Given Certain Nitrogenous Substances," *New England Journal of Medicine* 247 (1952): 239–46.

15. Laurens P. White, Elizabeth A. Phear, W. H. J. Summerskill, and Sheila Sherlock, with the technical assistance of Marjorie Cole, "Ammonium Tolerance in Liver Disease: Observations Based on Catheterization of the Hepatic Veins," *Journal of Clinical Investigation* 34 (1955): 158–68.

16. S. Krugman, M.D., Robert Ward, M.D., Joan P. Giles, M.D., Oscar Bodansky, M.D., and A. Milton Jacobs, M.D., "Infectious Hepatitis: Detection of Virus during the Incubation Period and in Clinically Inapparent Infection," *New England Journal of Medicine* 261 (1959): 729–34.

17. Elinor Langer, "Human Experimentation: Cancer Studies at Sloan-Kettering Stir Public Debate on Medical Ethics," *Science* 143 (1964): 551–53.

18. Edward F. Scanlon, M.D., Roger A. Hawkins, M.D., Wayne W. Fox, M.D., and W. Scott Smith, M.D., "Fatal Homotransplanted Melanoma: A Case Report," *Cancer* 18 (1965): 782–89.

19. P. R. Allison, F.R.C.S., and R. J. Linden, M.B., Ch.B., "The Bronchoscopic Measurement of Left Auricular Pressure," *Circulation* 7 (1953): 669–73.
20. Andrew G. Morrow, M.D., F.A.C.S., Eugene Braunwald, M.D., J. Alex Haller, Jr., M.D., and Edward H. Sharp, M.D., "Left Heart Catheterization by the Transbronchial Route: Technic and Applications in Physiologic and Diagnostic Investigations," *Circulation* 16 (1957): 1033–39.

21. John B. Hickam and Walter H. Cargill, "Effect of Exercise on Cardiac Output and Pulmonary Arterial Pressure in Normal Persons and in Patients with Cardiovascular Disease and Pulmonary Emphysema," *Journal of Clinical Investigation* 27 (1948): 10–23.

22. Robert Lich, Jr., Lonnie W. Howerton, Jr., Lydon S. Goode, and Lawrence A. Davis, "The Ureterovesical Junction of the Newborn," *Journal of Urology* 92 (1964): 436–38.

NOTES

Introduction

1. Hans Jonas, "Philosophical Reflections on Experimenting with Human Subjects," *Daedalus* 98 (1969): 219.
2. Marie R. Haug and Bebe Lavin, "Practitioner or Patient—Who's in Charge?" *Journal of Health and Social Behavior* 22 (1981): 215; Boston Women's Health Book Collective, *Our Bodies, Ourselves* (New York: 1973), xx.
3. Letter from Dr. William Bartholome of the University of Kansas Medical School to Mrs. Samuel Mayer, 9 December 1971.
4. See, for example, the discussion in Jeanne Harley Guillemin and Lynda Lytle Holmstrom, *Mixed Blessings: Intensive Care for Newborns* (New York: 1986), chap. 5.

Chapter 1

1. Henry K. Beecher, "Ethics and Clinical Research," *New England Journal of Medicine* 74 (1966): 1354–60 (hereafter cited as *NEJM*). All quotations from Beecher are to this article unless otherwise cited. A synopsis of the argument that follows appeared in my *NEJM* article, "Ethics and Human Experimentation: Henry Beecher Revisited," 317 (1987): 1195–99.
2. C. L. Kaufman, "Informed Consent and Patient Decision Making: Two Decades of Research," *Social Science and Medicine* 17 (1983): 1657–64.
3. Beecher to Richard Field, 3 August 1965, Henry Beecher Manuscripts, Francis A. Countway Library of Medicine, Harvard University (hereafter cited as Beecher MSS).
4. Beecher to Arnold Relman, 21 June 1966, Beecher MSS.

NOTES

5. See the letters of Beecher to these publications, May–June 1966, Beecher MSS.

6. See Beecher to George Burch, 27 June 1966, Beecher MSS.

7. For two useful surveys see Norman Howard-Jones, "Human Experimentation in Historical and Ethical Perspective," *Social Science Medicine* 16 (1982): 1429–48; J. C. Fletcher, "The Evolution of the Ethics of Informed Consent," in *Research Ethics*, ed. K. Berg and K. E. Tanoy (New York: 1983), pp. 187–228. See also Lawrence K. Altman, *Who Goes First: The Story of Self-Experimentation in Medicine* (New York: 1987).

8. J. P. Bull, "The Historical Development of Clinical Therapeutic Trials," *Journal of Chronic Diseases* 10 (1959): 218–48.

9. Bull, "Clinical Therapeutic Trials," p. 222.

10. D. Baxby, *Jenner's Smallpox Vaccine* (London: 1981), esp. pp. 22–23, 58–63; Lewis H. Roddis, "Edward Jenner and the Discovery of Smallpox Vaccination," *Military Surgeon* 65 (1929): 853–61.

11. Edward Jenner, "Vaccination against Smallpox" (1798; reprint, Harvard Classics, *Scientific Papers* vol. 38, 1910), pp. 164–65.

12. Roddis, "Edward Jenner," pp. 861–64.

13. Howard-Jones, "Human Experimentation," p. 1429.

14. Ibid., pp. 1429–31.

15. William Beaumont, "Experiments and Observations on the Gastric Juice and Physiology of Digestion" (1833; reprint, New York: Peter Smith, 1941), pp. xii–xiii.

16. R. Vallery-Radot, *The Life of Pasteur* (New York: 1926), pp. 404–5. See also Gerald Geison, "Pasteur's Early Work on Rabies: Reexamining the Ethical Issues," *Hastings Center Report* 8 (1978): 26–33; Stephen Paget, *Pasteur and after Pasteur* (London: 1914), p. 79. The recent work of Bruno Latour on Pasteur does not address the ethics of human experimentation: *The Pasteurization of France* (Cambridge, Mass.: 1988).

17. Vallery-Radot, *Pasteur*, pp. 414–17.

18. Pasteur recommended that convicted criminals be the subjects of human experimentation. As he wrote to the emperor of Brazil: "If I were a King, an Emperor, or even the President of a Republic . . . I should invite the counsel of a condemned man, on the eve of the day fixed for his execution, to choose between certain death and an experiment which would consist in several preventive inoculations of rabic virus. . . . If he survived this experiment—and I am convinced that he would—his life would be saved" (Vallery-Radot 1926, p. 405).

19. Claude Bernard, *An Introduction to the Study of Experimental Medicine*, trans. H. C. Greene (New York: 1927), pp. 101–2.

20. J. H. Salisbury, "On the Causes of Intermittent and Remittent Fevers," *American Journal of Medical Science* 26 (1866): 51–68.

21. Cited in Howard-Jones, "Human Experimentation," p. 1430.
22. J. P. Bull, "The Historical Development of Clinical Therapeutic Trials," *Journal of Chronic Disease* 10 (1959): 235.
23. Michael Bliss, *The Discovery of Insulin* (Chicago: 1982).
24. Bull, "Clinical Therapeutic Trials," p. 237.
25. Cited in Walter B. Bean, *Walter Reed; A Biography* (Charlottesville, Va.: 1982), p. 128.
26. Cited in Bean, *Reed*, pp. 131, 147.
27. Ibid.
28. Ibid., pp. 146–47, 165.
29. V. Veeressayev, *The Memoirs of a Physician*, trans. Simeon Linder (New York: 1916), app. B.
30. George M. Sternberg and Walter Reed, "Report on Immunity against Vaccination Conferred upon the Monkey by the Use of the Serum of the Vaccinated Calf and Monkey," *Transactions of the Association of American Physicians* 10 (1895): 57–69.
31. Joseph Stokes, Jr., et al., "Results of Immunization by Means of Active Virus of Human Influenza," *Journal of Clinical Investigation* 16 (1937): 237–43. This was one in a series of his investigations that used institutionalized populations. See, for example, Stokes et al., "Vaccination against Epidemic Influenza," *American Journal of the Medical Sciences* 194 (1937): 757–68.
32. My account here follows the excellent analysis of Susan Lederer, "Hideyop Noguchi's Luetin Experiment and the Antivivisectionists," *Isis* 76 (1985): 31–48.
33. All quotations cited in Lederer, "Noguchi's Luetin Experiment," pp. 321–48.

Chapter 2

1. Chester S. Keefer, "Dr. Richards as Chairman of the Committee on Medical Research," *Annals of Internal Medicine* 71, supp. 8 (1969): 62.
2. E. C. Andrus et al., eds., *Advances in Military Medicine*, 2 vols. (Boston: 1948). For a summary of the work of the CMR, see the foreword to volume 1.
3. Andrus et. al., *Advances*, vol. 1, p. 7.
4. Records of the Office of Scientific Research and Development, Committee on Medical Research, Contractor Records (Contract 120, Final Report), Principal Investigator Stuart Mudd (University of Pennsylvania), 3 March 1943, Record Group 227, National Archives, Washington, D.C., (hereafter cited as Records of the OSRD, CMR; C = Contract, R = Report, PI = Principal Investigator).
5. Records of the OSRD, CMR, Summary Report, Division of Medicine, Status Report, PI E.C. Anderson, 14 December 1944.

NOTES

6. Records of OSRD, CMR, Contractor Records (Children's Hospital), June 1946, 293, L27, pp. 24–45.
7. Ibid.
8. Ibid.
9. Records of the OSRD, CMR, Contractor Records, 120, Monthly Progress Report 18, PI Stuart Mudd, 3 October 1944.
10. A. V. Hardy and S. D. Cummins, "Preliminary Note on the Clinical Response to Sulfadiazine Therapy," *Public Health Reports* 58 (1943): 693–96.
11. J. Watt and S. D. Cummins, "Further Studies on the Relative Efficacy of Sulfonamides in Shigellosis," *Public Health Reports* 60 (1945): 355–61.
12. Andrus et al., *Advances*, vol. 1, p. xlix.
13. Records of the OSRD, CMR, Contractor Records, C 450, R L2, Bimonthly Progress Report, PI Alf S. Alving (University of Chicago), 1 August 1944.
14. Records of the OSRD, CMR, Contractor Records, C 450, R L36, 21 December 1945; Reports L50, L49.
15. *New York Times*, 5 March 1945, pp. 1–3.
16. Andrus et al., *Advances*, vol 1, p. 17.
17. Records of the OSRD, CMR, Contractor Records, C 360, R L 14, Bimonthly Progress Report 8, PI Werner Henle (Children's Hospital of Philadelphia), 1 December 1944.
18. Werner Henle et al., "Experiments on Vaccination of Human Beings against Epidemic Influenza," *Journal of Immunology* 53 (1946): 75–93.
19. For similar research at Ypsilanti State Hospital, see Jonas E. Salk et al., "Immunization against Influenza with Observations during an Epidemic of Influenza A One Year after Vaccination," *American Journal of Hygiene* 42 (1945): 307–21.
20. Thomas Francis, Jr., Jonas E. Salk et al., "Protective Effect of Vaccination against Induced Influenza A," *Proceedings of the Society for Experimental Biology and Medicine* 55 (1944): 104. For details on the research reports, see Jonas E. Salk et al., "Protective Effects of Vaccination against Induced Influenza B," *Journal of Clinical Investigation* 24 (1945): 547–53; see also Francis, Salk, et al., 536–46.
21. Commission on Influenza, "A Clinical Evaluation of Vaccination against Influenza," *Journal of the American Medical Association* 124 (1944): 982–84; see also Monroe D. Eaton and Gordon Meiklejohn, "Vaccination against Influenza: A Study in California during the Epidemic of 1943–44," *American Journal of Hygiene* 42 (1945): 28–44.
22. The account here is based on the material in Records of the OSRD, CMR, General Correspondence, A–F, box 59. See especially the policy memorandums of 16 July 1943; 22 September 1943 (Summary, Penicillin Procedures, Industry Advisory Committee); 13 January 1944; 15 January 1944; 20 January 1944. See also A. N. Richards, "Production of Penicillin in the United States (1941–1946)," *Nature* 201 (1964): 441–45.

23. On the COs' experience, see Records of the OSRD, CMR, box 18. Contracts 206 and 483 provide typical examples, as does the correspondence of E. F. Adolph (University of Rochester) with E. C. Andrus, 14 December 1943 and 6 April 1944. See also Administrative Document 18, Camp Operations Division, 1 October 1943. The seawater experiments are reported in Contract 180, PI Allan Butler, 14 September 1942. Records of the OSRD, CMR, "Human Experiments," box 36.

24. Records of the OSRD, CMR, General Correspondence, "Human Experiments—Venereal Disease" (hereafter cited as Records of the OSRD, CMR, "Human Experiments"), box 39, Moore to Richards, 1 February 1943. Parran to Richards, 9 February 1943.

25. J. E. Moore to A. N. Richards, 6 October 1942. Richards to Moore, 9 October 1942.

26. Richards to Moore, Ibid., 31 October 1942, box 39.

27. R. E. Dyer to Richards, 18 January 1943.

28. Records of the OSRD, CMR, General Correspondence, "Statement of Explanation of the Experiment and Its Risks to Tentative Volunteers," Minutes of a Conference on Human Experimentation in Gonorrhea, filed with Subcommittee of Venereal Disease of the Committee of Medicine, box 39, 29 December 1942. The document may have exaggerated the efficacy of sulfanilamide treatment; there was much dispute about the actual cure rate, and recurrence was noted to be a problem, as was the existence of resistant strains. Indeed, this uncertainty was one of the reasons for the CMR research.

29. Records of the OSRD, CMR, "Human Experiments," box 39, Moore to Richards, 1 February 1943.

30. Ibid., Frank Jewett and Ross Harrison to Vannevar Bush, 5 March 1943.

31. Ibid., Thomas Parran to A. N. Richards, 9 February 1943.

32. James Bennet to J. E. Moore, 26 February 1943; Contractor Records, M3169, Report L7, 7 September 1945–50, pp. 45–50.

Chapter 3

1. For an overview of this history, see Donald C. Swain, "The Rise of a Research Empire: NIH, 1930 to 1950," *Science* 138 (1962): 1233–37; V. A. Harden, *Inventing the NIH: Federal Biomedical Research Policy, 1887–1937* (Baltimore, Md.: 1986), esp. pp. 179–91; Stephen P. Strickland, *Politics, Science, and Dread Disease* (Cambridge: 1972).

2. For a detailed analysis of the transfer of authority from the CMR to the NIH, see Daniel M. Fox, "The Politics of the NIH Extramural Program, 1937–1950," *Journal of the History of Medicine and Allied Sciences* 42 (1987): 447–66. As he makes clear, the transfer was easiest at the ideological level and far more complicated at the contract-grant level.

3. George Rosen, "Patterns of Health Research in the United States, 1900–1960," *Bulletin of the History of Medicine* 39 (1965): 220.

4. Vannevar Bush, "Science, the Endless Frontier: Report to the President on a Program for Scientific Research," (1945): esp. pp. 46–47, 53. In addition to Fox, "The Politics of the NIH," see also *New York Times*, 21 July 1945, 13 August 1945.

5. *New York Times*, 4 July 1945, p. 13.

6. "The National Institutes of Health: A Concerted Effort to Investigate and Study the Many Unconquered Diseases which Afflict Mankind," distributed by the Chemical Foundation, New York (n.d.), pp. 18–19, quoting from the *Congressional Record*.

7. *New York Times*, 6 February 1945, p. 18.

8. Ibid., 12 September 1944, p. 12.

9. Ibid., 21 November 1944, p. 24; see also 29 October 1945, sec. 4, 9.

10. J. E. Rall, epilogue, in *NIH: An Account of Research in Its Laboratories and Clinics*, ed. Dewitt Stetten, Jr., and W. T. Carrigan (New York: 1984), p. 527.

11. "Handbook for Patients at the Clinical Center," Public Health Service (PHS) Publication 315 (1953), esp. p. 2; "Clinical Center: National Institutes of Health," PHS Publication 316 (1956), esp. p. 13; "The Patient's Part in Research at the Clinical Center," PHS Publication (n.d.), pp. 2–3.

12. Minutes, Ad Hoc Committee on Clinical Research Procedures, 28 May 1965, NIH Files, Bethesda, MD., p. 1 (hereafter cited as Minutes, NIH Ad Hoc Committee). "In only a small percentage of instances do patients sign a specific consent."

13. Minutes, NIH Ad Hoc Committee, 19 March 1965, pp. 1–5. The committee was brought together to revise the 1950 publication entitled "Group Consideration of Clinical Research Procedures Deviating from Acceptable Medical Practice or Involving Unusual Hazards." Under the chairmanship of Nathaniel Berlin, the committee members reviewed past procedures in order to make recommendations, which were approved in 1966.

14. Minutes, NIH Ad Hoc Committee, 16 February 1965, p.2.

15. Ibid., 28 May 1965, pp.1–3.

16. Ibid., 22 January 1965, p. 2.

17. Ibid., 19 March 1965, p. 4.

18. Ibid., p.3; 23 April 1965, p.4

19. Ibid., 2 June 1965, pp. 1–2.

20. Ibid., 2 June 1965, pp. 1–3.

21. Mark S. Frankel, *The Public Health Guidelines Governing Research Involving Human Subjects*, George Washington University Program of Policy Studies in Science and Technology Monograph no. 10 (Washington, D.C.: 1972), pp. 6–12.

22. L. G. Welt, "Reflections on the Problems of Human Experimentation," *Connecticut Medicine* 25 (1961): 75–78.

23. Law–Medicine Research Institute of Boston University, Report to the U.S. Public Health Service; Frankel, *Guidelines Governing Research*, p.18

24. Welt, "Human Experimentation," pp. 78; Law–Medicine Institute, "Report." See also chapter 5, note 10.

25. The most useful and accessible compendium of relevant articles and codes is Irving Ladimer and Roger Newman, *Clinical Investigation in Medicine: Legal, Ethical, and Moral Aspects* (Boston: Law–Medicine Institute of Boston University, 1963). Ladimer and Newman were both on the staff of the Boston University Law–Medicine Institute. There was sufficient commentary on the history, ethics, and practice of human experimentation to enable the editors to assemble a 500-page book and a bibliography of 500 references. But several points must be made, quite aside from the tone of the articles and the limits of public action. First, the institute was altogether accurate in describing itself as "a program unique in the United States," and the importance of its own work should not be exaggerated. Second, the great majority of articles reprinted were from physicians—lawyers were second, Ph.D.s in other disciplines a distant third (the most notable were Renee Fox and Margaret Mead). Medical ethics and the ethics of human experimentation were still the province of physicians (see chapter 6), with lawyers making forays into this particular area.

26. *U.S. v. Karl Brandt*, Nuremberg Tribunal, Trials of War Criminals, vol. 2, pp. 71–73.

27. *New York Times*, 4 November 1945, p. 29.

28. Francis D. Moore as quoted in *Clinical Investigation in Medicine*, ed. Ladimer and Newman, p. 433.

29. On the realities of the matter, see the outstanding study by Robert N. Proctor, *Racial Hygiene: Medicine under the Nazis* (Cambridge: 1988). See also Robert Jay Lifton, *The Nazi Doctors* (New York: 1986). Note how recent these two studies are, reflective of how late the turn of attention to these issues has been.

30. See, for example, Cortez Enlow, "The German Medical War Crimes: Their Nature and Significance," *JAMA* 139 (1947): 801–5.

31. "Drug Industry Act of 1962," *Congressional Record*, 23 August 1962, p. 17391.

32. Ibid., pp. 17395, 17397.

33. Ibid., pp. 17398–99, 17401, 17404.

34. Ibid., p. 17400.

35. See National Society for Medical Research, *Report on the National Conference on the Legal Environment of Medical Science*, Chicago, 27–28 May 1959, pp. 5–90; Welt, "Human Experimentation," pp. 75–78; Stuart Sessions, "Guiding Principles in Medical Research Involving Humans, National Institutes of Health," *Hospitals* 32 (1958): 44–64. Even to read A. C. Ivy, who was so intimately involved with the prosecution at Nuremberg, is to feel this tone;

see, for example, "The History and Ethics of the Use of Human Subjects in Medical Experiments," *Science* 108 (1948): 1–5.

36. National Society for Medical Research, *Report on the Conference*, pp. 81–89. Otto Guttentag, a physician writing in *Science*, did describe the ultimate dilemma posed by human experimentation as "tragic in the classical sense," and he suggested a division of authority between the "physician-friend" and the "physician-experimenter." But his recommendation captured little attention in the literature and had no influence on practice. See Guttentag's commentary on Michael Shimkin, "The Problem of Experimentation on Human Beings: The Physician's Point of View," *Science* 117 (1953): 205–10.

37. Ladimer and Newman, in their *Clinical Investigation in Medicine*, list only four American codes: those of the American Medical Association (AMA), the NIH Clinical Center, the American Psychological Association, and the Catholic Hospital Association.

38. "Requirements for Experiments on Human Beings," Report of the Judicial Council, adopted by the House of Delegates of the AMA, December 1946, *JAMA* 132 (1946): 1090.

39. AMA, *Digest of Official Actions* (Adopted December 1952) (Chicago: Author, 1959), pp. 617–18.

Chapter 4

1. In the absence of any biography or scholarly articles about Beecher, one must turn to obituaries and the like. See, for example, the *New England Journal of Medicine* 295 (1976): 730.

2. Henry K. Beecher and Donald P. Todd, "A Study of the Deaths . . . ," *Annals of Surgery* 140 (1954): 2, 5, 17.

3. For Beecher's wartime experience, see his letters to Edward Mallinkrot, 22 December 1943 and 19 June 1945, Henry Beecher manuscripts, Francis A. Countway Library of Medicine, Harvard University (hereafter cited as Beecher MSS). See also his notes to a lecture delivered in Sanders Theater, 16 October 1946, "The Emergence of Anesthesia's Second Power." In his papers there is also an undated memorandum describing the research he wished to carry out: "We have been asked by the Army to study the compounds that have . . . in common: they give access to the subconscious. The Army has a further interest as well: It can be indicated in the question: Can one individual obtain from another, with the aid of these drugs, willfully suppressed information? If we undertake the study this latter question will not be mentioned in the contract application. We request that it not be referred to outside this room." Beecher's rationalization for carrying out the study fit perfectly with the researchers' orientation discussed in chapter 2: "In time of war, at least, the importance of the other [army] purpose hardly appears

debatable." Henry K. Beecher, *Measurement of Subjective Responses* (New York: 1959), esp. pp. viii, 65–72.

4. The link for Beecher between placebo trials and the ethics of experimentation studies is most clearly made in his editorial, "Ethics and Experimental Therapy," *Journal of the American Medical Association* 186 (1963): 858–59 (hereafter cited as *JAMA*).

5. *New York Times*, 24 March 1965; *Wall Street Journal*, 10 June 1965.

6. Beecher to George Burch, 27 June 1966, Beecher MSS.

7. Beecher to John Talbott, 20 August 1965, 30 August 1965, and Talbott to Beecher, 25 August 1965, Beecher MSS.

8. Talbott to Beecher, 25 October 1965, Beecher MSS.

9. Joseph Garland to Beecher, 30 March 1966, 7 April 1966, and Beecher to Garland, 1 April 1966, Beecher MSS.

10. Beecher to John Knowles, 10 June 1966, Beecher MSS.

11. Henry K. Beecher, "Ethics and Clinical Research," *NEJM* 274 (1966): 1354–60.

12. Beecher to Joseph Sadusk, 7 June 1965, Beecher MSS. Sadusk was the medical director of the FDA. See also Beecher to Geoffrey Edsall, 3 August 1966, Beecher MSS.

13. An excellent compilation of materials in the Southam case can be found in *Experimentation with Human Beings*, ed. Jay Katz (New York: 1972), pp. 9–65.

14. Beecher, "Ethics of Clinical Research," pp. 1354–55.

15. In a personal interview (April 19, 1988), Dr. Braunwald said that he did seek the permission of the patients but did not then or later supply evidence for the assertion. Note the comments of Donald Fredrickson in chapter 3 on these experiments as well. When I asked Dr. Braunwald why he never entered a protest against Beecher's statements about him, he declared (in a point that strengthens my general arguments about the state of research ethics in the period) that no one ever queried him about it. Despite the absence of footnotes in the Beecher article, there could be little doubt about who was doing such research.

16. David J. Rothman and Sheila M. Rothman, *The Willowbrook Wars* (New York: 1984), chap. 11.

17. Henry K. Beecher, "Experimentation in Man," *JAMA* 169 (1959): 461–78.

18. Ibid.

19. Beecher, "Ethics of Clinical Research," p. 1360. This was also the position of his contemporary, Louis Welt; see "Reflections on the Problem of Human Experimentation," *Connecticut Magazine* 25 (1961): 78.

Chapter 5

1. Mark S. Frankel, *The Public Health Service Guidelines Governing Research Involving Human Subjects*, George Washington University Program of Policy Studies

in Science and Technology Monograph no. 10 (Washington, D.C.: 1972), pp. 20–21.

2. Ibid., pp. 23–24.

3. John Sherman to Roman Pucinski, 1 July 1966, National Institutes of Health Files, Bethesda, Md.

4. Frankel, *Guidelines Governing Research*, pp. 23, 31.

5. Ibid., p. 30.

6. Committee on Government Operations report to the Senate Subcommittee on Government Research, *Hearings on the National Commission on Health Science and Society*, 90th Cong., 2d sess., 1968, pp. 211, 212 (hereafter cited as Hearings on Health).

7. Henrik Bendixen to Henry Beecher, March 1966, Henry Beecher Manuscripts, Francis A. Countway Library of Medicine, Harvard University (hereafter cited as Beecher MSS).

8. *Handbook on the Normal Volunteer Patient Program of the Clinical Center*, March 1967, NIH Files, Bethesda, Md., p. 15.

9. In May 1969, PHS-NIH officials did provide a more specific definition of consent; see Frankel, *Guidelines Governing Research*, pp. 38–39. See also Ruth R. Faden and Tom L. Beauchamp, *A History and Theory of Informed Consent* (New York: 1986), pp. 205–15, for a more positive view of the 1966 document as well as the 1969 revisions.

10. The most acute analysis of the FDA regulations in human experimentation remains William J. Curran's "Governmental Regulation of the Use of Human Subjects in Medical Research: The Approach of Two Federal Agencies," *Daedalus* 98 (1969): 542–94; I have relied on it in the paragraphs that follow.

11. Curran, "Governmental Regulation," pp. 558–69.

12. Hearings on Health, pp. 211–12.

13. Paul Ramsey, *The Patient as Person* (New Haven, Conn.: 1970), p. 1.

14. Ibid., p. xiv.

15. Ibid., p. xv.

16. Ibid., pp. xvi, 5–7, xvii.

17. The resulting publication, *Ethical Aspects of Experimentation with Human Subjects*, appeared as vol. 98, Spring 1969.

18. Hans Jonas, "Philosophical Reflections on Experimenting with Human Subjects," *Daedalus* 98 (1969): 219.

19. Jonas, "Philosophical Reflections," p. 245.

20. David J. Rothman, "The State as Parent," in *Doing Good*, ed. Willard Gaylin, Steven Marcus, David J. Rothman, and Ira Glasser (New York: 1978), pp. 84–85.

Chapter 6

1. Hans Jonas, "Philosophical Reflections on Experimenting with Human Beings," *Ethical Aspects of Experimentation with Human Subjects* 98 (1969): 1.

2. Joseph Fletcher, *Morals and Medicine* (Princeton, N.J.: 1954), pp. x–xi, xx.

3. The Rush essay is in his *Sixteen Introductory Lectures* (Philadelphia: 1811), pp. 125–32; see esp. p. 127.

4. Richard Cabot, *Adventures on the Borderlands of Ethics* (New York: 1926), p. 23. See also his "The Use of Truth and Falsehood in Medicine," *American Medicine* 5 (1903): 344–49.

5. American Medical Association, Bureau of Medical Economics, "Economics and the Ethics of Medicine," *Bulletin of the American Medical Association* (May 1936): 58, 59, 61.

6. "Ectopic Gestation," *Linacre Quarterly* 10 (1942): 6–23.

7. Paul Blanshard, *American Freedom and Catholic Power* (Boston: 1950), ch. 6.

8. Joseph Fletcher, *Morals and Medicine*, pp. 18, 35.

9. Ibid., pp. 97, 142, 191.

10. John Burnham, "American Medicine's Golden Age: What Happened to It?" *Science* 215 (1982): 1474–79.

11. Compare the analysis that follows with Edward Shorter, *Bedside Manners* (New York: 1985).

12. Jay Katz, *The Silent World of Doctor and Patient* (New York: 1984). See, too, the perceptive discussion of his approach, as against that of Martin Pernick ("The Patient's Role in Medical Decision-Making," in the President's Commission for the Study of Ethical Problems in Medicine . . . , *Making Health Care Decisions* [Washington, D.C.: 1982], vol. 3), in Faden and Beauchamp, *Informed Consent*, pp. 76–101. I join with them in finding the Pernick case more persuasive, although the argument I make here is a different one.

13. On the history of the medical profession, see John S. Haller, Jr., *American Medicine in Transition* (Urbana, Ill.: 1981), chap. 7.

14. Oliver Wendell Holmes, "The Young Practitioner," *Medical Essays*, vol. 9 of the *Writings of Oliver Wendell Holmes* (Boston: 1891).

15. Quoted in Richard Shryock, *Medicine in America* (Baltimore: 1966), p. 163. See also Joseph McFarland, "How to Choose a Doctor," *Hygea* (August 1931): 743–45, for counsel that patients would not go wrong if they "choose a doctor of whom doctors think highly."

16. Carlo M. Cippola, *Public Health and the Profession of Medicine in the Renaissance* (Cambridge: 1976), p. 115.

17. See, for example, Jacob A. Goldberg, "Jews in Medicine," *Medical Economics*, March 1940, pp. 54–56. Many rural areas did their best to found some sort of medical institution, not only to have a facility nearby but to have as staff familiar, like-minded people. Even when good roads and connections made travel to nearby urban centers practical, the incentive remained to organize

community hospitals to ensure such ties. See, for example, Arthur E. Hertzler, *The Horse and Buggy Doctor* (New York, 1938), pp. 254–56.

18. Selwyn D. Collins, "Frequency and Volume of Doctors' Calls . . . ," *Public Health Reports* 55 (1940): 1977–2012.

19. Commission on Medical Education, *Final Report* (1932), p. 73; 55 percent of doctor–patient contacts were in the office, and 10 percent in the hospital.

20. Francis Weld Peabody, *Doctor and Patient* (New York: 1930), pp. 32–33. Peabody worried that hospital visits were liable to confound matters: "The difficulty is that in the hospital one gets into the habit of using the oil immersion lens instead of the low power, and focuses too intently on the center of the field." Using technology as a metaphor for hospital conditions was clever and suggestive of still larger problems.

21. Lane Gerber, *Married to Their Careers*, p. xiv. Since Gerber was more than a little unhappy about the neglect he believes his family suffered from his father, his account may have less romance about it; this is not a son celebrating his father.

22. Lewis Thomas, *The Youngest Science* (New York: 1983), p. 9.

23. S. J. McNeill, "Where Is the Family Doctor and What Is the Matter with the Public?" *Illinois Medical Journal* (February 1928): 145–146. "The doctor would enter the home, revered and respected, his every wish and judgment acquiesced, for his advice and dictation was paramount and the family . . . had all confidence in his ability as a doctor."

24. Rosemary Stevens, as quoted in Irvine Loudon, "The Concept of the Family Doctor," *Bulletin of the History of Medicine* 58 (1984): 347. Loudon, incidentally, finds both the concept and reality of the family doctor very much alive in pre–World War II England, and uses Stevens's remark as a point of departure. See also Selwyn Collins, "Frequency and Volume of Doctor's Calls," p. 1998.

25. Peabody, *Doctor and Patient*, p. 25. He also feared that doctors were becoming too scientific in their approach to patients; but here, too, he was anticipating a problem, not giving persuasive evidence that it already existed. In addition to the citations below, see also J. Lue Sutherland, "The Passing of the Family Physician," *The Nebraska State Medical Journal* 6 (1921): 305–6.

26. *Final Report of the Commission on Medical Education* (New York: 1932), pp. 65, 115, 173. By now, however, over one-third of the medical school classes were beginning to specialize, which is what made medical educators so sensitive to the change; and the better schools did have higher rates: the percentage of Harvard Medical School graduates entering specialty training and practice was 64 percent; at Johns Hopkins, 75 percent; at Stanford, 55 percent.

27. Daniel Funkenstein, *Medical Students, Medical Schools and Society during Five Eras* (Cambridge: 1968), p. 12.

28. Robert S. Veeder, "Trend of Pediatric Education and Practice," *American Journal of Diseases of Children* 50 (1935): 1–10.

29. J. D. Brook, "The Passing of the Family Doctor and Practice of the Future," *Journal of the Michigan State Medical Society* 29 (1930): 694.

30. Earl L. Koos, *The Health of Regionville* (New York: 1954), pp. 53–59. See also the study by Harold Frum, probably based on Columbus, Ohio ("Choice and Change of Medical Service," Master's thesis, Ohio State University, 1939). He reports that 72.5 percent of the families in his survey saw only one or two physicians in the course of a year; fully 67 percent saw only one or two physicians over five years (p. 49). Frum does add that few families—perhaps 60 of 200—had "family doctors," as very narrowly defined. Even so, he concluded that having a family doctor was the pattern for 40 percent of the population, and certainly more for the middle class than the lower class.

31. Gladys V. Swackhamer, *Choice and Change of Doctors*, Committee on Research in Medical Economics (New York: 1939), esp. pp. 6–23, 27–28, 31.

32. *New York Times*, 14 May 1934, sec. 4, p. 8.

33. Holmes, *Medical Essays*, p. 377. We will return later to the end of the phrase: "and whether they had better live at all or remain unrealized possibilities, as belonging to a stock not worth being perpetuated."

34. Quoted in Robert K. Merton et al., *The Student-Physician* (Cambridge: 1957), p. 26, footnote 12. See also the remark of D. N. Cathell: "You are supposed to know the family's constitution. You will find that 'knowing people's constitutions' is a powerful acquisition" (*The Physician Himself and What He Should Add to His Scientific Acquirements* [Baltimore, Md., 1882], p. 66).

35. Walter L. Bierring, "The Family Doctor and the Changing Order," *Journal of the American Medical Association* 102 (1934): 1996.

36. John Stoeckle and J. Andrew Billings, "A History of History-Taking: The Medical Interview" (Unpublished manuscript, Department of Medicine, Harvard Medical School, 1989).

37. The study of literature and medicine has burgeoned over the past five years, another manifestation of the changes that this book is analyzing. A useful introduction to the nineteenth-century literature is Richard R. Malmsheimer, "From Rappaccini to Marcus Welby: The Evolution of an Image" (Ph.D. diss., University of Minnesota, 1978).

38. George Eliot, *Middlemarch* (New York: Penguin, [1871–72] 1965), esp. pp. 178–80, 193–95.

39. Anton Chekhov, *Uncle Vanya: Scenes from Country Life* (New York: Signet, [1899] 1964), esp. pp. 174, 194, 197, 201, 209, 225.

40. Sidney Kingsley, *Men in White* (New York: 1933).

41. Charles E. Rosenberg, "Martin Arrowsmith: The Scientist as Hero," *American Quarterly* 15 (1963): 447–58.

42. Joseph Jerger, *Here's Your Hat! The Autobiography of a Family Doctor* (New York: 1939), esp. pp. 51, 223; William Allen Pusey, *A Doctor of the 1870s and 80s* (Baltimore: 1932), esp. pp. xi, 85; Robert T. Morris, *Fifty Years a Surgeon* (New York: 1935), esp. p. 7; James B. Herrick, *Memories of Eighty*

Years (Chicago: 1949), esp. pp. 86, 155. The New York Academy of Medicine has an excellent guide to these autobiographies, and an excellent collection of them.

43. Frederic Loomis, *Consultation Room* (New York: 1939), pp. 74–76.
44. D. W. Cathell, *The Physician Himself and What He Should Add to His Scientific Acquirements* (Baltimore: 1882), p. 12. Cathell was professor of pathology at the College of Physicians and Surgeons in Baltimore and the president of its Medical and Surgical Society. Over the course of these decades, it was also common to find physicians in the leadership ranks of the boosters and promoters of new towns and cities. Such political involvement was not without its critics. Holmes, for example, advised that physicians "do not dabble in the muddy sewer of politics." But the general practitioners commonly ignored such advice.
45. Holmes, *Medical Essays*, p. 388.
46. Ibid., p. 377.
47. Alphonso Schwitalla and M. R. Kneift, "The Catholic Hospital of the United States, Canada, and Newfoundland at the Beginning of 1934," *Hospital Progress* 15 (1934): 69–71, 74–75.
48. Ibid., 81–93; Mary Hicks, *Hospitals of Cincinnati, A Survey* (n.p., 1925), chap. 2, pp. 51–53. See also *Story of the First Fifty Years of the Mt. Sinai Hospital, 1852–1902* (New York: 1944).
49. Peter Joseph Barone, "Practical Advice by a Catholic Doctor," *Hospital Progress* 4 (1923): 177; John P. Boland, "Religious Aspects of Sisters' Hospitals," *Hospital Progress* 2 (1921): 285. See also Haven Emerson, *The Hospital Survey for New York*, vol. 1 (New York: 1937), p. 36; E. H. Lewinski-Corwin, *The Hospital Situation in Greater New York* (New York: 1924).
50. Tina Leviton, *Islands of Compassion: A History of the Jewish Hospitals of New York* (New York: 1964), esp. pp. 89–91, 113.
51. Emerson, *Hospital Survey*, vol. 1, pp. 19–31.
52. Ibid., p. 29. See also Haven Emerson et al., *Philadelphia Hospital and Health Survey—1929* (Philadelphia: 1929), pp. 574–79; Michael M. Davis, "Are There Enough Beds? Or Too Many?" *The Modern Hospital* 48 (1937): 149–52; C. Rufus Rorem, "The Percentage of Occupancy in American Hospitals," *JAMA* 98 (1932): 2060–61.
53. Emerson, *Hospital Survey*, vol. 1, p. 27. Length of stay ranged from 12.2 days in voluntary hospitals to 17.8 in municipal hospitals.

Chapter 7

1. Meg Greenfield, "The Land of the Hospital," *Newsweek*, 30 June 1986, p. 74.

2. Eliot Freidson, *Patients' Views of Medical Practice* (New York: 1961), pp. 58–59, 66–67.

3. Charles Rosenberg, *The Care of Strangers: The Rise of America's Hospital System* (New York: 1987), pp. 173–75, 253–57.

4. For an elaboration of this point see David J. Rothman, "The Hospital as Caretaker," *Transactions and Studies of the College of Physicians of Philadelphia* 12 (1990): 151–74.

5. United Hospital Fund, "Hospital Closures in New York City," *Proceedings of the Health Policy Forum* (New York: 1978), pp. 28–31.

6. *New York Times*, 6 June 1987, pp. 1, 11.

✓ 7. Elisabeth Kübler-Ross, *On Death and Dying* (New York: 1969), pp. 5, 7, 8, 146–47. See also Terry Mizrachi, *Getting Rid of Patients: Contradictions in the Socialization of Physicians* (New Brunswick, N.J.:1986).

8. Natalie Rogoff, "The Decision to Study Medicine," in *The Student-Physician*, ed. Robert K. Merton et al. (Cambridge: 1957), pp. 110–11.

9. Reported by Alan Gregg, *Challenges to Contemporary Medicine* (New York: 1956), p. 103. Gregg, himself a vice-president of the Rockefeller Foundation, would ask physicians how old they were when they decided on their profession; he reported, "The majority has confirmed the impression that the decision is often made early."

10. Wagner Thielens, Jr., "Some Comparisons of Entrants to Medical and Law School," in *The Student-Physician*, ed. Merton et al., pp. 132–33.

11. Ibid., p. 143.

12. Gregg, *Challenges to Contemporary Medicine*, p. 105.

13. Melvin Konner, *Becoming a Doctor: A Journey of Initiation in Medical School* (New York: 1987), pp. 1–5.

14. Daniel Funkenstein, *Medical Students, Medical Schools, and Society during Five Eras* (Cambridge: 1968), p. 17. He reports much higher percentages for the class of 1971 (68 percent), but then the start of a drop-off by the class of 1976 (down to 59 percent). See also John Colombotos and Corinne Kirchner, *Physicians and Social Change* (New York: 1986).

15. Louis Harris and associates, "Medical Practice," pp. 30–39.

16. Lane A. Gerber, *Married to Their Careers* (New York: 1983), pp. 51, 58, 63, 67, 70.

17. Alice Adams, *Superior Women* (New York: 1984), pp. 234–35.

18. Philip Roth, *The Anatomy Lesson* (New York: Ballantine, 1983), esp. pp. 163, 170, 217, 225, 230–31.

19. C. E. Poverman, *Solomon's Daughter* (New York: Penguin, 1981), p. 256.

✓ 20. John Irving, *The Cider House Rules* (New York: 1985).

21. John Burnham, "American Medicine's Golden Age: What Happened to It?" *Science* 215 (1982): 1474–79.

22. Richard Carter, *The Doctor Business* (New York: 1958), pp. 11–17.

23. Selig Greenberg, *The Troubled Calling* (New York: 1965), pp. xi, 1–3.
24. Daniel M. Fox, "Who We Are: The Political Origins of the Medical Humanities," *Theoretical Medicine* 6 (1985): 329, 334, 338.
25. Boston Women's Health Book Collective, *Our Bodies, Ourselves* (New York: 1971), pp. 252–53.
26. Sylvia Law and Steven Polan, *Pain and Profit: The Politics of Malpractice* (New York: 1978). The quotation is from R. Crawford Morris, "Law and Medicine: Problems of Malpractice Insurance," *Journal of the American Medical Association* 215 (1971): 843. See also *Medical Malpractice*, Report of the Secretary's Commission on Medical Malpractice, Department of Health, Education and Welfare (Washington, D.C.: 1973), esp. pp. 3, 69, 71–72, 667–68.
27. Joint Commission on Accreditation of Hospitals, *Accreditation Manual for Hospitals*, Preamble 1–2 (1970).
28. George J. Annas and Joseph M. Healey, Jr., "The Patient Rights Advocate: Redefining the Doctor–Patient Relationship in the Hospital Context," *Vanderbilt Law Review* 27 (1974): 254–57.
29. Willard Gaylin, "The Patient's Bill of Rights," *Saturday Review of Science* 1 (1973): 22.
30. William J. Curran, "The Patient Bill of Rights Becomes Law," *New England Journal of Medicine* 290 (1974): 32–33.
31. D. Oken, "What to Tell Cancer Patients: A Study of Medical Attitudes," *JAMA* 175 (1961): 1120–28; Howard Waitzkin and John D. Stoeckle, "The Communication of Information about Illness," *Advances in Psychosomatic Medicine* 8 (1972): 185–89.

Chapter 8

1. Shana Alexander, "They Decide Who Lives, Who Dies," *Life*, 9 November 1962, p. 103.
2. Delford L. Stickel, "Ethical and Moral Aspects of Transplantation," *Monographs in the Surgical Sciences* 3 (1966): 267–72. As would be expected in 1966, Stickel was a surgeon interested in medical ethics, not a lay ethicist. Moreover, he framed the transplantation issues in the context of human experimentation. See also "Moral Problems in the Use of Borrowed Organs, Artificial and Transplanted," *Annals of Internal Medicine* 60 (1964): 310–13.
3. Thomas E. Starzl, "Ethical Problems in Organ Transplantation," *Annals of Internal Medicine* 67, supplement 7 (1967): 35–36.
4. G. E. W. Wolstenholme and Maeve O'Connor, eds., *Ethics in Medical Progress: With Special Reference to Transplantation* (Proceedings of the CIBA Foundation Symposium, Boston, 1966), p. 6.
5. Ibid., p. 19.

6. Ibid., p. 59. The recognition of this point was widespread; see, for example, the *Annals of Internal Medicine* editorial cited in note 2 ("Borrowed Organs," p. 312), noting that the problem of risk to the donor raised an ethical problem that was "frighteningly real."

7. Wolstenholme and O'Connor, *Ethics in Medical Progress*, pp. 66, 81. William J. Curran, "A Problem of Consent: Kidney Transplantation in Minors," *New York University Law Review* 34 (1959): 891–98.

8. Wolstenholme and O'Connor, *Ethics in Medical Progress*, p. 71.

9. Francis D. Moore, *Give and Take: The Development of Tissue Transplantation* (Philadelphia: 1964).

10. Francis D. Moore, "Medical Responsibility for the Prolongation of Life," *Journal of the American Medical Association* 206 (1968): 384 (hereafter cited as *JAMA*).

11. Howard P. Lewis, "Machine Medicine and Its Relation to the Fatally Ill," *JAMA* 206 (1968): 387.

12. John Shillito, "The Organ Donor's Doctor: A New Role for the Neurosurgeon," *New England Journal of Medicine* 281 (1969): 1071–72 (hereafter cited as *NEJM*).

13. *Newsweek*, 18 December 1967, p. 86. Just how persistent this idea was, is evident in the United Nations Report from the Secretary General that concluded that "human rights need to be protected in the field of surgical transplants," because the rights of the donor might be too easily violated (*New York Times*, 19 April 1970, p. 36).

14. Rene Menguy, "Surgical Drama," *NEJM* 278 (1968): 394–95.

15. John D. Arnold, Thomas F. Zimmerman, and Daniel C. Martin, "Public Attitudes and the Diagnosis of Death," *JAMA* 206 (1968): 1949–54, esp. pp. 1950–51.

16. Ad Hoc Committee of the American Electroencephalographic Society, "Cerebral Death and the Electroencephalogram," *JAMA* 209 (1969): 1505–9, esp. p. 1508.

17. Clarence C. Crafoord, "Cerebral Death and the Transplantation Era," *Diseases of the Chest* 55 (1969): 141–45, esp. p. 142. (Crafoord was a professor of thoracic surgery in Stockholm and the recipient of a 1968 gold medal from the American College of Chest Physicians.) See also "When Is a Patient Dead?" *JAMA* 204 (1968): 142.

18. Henry Beecher to Robert H. Ebert, 30 October 1967, Henry Beecher Manuscripts, Francis A. Countway Library of Medicine, Harvard University (hereafter cited as Beecher MSS).

19. Ebert to Joseph Murray, 4 January 1968, Beecher MSS.

20. Ad Hoc Committee to Examine the Definition of Death, Harvard Medical School, "A Definition of Irreversible Coma," *JAMA* 205 (1968): 337–40.

21. George H. Williams to Henry K. Beecher, 23 January 1968, Beecher MSS.

22. Draft of 11 April 1968; for this and other materials on the Harvard Brain Death Committee, see the file in the Beecher MSS.

23. Ad Hoc Committee, "Definition of Irreversible Coma," pp. 338–39.

24. Henry Beecher, "After the 'Definition of Irreversible Coma,'" *NEJM* 281 (1969): 1070–71. It was accepted, for example, by the Committee on Ethics of the American Heart Association. In this article, Beecher quoted Peter Medawar's brilliant definition of death: A man is legally dead "when he has undergone irreversible changes of a type that make it impossible for him to seek to litigate."

25. "What and When Is Death?" *JAMA* 204 (1968): 219–20.

26. Ebert to Beecher, 1 July 1968, Beecher MSS.

27. Ad Hoc Committee, "Definition of Irreversible Coma," p. 339.

28. Leonard A. Stevens, "When Is Death?" *Reader's Digest* 94 (1969): 225–32; *Time*, 16 August 1968 and also 27 May 1966.

29. *Annals of Internal Medicine* 68 (1968): 695–99.

30 Kenneth Vaux, "A Year of Heart Transplants: An Ethical Valuation," *Postgraduate Medicine* (1969): 201–5.

31. J. Ernest Breed, "New Questions in Medical Morality," *Illinois Medical Journal* 135 (1969): 504–26, esp. p. 506, on a meeting at Perry Hospital. See also "Symposium on Death," *North Carolina Medical Journal* 28 (1967): 457–68; "Clergy–Physician Dialogues," *Maryland State Medical Journal* 18 (1969): 77–84. Religious spokespeople were alert to the issue the moment that the first transplant occurred; see *Newsweek*, 18 December 1967.

32. Irvine H. Page, "The Ethics of Heart Transplantation," *JAMA* 207 (1969): 109–13.

33. Jordan D. Haller and Marcial M. Cerruti, "Progress Report: Heart Transplantation in Man," *American Journal of Cardiology* 124 (1969): 554–63.

34. Quoted in Renee C. Fox and Judith P. Swazey, *The Courage to Fail* (Chicago: 1974), p. 110.

35. "Cardiac Transplantation in Man," *JAMA* 204 (1968): 147–48; "A Plea for a Transplant Moratorium," *Science News* 93 (1968): 256.

36. "Too Many Too Soon," 29 June 1968, pp. 1413–14.

37. Fox and Swazey, *The Courage to Fail*, p. 132.

38. See, for example, *Time*, 15 March 1968, p. 66; 6 December 1968, pp. 59–60; *Newsweek*, 21 April 1969, pp. 76–78; *The Nation*, 30 December 1968, pp. 719–20.

39. Page, "Heart Transplantation," p. 113.

40. Lyman A. Brewer, "Cardiac Transplantation, An Appraisal," *JAMA* 205 (1968): 101–2.

41. Michael E. DeBakey, Editorial, *Journal of Thoracic and Cardiovascular Surgery* 55 (1968): 449.

Chapter 9

1. The resolution prompted hearings and testimony: Committee on Government Operations report to the Senate Subcommittee on Government Research, *Hearings on the National Commission on Health Science and Society*, 90th Cong., 2d sess., 1968 (hereafter cited as Hearings on Health), pp. 315–19.
2. Ibid., p. 24.
3. Ibid., p. 149.
4. Ibid., p. 121.
5. Ibid., p. 200. David Bazelon, the federal judge who had pioneered in creating mental health law, made this same distinction: in his terms, experts decided the degree of a patient's dangerousness, and society decided whether that degree of dangerousness was sufficient to warrant confining the individual (Hearings on Health, p. 280).
6. Hearings on Health, p. 138.
7. Ibid., Beecher, p. 104; Braver, p. 121; Vaux, p. 138; Mendelsohn, pp. 200–201; Bazelon, p. 276.
8. Hearings on Health, p. 70.
9. Ibid., p. 80.
10. Ibid., pp. 81–82.
11. Ibid., p. 77.
12. Ibid., p. 98.
13. Ibid., pp. 100–101.
14. Ibid., pp. 310–17.
15. Ibid., p. 9.
16. Ibid., pp. 41–43.
17. Ibid., pp. 45–52.
18. Ibid., p. 333.
19. Ibid., pp. 292, 333, 338.
20. Report of the National Advisory Commission on Civil Disorder, March 1968, Bantam ed., 269–72.
21. National Advisory Commission on Health Science and Society, Joint Hearing before the Senate Subcommittee on Health . . . of the Committee on Labor and Public Welfare, 92d Cong., 1st sess., 9 November 1971, pp. 49, 112.
22. Hearings on Health, pp. 5–6.
23. Ibid., p. 315.
24. Ibid., pp. 315, 317, 319.
25. Ibid., pp. 46, 53, 55.
26. Ibid., p. 29.
27. Ibid., p. 45.
28. Mark S. Frankel, "Public Policy Making for Biomedical Research: The Case of Human Experimentation" (Ph.D. diss., George Washington University, 1976) p. 293, footnote 85.

NOTES

29. James Jones, *Bad Blood* (New York, 1981); David J. Rothman, "Were Tuskegee and Willowbrook 'Studies in Nature'?" *Hastings Center Report* (April 1982), pp. 5–7.
30. Jerone Stephens, "Political, Social, and Scientific Aspects of Medical Research on Humans," *Politics and Society* 3 (1973): 409–27; Richard N. Little, Jr., "Experimentation with Human Subjects: Legal and Moral Considerations Regarding Radiation Treatment of Cancer at the University of Cincinnati College of Medicine," *Atomic Energy Law Journal* 13 (1972): 305–30. See also Frankel, "Public Policy Making," pp. 178–83.
31. *Congressional Record*, 24 March 1971 (92nd Cong., 1st sess.), pp. 7670–7678.
32. "Quality of Health Care—Human Experimentation, 1973," pts. 1–4, Hearings before the Senate Subcommittee on Health of the Committee on Labor and Public Welfare, 93d Cong., 1st sess., 1973 (hereafter cited as Hearings on Human Experimentation).
33. Ibid., p. 1055.
34. Ibid., pt. 1, 21 February 1973, p. 2.
35. The alternative policy, to have the FDA monitor actual physician usage, has never been implemented on the grounds that it would restrict physicians' prerogatives too much.
36. Hearings on Human Experimentation, pt. 1, 22 February 1973, pp. 65–66.
37. Ibid., pt. 2, 23 February 1973, p. 354.
38. Ibid., pt. 3, 7 March 1973, p. 841.
39. Ibid., p. 795.
40. Ibid., 8 March 1973, pp. 1045, 1049.
41. Ibid., pt. 2, 23 February 1973, pp. 378–79.
42. Ibid., pt. 3, 7 March 1973, p. 843.
43. Ibid., pt. 4, pp. 1264–65. For evidence of how persistent a theme this was for Kennedy, see also National Advisory Commission on Health Science and Society, Joint Hearings, 9 November 1971, 92d Cong., 1st sess., p. 2.

Chapter 10

1. One of the first analyses of ethics of the case was James Gustafson, "Mongolism, Parental Desires, and the Right to Life," *Perspectives in Biology and Medicine* 16 (1972–73): 529–57.
2. The press reports on the film either missed the fact that this was a re-creation or took the baby to be the actual baby. See, for example, *New Haven Register*, 20 October 1971: "The film opened with the baby's birth."
3. The lead for the story of the conference in the *New York Times*, for example, was "Film Ponders the Right to Life of a Mentally Retarded Infant," 15 October 1971, p. 31.

4. *Annapolis Evening Capital*, 16 October 1971, p. 1; letters to the *Washington Post*, 23 October 1971.

5. D. M. to William Bartholome, 28 October 1971; Mrs. R. H. to Robert Cooke, 18 October 1971. These were part of the letters saved by Bartholome and kindly shared with me.

6. Seemingly, the first use of the term *bioethics* was in an article by Van Rensselaer Potter, "Bioethics, the Science of Survival," *Perspectives in Biology and Medicine* 14 (1970): 127–53. But his use of the term was not what it came to be: "We are in great need of a land ethic, a wildlife ethic, a population ethic, a consumption ethic, an urban ethic, an international ethic, a geriatric ethic, and so on. . . . All of them involve *bioethics*, and survival of the total ecosystem is the test of the value system" (p. 127).

7. *Washington Post*, 2 October 1971, p. 1; and 13 October 1971, "Can Science and Ethics Meet?"

8. William Bartholome to Mrs. S. M., 9 December 1971.

9. *Baltimore Sun*, 21 October 1971.

10. "Ethical Dilemmas in Current Obstetric and Newborn Care," Report of the Sixty-Fifth *Ross Conference on Pediatric Research* (Columbus, Ohio, 1973) (hereafter cited as Ross Conference, "Ethical Dilemmas").

11. Ibid., pp. 12, 16–17.

12. Ibid., p. 18.

13. The "new barbarianism" phrase was Raymond Duff's. "Medical Ethics: The Right to Survival, 1974," Hearings before the Senate Subcommittee on Health of the Committee on Labor and Public Welfare, 93d Cong., 2d sess., 11 June 1974 (hereafter cited as Medical Ethics: The Right to Survival), p. 4.

14. Ross Conference, "Ethical Dilemmas," pp. 58–59, 63, 70–71, 73–74.

15. Ibid., pp. 20, 91.

16. Ibid., p. 77.

17. Ibid., pp. 89–91.

18. Raymond Duff and Alexander Campbell, "Moral and Ethical Dilemmas in the Special-Care Nursery," *New England Journal of Medicine* 289 (1973): 890–94.

19. Ibid., p. 893.

20. Ibid., pp. 893–94.

21. Ibid., p. 894.

22. Anthony Shaw, "Dilemmas of 'Informed Consent' in Children," *NEJM* 289 (1973): 885–90. Shaw later observed that he actually received very few letters in response to the article.

23. Franz Ingelfinger's editorial remarks appeared in the same *NEJM* issue: "Bedside Ethics for the Hopeless Case," 289 (1973): 914–15.

24. In reviewing these lines, one wonders whether it was Ingelfinger who suggested that Shaw add to his article the awkward closing line, "Or should they?"

25. "Correspondence," *NEJM* 290 (1974): 518.
26. Hearings on "Medical Ethics: The Right to Survival," pp. 16–19.
27. Fost's remarks are quoted in Chester Swinyard, ed., *Decision Making and the Defective Newborn* (Proceedings of a [1975] Conference on Spina Bifida and Ethics, Springfield, Illinois, 1978), pp. 228, 247, 562.
28. Ibid., pp. 59–67, esp. pp. 63, 66–67.
29. Ibid., pp. 592–93.
30. The coincidental developments in 1973 first came to my attention in Nelson Lund, "Infanticide, Physicians, and the Law," *American Journal of Law and Medicine* 11 (1985): 1–29.
31. See the discussion in John Fletcher, "Abortion, Euthanasia, and Care of Defective Newborns," *NEJM* 292 (1975): 75–77.
32. Material in this and the next paragraph is drawn from Richard K. Scotch, *From Good Will to Civil Rights: Transforming Federal Disability Policy* (Philadelphia: 1984).
33. Scotch, *From Good Will to Civil Rights*, pp. 43, 55.
34. "Medical Ethics: The Right to Survival," pp. 1–2, 11, 22.
35. Ibid., pp. 17, 19.
36. Ibid., p. 25.
37. Interview with Daniel Callahan, 17 March 1977, conducted by Allan Brandt (who shared the transcript with me); quotations are from pp. 2–6, 49.
38. Joseph Fletcher, *Situation Ethics: The New Morality* (Philadelphia: 1966), p. 261. See also Harvey Cox, *The Situation Ethics Debate* (Philadelphia: 1968), pp. 12–13.
39. A. R. Jonsen et al., "Critical Issues in Newborn Intensive Care: A Conference Report and Policy Proposal," *Pediatrics* 55 (1975): 756–68.
40. Ibid., p. 761.
41. Ibid., p. 763.
42. Ibid., p. 764.
43. Ibid., p. 760.
44. Ibid., p. 764.
45. Robert and Peggy Stinson, *The Long Dying of Baby Andrew* (Boston: 1983). The book is an expansion of an article that originally appeared in *Atlantic Monthly* (July 1978) entitled "On the Death of a Baby."
46. Robert and Peggy Stinson, *Baby Andrew*, p. xi.
47. Ibid., p. 71.
48. Ibid., pp. xii–xiv.
49. Ibid., p. 62.
50. Ibid., pp. 145, 62, 115, 142.
51. Ibid., pp. 57, 145.
52. Ibid., pp. 93, 115, 46–47.
53. Ibid., pp. 301, 358.
54. "The Future of Baby Doe," *New York Review of Books*, 1 March 1984, p. 17.

55. Alistair G. Philip et al., "Neonatal Mortality Risk for the Eighties: The Importance of Birth Weight/Gestational Age Groups," *Pediatrics* 68 (1981): 128; Maureen Hack et al., "The Low-Birth-Weight Infant—Evolution of a Changing Outlook," *NEJM* 301 (1979): 1163.

56. Robert and Peggy Stinson, *Baby Andrew*, pp. 147, 187.

Chapter 11

1. Daniel R. Coburn, *"In Re Quinlan*: A Practical Overview," *Arkansas Law Review* 31 (1977): 63.

2. Joseph and Julia Quinlan with Phyllis Battelle, *Karen Ann* (New York: 1977), pp. 117–18, 127.

3. The briefs, the court argument, and the decision are conveniently collected in *In the Matter of Karen Quinlan*, vol. 2 (Arlington, Va.: University Publications of America, 1976). For appellant brief, see pp. 1–40. See also Transcript of Proceedings, 26 January 1976, p. 237 (hereafter, all references to documents from the case refer to this source).

4. Brief and Appendix on Behalf of the Attorney General of New Jersey, p. 51. Defendants brought in Dr. Sidney Diamond, professor of neurology at Mt. Sinai, to testify: "No physician to my knowledge will ever interrupt a device which is performing a life-saving measure at any time at all" (p. 117).

5. Brief on Behalf of Defendants-Respondents, p. 145.

6. Supplemental Brief on Behalf of . . . St. Clare's Hospital, pp. 187–88.

7. Transcript of Proceedings, pp. 284, 258–59.

8. Docket no. A-116, Supreme Court, State of New Jersey, 31 March 1976.

9. *In the Matter*, p. 305.

10. Ibid., pp. 306–8.

11. Ibid., p. 309.

12. Ibid., p. 310.

13. Ibid., pp. 278–79, 311.

14. Karen Teel, "The Physician's Dilemma: A Doctor's View: What the Law Should Be," *Baylor Law Review* 27 (1975): 6–9.

15. *In the Matter*, p. 312.

16. Michael Halberstam, "Other Karen Quinlan Cases Never Reach Court," Op-Ed, *New York Times*, 2 November 1975.

17. *Journal of the American Medical Association* 234 (1975): 1057.

18. *Time*, 27 October 1975, p. 41.

19. *Time*, 3 November 1975, p. 58. See also Transcript of Proceedings, p. 257, where

counsel for the guardian observed: "If one thing has occurred as a result of this case, I think at least the doctors involved, and probably other doctors, are now going to be much more concerned about judicial approval than might have occurred before this."

20. Quoted in Stephan Bennett, "In the Shadow of Karen Quinlan," *Trial* 12 (1976): 40.
21. "Optimal Care for Hopelessly Ill Patients," Report of the Critical Care Committee of the Massachusetts General Hospital, *New England Journal of Medicine* 295 (1976): 362–64 (hereafter cited as *NEJM*).
22. M. T. Rapkin et al., "Orders Not to Resuscitate," *NEJM* 295 (1976): 364–66.
23. Letter of Jean Pierre Raufmann (Montefiore Medical Center, New York), *NEJM* 295 (1976): 1140.
24. Letter of Allan Parham (Medical University of South Carolina), *NEJM* 295 (1976): 1139.
25. Charles Fried, "Terminating Life Support: Out of the Closet!" *NEJM* 295 (1976): 390–91. And not only patients but medical institutions needed lawyers' help, for both the MGH and Beth Israel drew on lawyers to design their new procedures.
26. Harold L. Hirsch and Richard E. Donovan, "The Right to Die: Medico-Legal Implications of *In Re Quinlan*," *Rutgers Law Review* 30 (1977): 267–303, esp. p. 274.
27. *Superintendent of Belchertown State School v. Saikewicz*, 373 Mass. 728; 370 N.E. 2d 417 (1977).
28. Arnold Relman, "The *Saikewicz* Decision: Judges as Physicians," *NEJM* 298 (1978): 508–9.
29. Supreme Court of the State of New York, "Report of the Special January 3rd, Additional 1983 Grand Jury Concerning 'Do Not Resuscitate' Procedures at a Certain Hospital in Queens County," esp. pp. 4, 14, 23–24.
30. For the Brother Fox case, see *In Re Storer*, 52 N.Y., 2d 363; 420 N.E. 2d 64 (1981).
31. The Harris Survey, 4 March 1985, no. 18, "Support Increases for Euthanasia." In a Gallup poll of 1985, over 80 percent favored the court position in *Quinlan*: Gallup Report, no. 235, April 1985, p. 29. See also John M. Ostheimer, "The Polls: Changing Attitudes toward Euthanasia," *Public Opinion Quarterly* 44 (1980): 123–28.
32. David Dempsey, "The Living Will," *New York Times*, Magazine, 23 June 1974, pp. 12–13; Walter Modell, "A 'Will' to Live," *NEJM* 290 (1974): 907–8; "Death with Dignity," *Hearings before the Special Committee on Aging*, U.S. Senate, 92nd Cong., 2d sess., 7 August 1972, pp. 23–24, 33.
33. Sissela Bok, "Personal Directions for Care at the End of Life," *NEJM* 295 (1976): 367–69.

34. Donald J. Higby, "Letter to the Editor," *NEJM* 295 (1976): 1140.
35. Marquis Childs, "Ethics and Illness," *Washington Post*, 18 November 1985.
36. "The Right to Die a Natural Death," *University of Cincinnati Law Review* 46 (1977): 192–98; "Note: The Legal Aspects of the Right to Die: Before and after the Quinlan Decision," *Kentucky Law Journal* 65 (1976–77): 831–33; Donald Collester, "Death, Dying and the Law: A Prosecutorial View of the Quinlan Case," *Rutgers Law Review* 30 (1977): 328.
37. Renee C. Fox, "Advanced Medical Technology—Social and Ethical Implications," *Annual Review of Sociology* 2 (1976): 231–68.
38. Ibid., p. 414.
39. Renee C. Fox and Judith P. Swazey, "Medical Morality Is Not Bioethics: Medical Ethics in China and the United States," in *Essays in Medical Sociology*, ed. Renee C. Fox (New Brunswick, N.J.: 1988), pp. 645–70, esp. pp. 668–70.
40. Joseph and Julia Quinlan, *Karen Ann*, pp. 252–53.
41. Edmund Pellegrino, Interview, *U.S. News and World Report*, 3 November 1975, p. 53.
42. Tristram Engelhardt, Jr., "But Are They People?" *Hospital Physician* (February 1976): 7. In this same spirit, Sisela Bok promoted living wills so that the patient could "retain some control over what happens at the end of one's life."
43. Robert Veatch, *Death, Dying, and the Biological Revolution* (New Haven, Conn.: 1976), p. 140.

Epilogue

1. United States Senate, 1978. Congressional Hearings.
2. Morris Abram, *The Day is Short* (New York: 1982), ch. 12.
3. There has been little scholarly attention to how the Commission worked, its strengths and weaknesses, and its overall impact. This point is aptly made by Alan Weisbard and John Arras in their introduction to the "Symposium: Commissioning Morality: A Critique of the President's Commission for the Study of Ethical Problems in Medicine and Biomedical and Behavioral Research," *Cardozo Law Review* 6 (1984): 223–355 (hereafter cited as "Commissioning Morality").
4. Alexander M. Capron, "Looking Back at the President's Commission," *Hastings Center Report* (October 1983), pp. 7–10.
5. President's Commission for the Study of Ethical Problems in Medicine and Biomedical and Behavioral Research (hereafter cited as "President's Commission"), *Summing Up: The Ethical and Legal Problems in Medicine and Biomedical and Behavioral Research* (Washington, D.C.: 1983), pp. 20–21.

NOTES

6. President's Commission, *Deciding to Forego Life-Sustaining Treatment* (Washington, D.C.: 1983), p. 44.

7. Ibid., pp. 2–5.

8. Jay Katz, "Limping Is No Sin: Reflections on *Making Health Care Decisions*," in "Commissioning Morality," pp. 243–265. See also his book, *The Silent World of Doctor and Patient* (New York: 1984), and my comments above in chapter 6.

9. See the review article by Fredric Wolinsky, "The Professional Dominance Perspective, Revisited," in the *Milbank Quarterly* 66, Supplement 2 (1988): 33–47, esp. 40–41.

10. See, for example, Bradford H. Gray et al., "Research Involving Human Subjects," *Science* 201 (1978): 1094–1101; Jerry Goldman and Martin Katz, "Inconsistency and Institutional Review Boards," *JAMA* 248 (1982): 197–202.

11. For an elaboration of this point see Harold Edgar and David J. Rothman, "New Rules for New Drugs: The Challenge of AIDS to the Regulatory Process," *The Milbank Quarterly* 68, Supplement 1 (1990): pp. 111–42.

12. Susanna E. Bedell et al., "Do-Not-Resuscitate Orders for Critically Ill Patients in the Hospital," *JAMA* 256 (1986): 233–38; Palmi V. Jonsson et al., "The 'Do not Resuscitate' Order: A Profile of Its Changing Use," *Archives of Internal Medicine* 148 (1988): 2373–75.

13. President's Comission, *Deciding to Forego Life-Sustaining Treatment*, pp. 169–70, 227. To buttress the case for ethics committees, the commission cited the positive contributions of the IRB. However, it also noted how little was known about the actual operation of IRBs, and hoped that as ethics committees proliferated, their functioning would be evaluated more systematically.

14. See the report "Ethics Committees Double Since '83: Survey," *Hospitals* 59 (1985): 60. The literature on the advantages and disadvantages of ethics committees is huge—testimony to the prominence of the "Baby Doe" cases and the number of commentators interested in bioethical questions. A useful guide to the material is "Ethics Committee: Core Resources," available through the Hastings Center. Among the books and articles I found most useful are: Ronald E. Cranford and A. Edward Doudera, *Institutional Ethics Committees and Health Care Decisions* (Ann Arbor: 1984); Bernard Lo, "Behind Closed Doors: Promises and Pitfalls of Ethics Committees," *NEJM* 317 (1987): 46–50; and Alan R. Fleischman, "Bioethical Review Committees in Perinatology," *Clinics in Perinatology* 14 (1987): 379–93.

15. Robert F. Weir, "Pediatric Ethics Committees: Ethical Advisors or Legal Watchdogs?" *Law, Medicine and Health Care* 15 (1987): 105.

16. Mark Siegler, "Ethics Committees: Decisions by Bureaucracy," *Hastings Center Report* (June 1986), pp. 22–24. Weir, "Pediatric Ethics Committees,"

p. 109, for the comment by Angela Holder, counsel for medicolegal affairs, Yale University School of Medicine and Yale-New Haven Hospital.

17. "Life Support Forcibly Cut, A Father Dies," *New York Times*, 11 January 1990, p. B1. The medical examiner later ruled that he believed that the man was dead before the incident occurred, and on these weak grounds, dismissed the case.

18. Saul S. Radovsky, "U.S. Medical Practice Before Medicare and Now—Differences and Consequences," *NEJM* 322 (1990): 263–67.

19. Lawrence Altman and Elisabeth Rosenthal, "Changes in Medicine Bring Pain to Healing Profession," *New York Times*, 18 February 1990, p. 1.

INDEX

INDEX

Hippocrates, 101, 122, 194
Holmes, Oliver Wendell, 110–11, 123
Hospital care: demographic changes and, 130–31; ethics committees and, 255–56; intensive care units, 133; psychological aspects, 127; *Quinlan* case, effect on, 229–32; rural areas, 277–78*n*17; sectarian hospitals, 123–26, 129, 258; terminally ill patients, 132–33. *See also* Health care
Hospital patients as research subjects: 74, 77, 81, 183
House calls by physicians, 112–13, 128
Human experimentation: blacks as research subjects, 183; cancer, research on, 74, 77, 78, 80–81, 87, 93, 183; cardiology, research on, 74, 77–78, 81; children as research subjects, 33–34, 38, 74, 77, 78, 81; compensation for injuries, 248; conscientious objectors as research subjects, 41; dysentery, research on, 32–36, 33–34, 34–35, 47–48, 79; exposés on, 10, 15–18; federal regulations on, 10–11; gonorrhea, research on, 28, 44–47; hepatitis, research on, 17, 74, 77, 78, 79, 81; hospital patients as research subjects, 74, 77, 81, 183; influenza, research on, 37–39, 47–48, 79; malaria, research on, 23–24, 79; media attention, 83; medical and dental students as research subjects, 39, 47, 67, 83; mentally handicapped as research subjects, 2, 10, 17, 34–35, 47, 49, 74, 77, 78, 85–86; mentally ill as research subjects, 36, 38–39; minorities, 10, 183, 186–87; "normal" volunteers, 83, 92; Pasteur, Louis, 168*n*18; poor as research subjects, 10, 183, 185–87; prisoners as research subjects, 10, 36–37, 38, 44–47, 68–69, 83, 198; public opinion, 83, 183; senile persons as research subjects, 77, 78, 80–81, 87, 93; World War II, human experimentation during, 93. *See also* Drug experiments

"Human Rights, Retardation, and Research" (film), 192
Humphrey, Hubert, 185, 206

ICUs. *See* Intensive care units
Immune response: transplantation of organs, 152–53
Influenza, research on, 37–39, 47–48, 79
Informed consent: Beecher's exposé on research protocols, 80; cancer research, 80–81; drug experimentation, 92–93; Food and Drug Administration, defined by, 93; formal process, need for, 100; laboratory personnel as research subjects, 83; medical students as research subjects, 67, 83; National Commission on Protection of Human Subjects, 248; National Institutes of Health, 56–58; neonatal ethics, 198–200; policy changes, 90–91; President's Commission for the Study of Ethical Problems in Medicine and Biomedical and Behavioral Research, 247–50; prisoners as research subjects, 45–46, 83; surgery, consent for, 55–58; transplantation of organs, donors, 155; World War II, human experimentation during, 47–48
Ingelfinger, Franz, 200, 205, 234
Institutional Review Board, 90–91, 101, 220, 242, 249, 251–52, 255–56
Insulin therapy, research on, 25
Intensive care units, 159–60, 260; neonatal, 205, 210–20; *Quinlan* case, 235–36
Investigator-subject relationship, 89, 107; conflict of interest, 95, 100
IRB. *See* Institutional Review Board
Irving, John, 140

Javits, Jacob, 64–66, 87, 92, 183–84
Jenner, Edward, 20–21
Jewett, Frank, 47
Jews: hospitals, sectarian, 123–26; social aspects of medicine, 111, 164.
Johns Hopkins University Hospital, 12;

297

INDEX

Poverman, C. E., 139–40

President's Commission for the Study of Ethical Problems in Medicine and Biomedical and Behavioral Research, 189, 247–50, 255

Prisoners as research subjects, 10, 38, 44–47; AMA condemnation of, 68–69; drug research, 198; informed consent, 45–46, 83; for malaria, 36–37

Protestants: hospitals, sectarian, 124, 126; medical ethics and, 106; on termination of treatment, 164

Psychiatry: Commission on Health Science and Society, 181; psychosurgery, 186–87. *See also* Behavior modification

Public opinion: human experimentation, 83, 99, 183; mentally handicapped, research on, 49, 86; neonatal ethics, 204; physicians, 107; transplantation of organs, 174

Publicity. *See* Media

"Quality of Health Care—Human Experimentation" (hearings), 185

Quinine, 36

Quinlan, Joseph and Julia, 222–25

Quinlan, Karen Ann, 3, 12, 160, 222–46, 259; bioethicists, solidification of group, 241–46; controversies of case, 257; court case, 223–27, 236–37, 244; decision making in medicine generally, effect of case on, 237–38; ethics committees, effect on forming, 233–34; facts of case, 222–23; hospitals, effect of decision on, 229–32; legal profession, effect of case on, 232–33, 237; media, 231, 237–38, 254; physicians' reactions to decision, 229; respirator, disconnection from, 223–24, 235–36; "right to die," 238–39; verdict in court case, 223. *See also* Termination of treatment

Rabies, experiments on, 22–23

Radovsky, Saul, 260

Ramsey, Paul, 95–98, 99, 105

Randolph, Judson, 195–96

Ransdell, Joseph, 52–53

Reagan, Ronald W., 254–55

Reed, Walter, 25–27, 47

Reemtsma, Keith, 153

Reich, Warren, 208

Religion. *See* Ethnicity and religion

Relman, Arnold, 234

Researcher-subject relationship. *See* Investigator-subject relationship

Respirators, artificial, 2, 13, 156, 159–60, 164, 254; neonatal intensive care, 213–19; *Quinlan* case, 222–23

Retarded persons. *See* Mentally handicapped

Rheumatic fever, research on, 16

Ribicoff, Abraham, 144, 172, 175–76, 180–81

Richards, A. N., 43–44, 46

"Right to die." *See* Termination of treatment

Rockefeller Institute for Medical Research, 28–29

Roe v. Wade decision, 204, 208–209, 216, 220, 224, 232

Roosevelt, Franklin D., 21

Rosenthal, Elisabeth, 260

Ross Conference on Pediatric Research, 194–97, 210–11

Roth, Philip, 138–39

Rush, Benjamin, 103

Rusk, Howard, 165

Rutstein, David, 72

Saikewitz case, 233–35, 241

Salisbury, J. H., 23–24

Salk, Jonas: influenza research, 38–39

"Science, the Endless Frontier" (Bush), 52

Scribner, Belding, 149–50

Sectarian hospitals. *See* Hospital care

Selective Service Administration, 41–42, 49

Self-help books, 3, 127, 135

INDEX

Senile persons as research subjects, 77, 78, 80–81, 87, 93

Shannon, James, 86–87, 88, 95, 99

Shaw, Anthony, 198–200, 203

Sheiner, Lewis, 207–208

Shreveport Charity Hospital (Louisiana), 35

Shriver, Sargent, 193

Shumway, Norman, 157, 166, 170

Silent Spring (Carson), 15

Simpson, James, 21

Sinclair, Upton, 15

Singer, Peter, 217

Situation Ethics (Fletcher), 209–210

Skinner, B. F., 192

Sloan-Kettering Institute for Cancer Research, 77

Smallpox research, 20–21, 28, 52, 173

Smallpox Hospital, Boston, 21

Smidovich, V. V., 27–28

Smith, Clement, 212

Society for Health and Human Values, 141–42

Soldiers and Sailors Orphanage (Ohio), 33–34

Soldiers as research subjects, 39

Solomon's Daughter (Poverman), 139–40

Southam, Chester, 77, 78, 80–81, 87, 88, 93

Specialization by physicians, 114, 129

Spina bifida, 202, 203

St. Clair Hospital (New Jersey), 222–23

St. Martin, Alexis, 22

Standing Committee on Human Studies, Harvard University, 160–65

Starzl, Thomas, 153

"Statement on Policy Concerning Consent for the Use of Investigational New Drugs on Humans" (FDA), 93

Stateville Pentitentiary, 36–37

Sternberg, George, 28

Stevenson, Robert Louis, 195

Stewart, William, 89

Stinson, "Baby Andrew," 213–29

Stinson, Peggy and Robert, 213–29

Stokes, Joseph, 28

Stowe, Harriet Beecher, 15, 70

Subject-investigator relationship. *See* Investigator-subject relationship

Sulfonamides, 25, 35

Superior Women (Adams), 138

Swackhamer, Gladys, 116

Swazey, Judy, 166

Syphilis, research on, 28, 183

Talbott, John, 73

Technology and medicine, 148–49; Commission on Health Science and Society, 179–81; focus on, 12; physician and patient relationship, 128, 131, 132; social definitions, artificial; transplanation of organs, 180. *See also* Dialysis; Respirators

Teel, Karen, 227–29, 233

Termination of treatment, 12; decision making, 163–74; formality of resolution, 252–53; "living wills," 239–41; media, 164; National Commission on Protection of Human Subjects, 248; neonatal ethics, 191–208, 218; physician-patient relationship, 261; pre-1976, 160; "right to die," 238–39. *See also* Quinlan, Karen Ann

Tetanus, research on, 52

Thalidomide, 63–64

Theology and medical ethics, 102, 105–106, 142; brain death decision making, 164–65

Teresa, Mother, 192

Thomas, Lewis, 113

Training of physicians: case approach, 8–9; history, 110–11, 123; isolation and, 134; "rounds," 5–6. *See also* Medical students

Transplantation of organs: animal organs transplanted to humans, 153; cadavers, use of, 159; controversy on, 165–67; death, effect on definition of, 156; decision making, 154–56; donors, 154–55; heart transplants, 11, 156–59, 165–67, 172, 181; immune response and, 152–53; kidney transplants, 11, 152–55, 157, 158, 159,

1970s expose Tuskegee syphilis research, & FDA-approved DES.
Criticism that groups such as the AMA could not police themselves
because they were "protective guilds" (Willard Gaylin, 188).

God squad committees
1973: Roe vs. Wade
Disability advocacy
Neonatal life-&-death decisions
Joseph Fletcher: Situational Ethics (1966)

The Karen Ann Quinlan case was the most dramatic &
publicly persuasive, & moved bedside control from
doctor to lawyer & judge (223).

Critique that bioethics emphasizes patient rights &
neglects the larger socio-economic inequalities of
medical care (242-5).

1966: Beecher ... & Medicare & Medicaid

ABOUT THE AUTHOR

David J. Rothman is Bernard Schoenberg Professor of Social Medicine, Director of the Center for the Study of Society and Medicine, and Professor of History at Columbia University. His books have explored the consequences of past and present social policies toward the poor, the criminal, and the mentally disabled. In 1971, his book *The Discovery of the Asylum* was co-winner of the Albert J. Beveridge Prize, and in 1987, he received a honorary Doctor of Law degree from the John Jay School of Criminal Justice.

His current research and writing analyzes the social and ethical issues in medical practice and hospital care. He chaired a New York City task force that has explored the advantages and disadvantages of single-disease hospitals and has examined the impact of AIDS on the regulation of new drugs. He is presently completing a study of American attitudes and policies toward the allocation of scarce medical resources.

David Rothman has served as Samuel Paley Lecturer at Hebrew University, as Distinguished Lecturer at the Kyoto American Studies Seminar, as Fulbright Professor to India, and most recently, as a fellow at the Rockefeller Foundation study center at Bellagio.

After WWII, researchers encouraged the govt. to continue its active role in supporting medical research, spurred on by the success of Alexander Fleming's penicillin. The NIH expanded, & its research w/human subjects blurred the line between therapy & experiment, & was often vague on getting informed consent... despite what the Nuremberg Trials revealed about human experimentation, or what the ensuing Nuremberg Code for medical research called for. The trials of the Nazi doctors got little media attention (51-63), & doctors were allowed to experiment largely at their discretion until Beecher's exposé in 1966 because, after WWII, results & not methods & ethics were what people focused on... & the results were often dramatic. Furthermore, their research subjects were usually devalued or marginal people: retarded, poor, senile, etc., soldiers, alcoholics. But the researchers genuinely felt their projects had minimal risks & high potential for benefits (63-84).

Still, the results of the exposé led to peer review groups for human research in NIH; more insistence on consent by FDA; & the involvement of non-medical outsiders in the debate (e.g. philosophers, lawyers), some of whom stressed the inherent conflict between researchers' search for knowledge & the human rights of their subjects (85-98), the social good vs. the personal good, thereby introducing "a language of rights" into the debate (as was characteristic of other struggles in the 1960s)(98-100).

This emphasis on the rights of subjects vis-à-vis researchers was extended to the rights of patients vis-à-vis doctors between 1966 & 1976 (106-7), largely as a result of a growing social distance bet. doctor & patient, & hospital & community after WWII (108-9). These included declines in home visits; & the declining significance of small, sectarian hospitals serving localized populations where patients often remained for longer periods (123-126); the increasing reliance on office- & hospital-based, sophisticated medical technologies for diagnosis & treatment; increased use of referrals to specialists; economies of scale; changing patterns for recruiting & training doctors that promoted insularity; increasing malpractice suits & books critical of doctors; the development of a Patient's Bill of Rights (127-47).

Kidney dialysis & organ transplants opened up the issue of who would make decisions about life- & -death access to scarce resources: doctors or outsiders? And how to define the death of a potential donor? (148-167).

For a person to act as a moral being, he has to have the freedom & knowledge to make 'choices;' otherwise, we are not moral agents. —Joseph Fletcher (106).

1966-76 was a critical period of change in medical ethics decision-making. It began in 1966 w/ exposés of abuses in human experimentation & closed in 1976 w/the Karen Ann Quinlan decision to remove life-supports. The cumulative result has been to replace individual doctors making very private decisions about care, experiments, life-support to a situation where such decisions have become public & collective ones involving activist & consumer-oriented patients, bioethics committees, lawyers, judges, legislators, insurers, community representatives, medical administrators, academics (1-4), HSR committees... ie, outsiders who generally agreed on the need to reduce physicians' discretion & increase patients' autonomy (5).

Medicine is as much art as science: clinicians rely on anecdotal exemplary case histories cases, to make specific decisions (7), ie, a particular case, rather they know from the past than a general model of clinical or ethical practice, guides their conduct. They are thus case-oriented, not rule- or principle-oriented (7), w/ a current case.

Outsiders are more likely to seek out general principles (7) for social or ethical questions

The transformation of bringing rules to medicine centered on a erosion of trust in & deference to doctors; This erosion began w/ 1966 exposés about the ethics of medical experiments that involved minorities, prisoners & the poor (9-10).

After WWII, the distance & distrust between doctors & patients, & hospital & community grew; Trust was eroded. Besides the exposés of experiments such medical innovations created unprecedented issues about life-&-death decisions & The use of scarce resources (11-12), & the spiralling costs of medical care. But underlying all attempts by doctors or hospitals "outsiders" to control & intervene in these issues was the erosion of trust (13). This basic shift from beside ethics to bioethics has been valid & necessary (13)

History of informed medical experimentation: eg Edward Jenner (18c) & Claude Bernard (19c), & Walter Reed on yellow fever on small pox

WWII: upsurge in war-related US medical experiments on influenza w/ orphans, the retarded, prisoners, mental patients, students, soldiers, CO with no consent obtained. The pressures of the war, & the idea that it was acceptable to compel both military & medical services, encouraged this pattern (30-50).